BITTER MEDICINE

The Challenge of Immaturity
in the Modern American Male

Rich Jewett MA

ISBN-10: 1506136826
ISBN-13: 978-1506136820

Also by Rich Jewett

Dance on Fire—The Art of Radical Experiences:
Upheaval, Crisis and Insight

Four Storms: True Confessions of an Insurance Adjuster

~Soon to be released~

The Magpie Chronicles

The Buddha and the Whale

Roger

Weavers

BITTER MEDICINE
The Challenge of Immaturity in the Modern American Male

RICH JEWETT MA

CONTENTS

DEDICATION

For Pamela, the light of my life.

PREFACE

All living things
contain a measure of madness.
~Yann Martel, *The Life of Pi*

If you have the courage to touch life for the first time,
you will never know what hit you.
~U.G. Krishnamurti

This is a book about choice, very tough choices at that. Moreover, it's a book by and about men, about the choices we so typically fail to make, and the price we pay for that failure. Considering the amount of literature hitting the market concerning women's issues, it has become painfully obvious that there's something missing for the male side. But then personal growth books are generally criticized for being too simplistic, and for good reason, although the best any one book or point of view can ever do is to provide one small piece of a very complex puzzle.

One incentive here is that while we see women seeking to improve their lives, we see so little available specifically for men; the men's movement seems to have little life left in it, not that it ever had much to begin with, to tell a painful truth. And to reverse the genders in a comment by Simone de Beauvoir, no one is born a man. The challenge is to become one.

Women have justifiably complained that men have for generations tried to dictate how girls are supposed to be raised accordingly to male notions, pathologizing female instincts, and the last few decades have seen female psychologist and psychotherapists coming forward voicing important concerns. But then we see books written by women advising parents how to raise boys, advising men on how to maintain their relationships, even on how to be sexual, and it leaves men facing what women have had to deal with for so long, namely a lack of adequate representation.

In general, men haven't had the same incentives toward personal growth that women have had in the last half century, partly because so many self-development trends are not especially well attuned to the male experience, causing men to see the notion of personal growth as irrelevant, if not just plain silly—men who focus on all that nonsense are seen as whiners and wimps, and as someone who has been a part of the psychotherapy/self-help arena, I can understand all too well why. In many ways, the therapy subculture has become a parody of itself, and the scenes we sometimes see in TV sitcoms are often excruciating to anyone familiar with the profession.

Yet there are important challenges for men, but there's an unfortunate trend in contemporary culture to disregard those challenges, hence the theme of this book. For my title to this book, I draw from a dialogue that took place in eighteenth century philosophy in which one argument affirmed a trivial truth of sorts that humans are motivated to avoid discomfort and seek pleasure (anticipating Freud by a long shot), only to provoke the response that a reasoning adult sometimes needs to be willing to take a bitter tasting medicine to cure an illness. In other words, while a child can focus only on immediate gratification (*Eeeeww! That's yucky!*), a mature person will tolerate discomfort in order to heal, to grow, to learn, to earn, to achieve, to improve their lot in life, or simply to do what needs to be done.

What we don't anticipate as children is that we've stepped (or crawled) onto a steep and difficult learning curve with no real idea of what we're facing. And there's no user's manual, no Quick Start guide, though many claim with great certainty to have one.

For all the notions we hear of personal change in the psychotherapy and self-actualization arena, sometimes our lives change dramatically, and we don't quite know how. For example, the famous psychiatrist Milton Erickson describes a young man in a rural community who'd gained a reputation as the town delinquent until the day he asked a girl to a dance. She replied that, yes, she'd go with him, but only if he'd be a gentleman, and that's all it took. His anti-social behavior ended, things he'd stolen showed up on people's doorsteps, and the young man went on to marry the girl and become a community leader. All it took was something he wanted more than being a punk.

In another example, a homeless man came to Erickson saying he didn't have any money for therapy, but didn't want to go on sleeping in a drainage ditch, having anonymous sex with other men while living on trash and alcohol. And with consistent small challenges, each a bit more difficult than the last, Erickson provided him a ladder to pull himself up with until he'd engaged with the world around him instead of living as an outcast in a ditch.

A large part of feeling that we're stuck in bad places in life is a feeling that we have no other choices. But that's a feeling rooted in fixed notions about ourselves, about others, and about life itself, and the major point of this book, then, is to bring to light how we rigidify our those notions and find choices we didn't know we had.

We're all good at justifying and explaining our stance in life, but rather than consistently trying to prove ourselves right for being the way we are, life challenges us to reach for something better, at which our psyches will surprise us by finding ways to get there. No matter what we may think about ourselves and what others may tell us about ourselves, we are extraordinarily resourceful, creative beings, and can surprise ourselves when we let our creativity come through.

And this isn't a matter of pointing out how we do things wrong. Rather, it's a matter of pointing out challenges we all face, for it's difficult to change without seeing what it is that needs changing. So, the thrust of this book, while it can be seen as critical, even accusatory, is to lay out the invisible challenges that lay before us just by being born into this life. The moment we take our first breath we step onto that steep, complex learning curve, and if we insist on holding onto a place on that learning curve appropriate for a younger person, we are likely to insist that life itself is somehow wrong. The bitter medicine, then, is in facing how life demands of us things we often don't want to deal with, and we are capable of fighting to defeat those demands without realizing we are defeating ourselves.

So, the purpose of this book isn't to tell anyone how to live their lives. Rather, it's about laying out the challenges that have confronted us all right from the start, challenges most of us foibled human beings would rather avoid.

T.S. Elliot once said humanity has trouble bearing too much hard reality, and we all learn ways of trying to evade difficulties. I have on my refrigerator an old Gahan Wilson cartoon in which two Zen monks, one old, one young, are sitting side by side, the younger with a distinctly worried look about him. And the older one is saying, *Nothing happens next. This is it.* And that's what we're all facing: the simple realities we've so often avoided dealing with. It goes against so many popular notions by implying that spiritual enlightenment is simply a matter of getting what's here, not what we want to be here; that wherever we are, this is it.

Freud, with his characteristic obsession, called this a conflict between the pleasure principle and the reality principle, meaning essentially that we have to stop obsessing on sex in order to wash the dishes and mow the lawn. But it's more than that, for it's a conflict that increasingly characterizes contemporary culture where our advantages of education and technology put us further and further out of touch with some of life's most basic realities. So, there's a challenge to stop focusing on comfort and ease in order to deal with our lives in a mature manner, discovering in the process that our deepest experience of life typically starts at the edge of our comfort zone.

Considering Ronald Reagan's famous comment that problems can't be solved by government because government itself is the problem, it's more to the point that our most basic problems from individual to international ones result from our failure to deal with life's challenges in a responsible way. This even applies to the age-old religious question as to the nature of evil, because so much of what get labeled as "evil" results from behaviors rooted in childhood and infancy. Moreover, left to our own devices, many of us are too often likely to remain irresponsible, except when life itself forces us otherwise, just as a good government and good parenting do, or at least try to. Said a bit differently, it seems our psyches sense a pull of gravity that holds us to an early stage of development, and will go on doing so unless we take up the incentive to keep moving. But then we also feel an opposing sense of gravity that draws us forward, and the thrust of this work is to highlight this tug-of-war between opposites that many of us feel.

By necessity, my approach is deliberately one of seeing the glass as half-empty, and while it may seem like critical finger-pointing, my intention is to point at the basic challenges that lie before us all. One issue is that whenever we back away from those challenges, we generate all manner of problems not just for ourselves, but for the people around us, for if we don't learn to adequately carry our own lives, we'll put a burden someone else's, usually without bothering to notice, and typically blaming them for it. If that sounds harsh, it's because it needs to be, for we need to say things that need to be said without regard for politeness or political correctness.

The basic tone of this book can be stated fairly simply, that while we all grow up with entrenched attitudes, we're challenged to look beyond what's familiar to us and find greater possibilities. Otherwise, we'll try to make our lives work by doing more of what we've already been doing even when it has become clear that it doesn't work very well. Often what works, then, is to take up the opposite of our habits and assumptions about ourselves and others, even about life itself. At the very least, we're challenged to see how our habitual attitudes and expectations can undermine our lives, not because they're wrong, but because they fail to work so often. That can be a difficult challenge to take on because, despite our failings which are probably obvious to anyone around us, we'll have been justifying and explaining ourselves to ourselves for years. At the extreme end of things, this is what psychotic people babbling semi-coherently on park benches are doing—downloading and justifying their versions of reality. Yet it's something we all do in our own way, although our inner babble generally isn't quite so disorganized, and we usually don't put it on vocal except maybe when we're driving alone, waving one hand in the air. You might see it in the car in the next lane.

The heart of the challenge goes to the core of how we define ourselves, how we build the thing that calls itself "Me," and that means taking a hard look at how we will defend our "Me-ness" even when it means frustrating our own lives. And if it feels that we're being taken to task for being the way we are, it's simply that life itself takes us to task, often in disastrous ways.

Parallel to this is a curious element associated with the popular notions of mindfulness. This curious element is one that tells us our minds are often noisy because our life circumstances are somehow compelling us to face something we don't want to face, to learn something we don't want to learn, and we are internally babbling in order to maintain our habitual norm. By the same token, if we're not feeling grounded in our lives, our minds will be noisy, and we're so often not grounded in the moment because we're consistently making it more important to tell ourselves—and the world at large—why things are supposed to be different.

So, the parsing-out we'll be doing can feel hurtful to many of us, but the underlying challenge is to claim a deeper sense of identity, one that is not so threatened by self-examination. F. Scott Fitzgerald once commented that if we spend our lives protecting other people's feelings by nurturing their fragility and feeding their self-importance, we'll no longer be able to distinguish what truly deserves respect.

Good manners, he writes, "is an admission that everyone is so tender that they have to be handled with gloves." He may have been talking about his wife, Zelda, among others, yet it says a good deal about how notions of political correctness can go so seriously awry, for people afraid of having to face up to their own lives will use it to justify an attitude we see all too often: *I have rights, you don't, and you're not allowed to say anything I don't want to hear.*

This is why it's sometimes important to look at the most extreme cases, because they demonstrate nuances that we all have, at least to a lesser degree. Seeing someone acting out a worse example of something we do ourselves can go a long way toward compelling us to improve our lot.

For all this, I respect the underlying goodness in humanity, but have to recognize how readily that goodness is thwarted by childish self-interest, even when we are convinced that we're operating for the highest good. And I can't help but think of one of Buddhist scholar Alexandra David-Neel's more cynical comments that "the great god of this world is imbecility."

There's a stark mirror presented in the Greek tragedy, *Oedipus Rex*, which, aside from Freud's rendering, presents us with faults we all share and the seemingly inevitable fate to which we seem doomed despite our best efforts—a fairly common theme in Greek tragedy. When all is said and done, we really are a rather mad lot, mad and a bit daft much of the time, and there's more than enough pain, blame, and resentment to go around.

We all have the same basic underlying faults, and we're all challenged to face both the misery we cause each other and the misery we cause ourselves—misery we generally love to blame on everyone else. Above all, we're challenged to understand that it's all grist for the mill, for without that perspective, this book will just become an excuse to treat others as human punching bags, priding ourselves in pointing out everyone else's faults while failing to face our own.

Alfred Adler said that we are both the painting and painter of our own lives, and there comes a time to get it how we grew up creating our lives while thinking they've been created for us by circumstances. When we're young, though, it's typically difficult to know we have choices available to us, so it's only when we've gained enough experience in life that we can gain a broader perspective on how we've been creating our lives and question the assumptions we've been making about ourselves, others and life at large.

And that's not easy, for it takes a high degree of ruthless honesty with ourselves, and it takes the willingness to dig deep. So, this is to be a vigorous stirring of the stewpot, and it's not meant to be likeable. Even I don't like this book, but I write it both as a way of reporting from the trenches, and as a matter of psychological archeology in search of fossils we all carry buried under layers of detritus; as a way of bringing things to light and making the invisible obvious. It's a matter of unraveling the nature of this thing that everywhere calls itself 'Me,' and there seems no way of doing that without being rather blunt.

One of the primary notions in Adlerian coaching is that the client, the "coachee," has to come up with their own solutions, but when we're immersed in our own lives it's often difficult to know what the issues are, how we've undermined our own lives without some way of dredging up some very deep issues. In other words, to make deep changes, we need to shine a strong light on what it is that needs to be changed, on where the stumbling blocks are. While it's said in leadership circles that it's more important to be a problem solver than a problem identifier, the issue here is that the problems are so deeply immersed in our culture and in our personal psyches that identifying them becomes of supreme importance: we need to see just how stuck we are before we can recognize how badly we need to get unstuck. Otherwise our attempts to solve cultural or personal issues will simply miss the mark, for we'll tend to aim at false targets. At the very least, it requires making some stark assessments of the humanity in which we all participate, for otherwise we're left fighting invisible opponents and bleeding from invisible wounds as we obliviously wound those around us.

Humanity, after all, is possessed of a magnificent madness that both enthralls and infuriates us. But then, to paraphrase that famous comment from Lord Acton, few ideas are as annoying as those that reveal the origins of our most precious notions. And many of those most precious notions stem from early childhood where we're trying to leave behind the amorphous blur of infancy to form a sense of identity all our own. That can have us feeling like we've been thrown into the deep end of the pool without knowing how to swim, left to thrash about trying to work thing out.

But no one tells us it's that thrashing about in the deep end that grows us up, and there's usually no one who can truly tell us how to do it, although they may try. Then, as Nathaniel Hawthorne once said, we have to experience a great loss, a great sadness at some point in life, a thing that will seem impossible to a child, and will seem impossibly wrong to the mind of a child living in an adult body. That's why we generally resist and resent the most important lessons life presents to us—it's one thing to resist and resent the adult world when we're kids, quite another to fight against the demands of life itself as adults, for fighting that battle will cost us any chance of having an authentic self.

One thing life confronts us with as we age is the challenge to look back and realize just how little we'd really known and understood in our younger years, despite our glowing pride in ourselves. It comes down to a matter of tearing the bandages away from some very old wounds, as this seems the only way for us to see each other honestly and equally, each of us bleeding in equal measure. And it comes down to laying out a full spectrum of human experience rather than assuming that our personal stance somehow defines life for the entire human race. Otherwise, things degenerate to where we're sticking knives into everyone else's soft underbelly while shielding our own.

This motif, of exposing some of the most basic underlying human dynamics that affect us all, will predominate throughout this work. We spend a good deal of time right from infancy simply trying to figure things out, only to move into early adulthood at least slightly bewildered by the world in which we find ourselves. But some of us want to go on as if we are still dependent children, some of us determining early on to rule everything and everyone in sight, others of us living as if dreading being assimilated by the Borg, perhaps imagining ourselves going down in a blaze of gunfire like Al Pacino in *Scarface*, raging against a world that's out to get us. And remember Roger Daltrey singing, "I hope I die before I get old?" Well, Roger...

So, we have to spread all the cards out on the table and take a hard look at things we don't like to see about ourselves, starting with the ten thousand small ways we all have of annoying each other to the profoundly atrocious things we are capable of. We love to see things like that in others, of course, but not ourselves, yet for all its grand notions about itself, humanity has been continually compelled to stare into the face of its own propensity for violence, depravity, obliviousness and irrationality, as well as its tendency to act like stampeding wildebeest, or like lemmings seeking a cliff.

I recall a TV show I saw as a kid called *The Cheaters* in which a mad scientist had created a pair of glasses through which other people were seen 'as they really are,' a variety of characters using them to generally dastardly effect. The opening scene, though, was of their creator making the fatal mistake of trying on his new specs (it was a dark and stormy night) and looking in a mirror, at which, screaming quite wonderfully, he tried to rip his face off with his fingernails.

For all our grand philosophies, the human psyche carries a deep dread of seeing itself, a fear of discovering some unknowable horror lurking there, yet that's the challenge we're confronted with, to put on those magic glasses and look in the mirror until we're strong enough not to be shattered by the experience.

Moreover, the question I have to ask is how much of the anxiety that TV show generated in me was due to my fear of seeing things about myself, and how much was the fear of other people at being seen. I had, after all, two grandmothers and a mother who had deep fears of being seen too deeply.

So, there's also the challenge to confront the common notion that: *I get to pick you apart and analyze you, but don't you dare try to do it to me!* Humanity is simultaneously a glorious, curious, frustrating and heartbreaking affair, one in which we are all afflicted with a form of what has been termed 'inattentional blindness,' making ourselves selectively blind to things that violate our personal sense of reality. And for all our philosophical notions, we can all be terribly persistent in undermining our own lives while blaming others, which is why it has been said that if people could sort out whose job was whose, most therapists would be out of a job.

That single piece lies at the heart of this book, requiring us to ask how we can truly take responsibility for our own lives. Yet that's only one of the many ways we distort our experience of simply being here, for it would seem that the most fundamental thing about life is simply that—to be here. The intention here is to expose humanity to itself, the challenge being to see our own part in the grand madness and do whatever we can to be more responsible, even if it means screaming in horror for a time.

This seems the only sure way to truly 'get' humanity whilst

stumbling about in the midst of it, gaining the personal strength to deal with the darker nature of this thing of which we're all a part, and to become mature enough to bear up to it with understanding and authentic compassion.

And there's really nothing new about any of this. The current issue, though, is that there seems to be something about modern culture with all its technological and economic development that undermines us. This makes modern life more of a conundrum than ever, a problem without a solution, and every attempted solution seems to create other problems. An obvious example is the environmental degradation our technological development has created, while we seem always ready to accept just a little bit more pollution, just a little more mess.

We are also presented with some basic questions as to how much of our character is a result of the way we were (or were not) nurtured as children, how much is a part of our inherent nature or our genes, and how much is a matter of our personal will to become the person we choose to be. There's really no solid answer to any of it, only a suggestion that we're subject to all three: nature, nurture, and personal will.

There's an old saying that life isn't about playing with a good hand, but rather about playing well with a poor one. Taking the notion a bit further, every emotional wound that we have taken on is a potential lesson, an obscure gift of sorts, so while much of life may feel like running a gauntlet, it's also what Stephen King describes as that "dark and unpredictable pool..." where we are challenged like fishermen to "go out to where the big ones swim."

That goes against the grain of many of the attitudes we find both in psychotherapy and contemporary spirituality where the hope is to recreate our lives as if all those painful things had never happened. Instead, it's the gauntlet with all its slings and arrows and bloody cudgels that is our greatest teacher.

A strong statement about affluent culture comes from the travel writer, Paul Theroux, in commenting on tourists so sheltered and naïve that they talk about the places they've been as if they've been sightseeing on another planet. Luxury, he says, infantilizes us, preventing us from seeing the world around us clearly, and that's a comment that can be equally made about many current notions of philosophy and self-actualization. Yet we all have a tendency to seek luxury to shield us from hard reality, and Western culture in general has been accused of all this and more, that we have all been infantilized by technology and luxury, and as someone who once spent a bit too much time around the New Age/personal development/spiritual seeker scene, I find a parallel in that far too many therapists, spiritual teachers and personal growth facilitators carry that same stamp of naïveté while posing as authorities in a life they don't comprehend anywhere near as well as they would like to think they do.

At times I wonder what it would be like for a Martian anthropologist observing human behavior, asking what in the world all these lunatic Earthlings are up to. It brings to mind Arthur C. Clarke's novel, *Childhood's End*, in which an alien race takes over Earth, declaring an end to all this human nonsense, and when two countries go to war with one another, the aliens turn their capital cities into ashtrays: *What didn't you understand about the word, "No!"?* Then there's the 'Prime Directive' from the old *Star Trek* television series where they are to observe other cultures without interfering. Some of us, though, might look up into the night skies wondering, *Won't someone please come down and interfere with us just this once?*

Conflict can make for higher-quality decisions, and the conflicts I'll be highlighting here carry the potential to make for a higher-quality appreciation of the challenges we all encounter rather than trying to gloss things over with philosophical platitudes. But the mature ability to face life in its most basic terms seems to be diminishing in contemporary Western culture, as demonstrated in a National Public Radio piece (aired in December, 2010) asking if narcissism isn't simply the new norm. Well, if it is, we're in serious trouble. Martin Kihn, in his book, *A$$hole*, quotes a study indicating that our culture has become more Machiavellian, and that's even more trouble.

While I don't feel qualified to speak about the female side of things, I can talk about the failure of boys to become men in a culture that seems driven to escape so many of life's most basic realities. This, though, is one of those themes where it's more important to face the questions than it is to have hard answers. John Steinbeck wrote that to be a man is to be half mad-half god, that it's only women's balancing influence that keeps a man from destroying himself; that while men may complain about hectoring women, a great many of them live lives that demonstrate just how much they need hectoring.

Then there's Athena famously berating Telemachus in the *Odyssey*, telling him he's no longer a boy, and that it's time for him to go looking for his long-missing father. And that's what we're all challenged to do, to look for the mature male within us rather than living as a mad gods, doomed perhaps to living wasted lives.

And Now For The Good News…

One complaint this work is bound to generate is that it focuses too much on issues and not enough on solutions. My first response is that clarifying the issues is necessary before we can gain any further insight into the lives we lead. Then, when we've gained enough insight into what has been right in front of us all along, we can start making new choices about our lives, for we can't make new choices if we can't clearly see the ground we've been standing on all along.

A greater objection is that many of us long to hear positive, uplifting messages about the human spirit and great spiritual truths to lift us out of the general human drudgery, and considering the deeply-troubled lives many of us live, that makes sense, especially if the best we can manage is baby steps. The difficulty is that the market for uplifting messages can keep us stuck in feeling good about being limited in the same old ways, while the intention here is to highlight ways we all have of limiting our lives.

Scenarios dubbed "LGATs" (large group awareness trainings) like Landmark Forum (originally EST) and Life Spring have held the same intention, although their methodologies have been questioned. What is significant about the LGAT appeal, nonetheless, is that many of us come to a point in life where we long to step out from behind our masks and be honest about ourselves and the lives we've been living. That can be both liberating and a bit excruciating, for after having stumbled through life long enough we come to a point where we realize we have to do something different. To put it perhaps a bit too poetically, what can seem at first to be dark and negative can in the long run turn out to be ultimately positive and filled with light while what had initially looked to be positive and light-filled can seem oppressive, even delusional.

The challenges can be daunting to say the least, yet the

assumption I hold is that we are all capable and resourceful, and when presented with the proper challenges, can rise to the occasion when called upon. It's just that we tend to not see the challenges and not recognize the call. This work, then, is a calling out to us all, and yes, we handle it. Moreover, so much of the helplessness we humans feel, aside from dire physical circumstances, is due to our not knowing how or what to change in ourselves, and this is the point of this book.

CHAPTER ONE

~BOYS~

Lather was thirty years old today,
they took away all of his toys...
~Grace Slick, *Lather*

Kid can't read at seventeen,
the words he knows are all obscene...
~Rob<u>ert</u> Hunter, *Touch of Grey*

We can see examples every day. We see a young man moving swiftly, gracefully down a city street, sallow skin embellished with tribal markings, silver body piercings and tattooed images of mystical power showing his individuality and his defiance of all those deadening demands of society. Music pounds through his ear buds, his body pulsing with the raw power of rage and electric guitars. He wears his cap turned backwards to demonstrate, like millions of others, his uniqueness, wears oversized clothes, pants that slide down over his hips and sweatshirts that come down over his hands as if to say: *See? I'm just a little guy.* He will bow to no authority, for he's an artist, a magician, a mystic warrior as—riding his skateboard like a god—he conquers pavement by the yard, tearing along with the emotional makeup of a twelve-year-old although he's actually twenty-seven.

We see another young man at his computer. He's accomplished at this, moves with precision and competence; in fact, he's something of a genius at it. His expertise fills him with a sense of raw power and pride that makes him feel he has exceeded mere humanity, rising above the foolishness that burdens the common dross, rising perhaps toward immortality. What he's doing is playing a computer game. He plays a lot of computer games. The cyber world he lives in is one of magic and power while the one outside his door baffles, overwhelms, and frightens him until he can regard it only with hostility, resentment, and rage. So, he closes the door and boots up, immersing himself all over again in Wonderland.

Then there's the thirty-five-year-old who has quit his job and moved back in with his folks, a classic 'boomerang child' lazing around in his childhood bedroom, brooding, getting stoned, and basically quitting everything, complaining that his last boss had been an asshole, expecting him to work like a dog for next to nothing, and the landlord had been a greedy son of a bitch who expected to be paid rent *every month for God's sake!* But he'd gotten even in the end by trashing the place before he left. Bastard had deserved it, hadn't he?

We see yet another man sitting with poise, seemingly absorbed in blissful meditation, although he's actually absorbed in a movie playing inside his head—a drama of which he's the unsurpassed hero. But it'll pass for meditation because it's so uplifting, and he smiles beatifically at the joy of it. He lives in a spiritual community where he gets to play an influential role if only because of the metaphysical teachings about which he can speak authoritatively for hours on end. He can go on and on about spiritual relationships and sacred sexuality although his own relationships last on average about three months, and most of his former partners didn't consider him especially good in bed, should the truth be told. And if his partner of the moment has a child, he will jealously compete for the mother's attention, for when confronted with it, he's overwhelmed by the challenge of parenting. He can work within a communal environment, but can't hold a job outside of it, and while the women in the community love his gentle, spiritual demeanor, other men steer away from his complaining, his manipulation, and his occasional tantrums.

Then there's the punk raging along in a battered heap of a car, the young tough in his oversized pickup, the suave dude in his muscle car, attacking the rear bumpers of other cars on the highway, lurching with theatrical stabs at the brakes and swerving back and forth in a rage because the guy ahead is only going ten miles an hour over the speed limit. And when he finally gets a chance to pass, it's not enough just to pull into the next lane. Instead, he has to charge straight at the car ahead, cutting within a foot or two of the nearest taillight like throwing a punch at the other guy's head only to pull it at the last second. Well, hey, those NASCAR guys do it all the time, don't they? So, when we see the right headlight on his car punched in, we can pretty well guess how he did that. Then, as he blasts on by, we see his hand out the window making the same middle finger gesture as the decal on his rear window. It's his mantra, raging *Fuck you!* at every other car on the road, at people on the streets, at his parents, the police, his boss, at women in general, even at his friends. Or he'll have one of those decals on the rear window of a kid urinating on anyone who defies his chronic tantrum against the world. When the local team wins the big game, he's the guy who throws a rock through a window and overturns a car, and when he sees someone outdoors using a cell phone, he'll lean on his horn as he goes by just to get them. And any woman he touches gets to taste the same contempt. What the hell's she worth, anyway? Why won't she just shut up and put out like she's supposed to?

Well, easy as it is to pick on the obvious punks, next we get to look at someone who is held in high regard, at least in some circles— a psychotherapist dedicated to the emotional healing and well-being of others. He speaks earnestly of living by one's personal truths, of living without limits, of openness and honesty, of reaching for the stars, yet those familiar with him know him to be smug, manipulative, self-righteous, and intolerant. He feels he has the answers that others lack, and can't help but hold a slight air of contempt. His therapeutic approach is his religion and he preaches it like a true believer, sometimes striking out at the infidel, ridiculing anyone with differing notions. He loves having authority over others' emotional 'process,' thrilling at being indispensable to others' lives, although his own relationships are a mess. Clients who struggle with their careers seek his guidance, although he knows very little about careers in general, his own being based on others' belief that they need him. He lives, after all, in a therapy-oriented culture without which he'd be helpless, and he privately fears his work is worthless, which it may well be. At best he may help people deal with a few issues while inflicting on them yet another—that of their dependency upon people like him.

Then there's the guy with his Lexus and his Armani suit, his $300 shoes and his Rolex, making a couple hundred grand a year selling himself, talking circles around the best of them, manipulating everyone like the pro that he is. He knows how to act like your best friend, like he has only your best interests at heart while secretly looking on you with a mild sense of scorn, and he can take you so cleanly that you'll never know you've been taken until it's too late. What he keeps hidden under his seductive glitz is that he's only out to make the next score, to slam his next sale, to carve the next notch in his gun. In college he'd styled himself as something of a playboy, and hadn't been above helping a young woman be a little more cooperative with a little something slipped into her drink. Date rape? Yeah, that's what those feminist bitches call it, but these days he only needs money and influence as an aphrodisiac. If he were in college today he'd be joining those guys chanting, "*No means yes!*" and "*No means anal!*" (meaning that "No" only means no to vaginal sex). After all, how dare some stupid little slut fail to give him what he wants. When we look around his office or home, we see a tasteful clutter of executive toys, expensive sound systems, trinkets and knickknacks from Hammacher-Schlemmer and The Sharper Image, and he treats everyone else, anyone not a customer or a woman he's trying to hustle, with casual disdain. And why should he be satisfied with a mere four thousand square foot house? Just look at the twelve thousand square foot castle the CEO has. Why not go for it all? And the CEO is likely just as bad. Consider the infamous boss who drove around his employees as they sat in a traffic jam leaving work, flipping them all 'the bird' as he went by. But that was before he was sent to prison for fraud in which he'd helped destroy his employees' pension funds along with the rest of the company.

We could go on. Overall, there's a trend in which more and more men at all levels of society are moving into adulthood with the expectations and sense of entitlement we normally find in young boys. They are boyish in their expectations of how they are to be treated by others, in their expectations of what they are supposed to have and in what they're allowed to get away with, and they live in a culture that has reinforced this thinking. We see it in the bumper stickers that stare back at us in traffic:

Yield to the princess!
Don't like the way I drive? Call 1-800-EAT-SHIT
As a matter of fact, I do own the road
It really is all about me!
Cowboy foreplay: Get in the truck!
I wanna be like Barbie. That bitch has everything!
Do I look like someone who cares?
So many things to do, so few people to do them for me
Never underestimate the power of a hissy fit
Or this on the back of an expensive SUV: Saw it, asked for it,

threw a fit, got it!

Then there's the Verizon ad declaring, *Get ready to rule the world!* Really? With just a cell phone?

Sure, they're just jokes, but then again, they're not, for they represent a childishly narcissistic view of the world. And some people will brag about getting their way by intimidating others with childish tantrums: *See how infantile I am? Isn't it great?* Worse is the bumper sticker for skateboarders: "Proudly annoying pedestrians for twenty years," leaving the rest of us wondering how anyone could be so (expletive deleted) stupid? Well, the answer is that that's the way we're prone to be when our psyches are too underdeveloped to know anything but our own impulses: unable to get it, able only to defend our obliviousness with childish spite against the rest of the world that expects us to pay attention. Yet, we've all done that a time or two before we'd grown up enough to realize our impact on others.

We see these attitudes in the road rage that has become an everyday experience, and we see it in TV ads where lawyers reassure us what victims we are when we get DUIs or don't pay our taxes. When I first moved to the Rocky Mountains, slow drivers on a twisting road would pull aside to let others by, what we used to call 'mountain etiquette,' but those days are gone, although I still see old timers moving over like that in west Texas where city instincts haven't gotten to them yet. And while it used to be that a person driving through a parking lot would stop for car backing out, now they're more likely to simply bully their way past with a *Fuck you* attitude. We see it in the salesman who justifies his manipulative tactics, we see it in the developer who treats an entire community with scorn as he trashes their environment, and we see it in corporate attitudes that see profit as the only goal, and to hell with the consequences. We hear how rape has become a major issue on college campuses, and we hear computer hackers philosophize that any software or music out there should be free to him, no matter the work and expense someone else had to put into creating it. We see it in the everyday insurance fraud that's only a little white lie or two, and we see it in the multi-millionaire executive who runs a corporation into the ground, then walks away with a fortune in real estate and luxury toys. We hear it from the car thief saying he needs that guy's Porsche more than its selfish owner does, and we hear it in the college grad interviewing for his first career position, refusing to do a half dozen things that are part of the job description, then throwing a fit when he doesn't get hired. We hear it in the idealism of people who've hardly worked a day in their lives, yet are convinced they have all the answers to life's problems, and we see it in people everywhere indignant at the expectation that they should do anything besides getting a handout.

As the old saying goes, some of us grow up while some of us only grow older. One of the sad things about the Woodstock generation (of which I'm a part) is that ex-hippies were declaring twenty and thirty years ago that, because they were such spiritual people, their children would be the most enlightened generation the world had ever seen. Sadly, though, many of their kids have been deeply damaged by parents who are themselves little more than children, resulting in a generation of marginally functional kids being labeled 'Indigo Children' as a way of explaining their pathology with metaphysics.

Now we see Jean M. Twenge's *Generation Me (Why Today's Young Americans Are More Confident, Assertive, Entitled—And More Miserable Than Ever Before)*, describing the narcissism carried by the current population of twenty- and thirty-somethings, and Tina Fey has complained about how terrible it is to constantly tell children how special they are because that's the way they already think. So now men in their late thirties talk about how they've had to struggle to face an adult world that expects them to prove themselves.

But I have to question Twenge's subtitle, for those notions of confidence and assertiveness seem a flimsy mask disguising the incompetence and brazen narcissism of an immature psyche trying to fake it. And that degree of entitlement almost always leads to misery, although it typically first goes to rage until a person learns that chronic outrage doesn't really get them anywhere.

Well, all civilizations have their slips showing to some extent, but the Woodstock Generation, the Generation X-ers and the Gen Me-ers have all had to face the challenge of moving into adulthood without adequate tools for dealing with it, full of grand notions about how wrong the world is for being the way it is, but with little ability to do much of anything constructive. And each generation has its collection of anti-incentives, its ways of justifying avoiding the challenges life throws at us all.

Yes, there are many from those age groups who have met those challenges, yet we generally don't see this degree of immaturity in other countries, implying something dire about the culture we've created for ourselves, and of which we're all a part. Nor do we typically see in other cultures such a high percentage of people struggling so hard for a sense of identity, feeling driven to extremes of dress and decoration in an attempt to fulfill on the outside what they are missing on the inside. Moreover, the Woodstock generation and the generations since are challenged to look back and see how they had embraced some fairly serious pathology at times, mistaking it for cosmic awareness or rebellion against injustice and oppression. We hear it in rock lyrics like the song that whines: "Despite my rage, I'm still just a rat in a cage!", the irony being that wallowing in adolescent rage will build that cage around us more than anything the rest of the world can do to us.

The fact that we generally don't see kids outside the technologically developed nations going to such extremes in an attempt to find a sense of identity leaves us to ask whether modern culture doesn't somehow leave us internally disjointed. More disturbing is the lyric (from a Nine Inch Nails song) about a young man deliberately hurting himself to assure himself he can still feel, a mentality we also find in tattooing and body-piercing where people speak of wanting another jolt of pain to make them feel more alive. Now we see young teens sharing over the internet how to cut themselves and how to perform 'suicide gestures' that are sure to get attention without actually killing themselves.

Maybe it's the lack of hard work that leaves kids feeling so numb, for no one who has raised honest blisters will feel a need for a pain fix. What's especially disturbing, though, is that self-inflicted harm is typical of the borderline personality disorder, characterizing an adult with the emotional development of an insecure child, and when that dynamic shows up on a large scale, when it's taken for granted by a sizeable portion of the population, it implies something grave for the health of the culture at large.

While it's fairly common for teenagers to go through a borderline-like period during which they feel overwhelmed by the basic challenges of life, having it show up in adults is a serious concern. Whether this is the result of their having been faced as children with stressors too great to handle, or if it's the result of not being provided enough psychological resources to grow into adulthood, seeing so many adults feeling compelled to back away from adulthood is disturbing.

There's also a disconcerting tendency for sociopathic tendencies to be taken for granted. Joseph Campbell, for example, commented how it was shortly after World War II that it became common to go to the library to look up a book only to find it had been stolen. And it was not that long ago that it was common to do business with a handshake while now we find electronic scanners everywhere, metal detectors in schools, security guards in supermarkets and libraries, and business is conducted with complex contracts that take a lawyer to understand. Criminal behavior is becoming an accepted norm to the extent that public restrooms, telephones, and postboxes are rare due to wanton vandalism, and when challenged, teenagers shrug off their police records saying that they'd only been hauled in five or six times, which is no big deal. Then we hear halfway-house counselors refusing to work with teens because so many of them figure, hey, why not kill the guy who pisses you off? It's only five years with good behavior, if even that. Besides, you get fed for free and don't have to work a lick.

All this has been a part of humanity throughout recorded history, as in the oft-quoted line from Socrates about children being obnoxious, disrespectful tyrants, but it seems a far greater tendency these days. There's an equally ancient admonition that children need to learn seemliness and that adolescents need to learn self-control—notions that modern culture doesn't seem to support very well.

And while every generation has had its issues with lingering immaturity (it's a theme in Greek mythology, such as in the legend of Icarus), it seems kids who went through high school only five years ahead of my class were more mature than we were. Is there, as many suggest, a worldwide trend for young adults in greater numbers to remain stuck as belligerent, resentful children with the expectation that they're supposed to be catered to instead of learning to carry their own weight? Do these children truly expect that they have a right to wreak revenge on anyone who fails to give them whatever they want as they try to force the adult world into compliance with their demands?

More importantly, we need to ask what it is about our culture that fails its young so drastically, for the punk, the crass manipulator, the aimless, and the shiftless have become that way largely as a product of their environment, for while there are individual differences, overall trends demonstrate our culture's failure to raise its young in realistic ways. And it's ironic that the problem shows up at its worst in the most affluent cultures, just as it's ironic that the well-off become anorexic or bulimic while others starve because they have no choice.

An adult with attitudes normal for a child is likely to carry deep-seated anxieties that emerge as rage, smugness, and a manipulative sense of entitlement. All that in turn is likely to cause him to see the world at large as an enemy while convincing him that mature behavior is somehow wrong, even stupid. The formal term is 'neotony,' meaning an adult of a species showing juvenile behavior (dogs, for example, can be seen as neotonic wolves), and we humans are particularly challenged because our physical and emotional development is so prolonged.

While luxury, ease, and technology tend to infantilize us, it has also been said that a culture that prizes its privileges more than its values will soon lose both. So, is it inherent in human life that we are compelled to undermine our emotional development as we improve our lot in life, and that we are compelled to feel so stubbornly self-righteous about it?

Our subject, then, is an unraveling of the ways we cling so aggressively to the very things that undermine us, for in order to know how to repair things, we have to know what to repair, especially when it comes to things we take for granted about ourselves and about life in general.

A Late Note:

During my most recent revisions to *Bitter Medicine*, I've found it important to address the current divisions in US society that, although rooted in long-term issues, have become exaggerated since the election of Donald Trump. Politics aside, we see Trump stating (in *The Art of the Deal*), that if you say something long enough, others will believe it. But while it's one thing to push a political agenda or a sales pitch that way, the dislocation in contemporary society is no longer about opinions, politics or personal agendas. Rather, it has become about how we determine what reality is.

It's common enough when we are young to assume that our personal reality is the only reality, and most of us move off that position as we engage in the world around us, experiencing wider and deeper aspects of this life we all share. Otherwise, we're likely to drift toward attitudes saying essentially: "If say it's true, then it's true and you shut up about it. And if I say it's not true, then it's not, and you shut up about it!"

While that attitude feeds the popularity of conspiracy theories, the issue revolves not so much around conspiracy theories in themselves as around the chronic suspicion, distrust, fear, gullibility and outright paranoia that drives people to believe them. Why are so many of us drawn to assume that some faceless "They" are out to deceive, abuse and control us all? It's well-understood why an individual would promote suspicion and fear, but as with cult figures throughout history, we have to wonder why others are drawn to follow them. And why do people who believe those theories tend to sound like the "sheeple" they say the rest of us are: *You know that earthquake that happened? They set off a nuclear warhead down in the fault line. We have proof. Why did that hurricane hit land? They seeded the clouds and forced it to change course. We have proof.* Then there's COVID-19 which didn't really exist although They wanted us to believe in it in order to control us, but, wait a minute, it is real and They created it to cull the human race, then They created a vaccine to either kill us outright or turn us into mindless robots. We have proof. And the resulting superstitious outrage has subjected medical researchers and dedicated public servants to death threats for being minions of the Great They who are out to get us all.

While a wider and deeper life experience gives us the tools to get past the naivete, gullibility and magical thinking of childhood, an adult adhering to modern day superstitions is likely to dread too much intellectual understanding, too much science, too much curiosity, too much hard reality just as religious fundamentalist do.

And in holding to the magical thinking and limited perceptions, we are likely to confuse irrationality with reality because the feelings are so strong, confusing feelings with hard facts: I feel it's true, then it's real.

This was the rationale behind the Inquisition and the Salem witch trials, a medieval flavor based not on belief in a deity, but in a commonly-shared paranoia where belief matters more than hard facts. The theme has been called "Conspirituality," for it takes the place of religion for many. And those who grow up with chronic suspicion toward the world around them will, as adults, no longer call it fear—instead, they'll call it reality. And just like cult followers, they will abandon rational dialogue with society at large to create a culture where only their own version of logic applies.

By the same token, many who have grown up living in fantasy will eventually regard their fantasy world as fact, making the hardscrabble world an enemy that in some ways really is out to get them, for science, intellect, honest research and open dialogue are all seen as threats.

Overall, the trend represents a complex developmental failure, a failure of a person's psyche to come together adequately, and it seems one of the great culprits in contemporary society is the digital world, everything from social media to computer games. The problem isn't the computer world in itself, but rather how some of us get lost in it, taking it as their source of reality, a reality created out of imagination, and devoid of any physical experience. That makes for a self-referencing version of reality, one that relates only to itself, consistently validating itself.

An added aspect, especially in computer games is that there are layers upon layers going on at once, and we now find people in their thirties and forties whose sense of reality and sense of themselves is so nebulous that they have trouble dealing with a world that fails to be fluid and can't be changed with a click of a mouse. That can be a scary way of living, but then add the popular conspiracy notions and we have the *Matrix* film series where the reality we know is out to deceive and enslave us all.

In other words, this is the stance of wounded psyches trying to explain their versions of reality to themselves, trying to validate and justify their distorted experience of life. And in the irony typical of such things, for all their accusations, the conspiracy culture has produced more lies and outright fabrications than any other source we've seen outside of paranoid totalitarian governments, all with the intention of proving themselves right.

One quirk that has shown up throughout history is that we humans don't like uncertainty, and for some of us, the excitement of discovering hidden realities that explain what's "really going on" can compel us to run off down the garden path in pursuit of self-righteous feelings and revenge against a life we really don't understand, but are certain is out to torture us.

The overall picture is one of a breakdown of rationality and common sense in the most powerful, presumably most advanced country in the world, although a large segment of our culture is looking oddly questionable if not delusional. As we'll be discussing throughout this work, one great challenge in this life is to engage with the world, and that requires us to get out of our internal realities. Otherwise, we'll find ourselves at war not with a hidden elite who are out to oppress us, but with life itself, and with a world that demands that we pull our heads out of the magical thinking of childhood, out of the digital world, and out of superstitions that keep us trapped and enslaved in hells of our own creation.

Confessions

To be completely honest, I'm guilty of most of what I'll be describing here, for as kids say in grade school, it takes one to know one. Well, yes it does, and I have at one point or another done, thought, or at least felt just about everything I'll be speaking of here. And I really don't think I'm at all unique. It's just that most of us are better at hiding it all from ourselves, the great joke we play on ourselves being that while we think we're good at hiding it from others, we're never as good at it as we think we are. More to the point, the more we act out at others' expense, the more we reveal everything we don't want anyone to know about us, especially things we don't want to know about ourselves.

So, it takes someone who held onto adolescence far too long, to know what it's like to live inside that experience and address it first-hand. I remember growing up feeling strangely paralyzed, struggling in a world that was overwhelming, confusing and threatening, and I grew up almost pathologically shy, a trait too often interpreted as arrogance by people who profess to be loving and understanding while acting with arrogance of their own. Yes, there's that curious touch of sadism running through humanity under the guise of wisdom, love, insight, and spirituality, four of the most abused words in our language.

Then I got to discover that with time we can turn our wounds into deep understanding, for learning about ourselves teaches us deeply about the neuroses of the people who'd done all that damage to us way back when. In the end, any emotional wounding can lead to a deeper understanding of humanity if we go at it with clear-enough hindsight.

I'm also part of a generation determined to throw itself into that exciting territory where there are no rules or structure, only to have to learn the need for rules and structure. We heard the adult world (remember: *don't trust anyone over thirty?*) telling us how we thought the world owed us a living, while we in turn waxed eloquent with hippie philosophy that actually understood very little about much of anything. And it's not just in the US, for as British novelist Tony Parsons writes, his was the generation that, contrary to their hardworking war-worn parents, learned to "fuck around, fuck off, and fuck up," realizing too late just how badly they'd shot themselves in the foot. It was the parents and grandparents of that generation, by the way, who having survived the blitz, rationing, and threats of imminent invasion would say that happiness is an overrated emotion, not something we're likely to hear today.

We were also the generation that was to fall headlong into widespread drug use, convinced it was a grand consciousness-expanding adventure, while now we see a world torn apart with drug-related mayhem from the US and Europe to the jungles of Columbia and Southeast Asia. Marianne Faithfull once said that watching the ideals of the sixties degenerate into a drug-hazed oblivion was like a

Mahler symphony swirling out of control, while Bob Dylan compared it to *The Night of the Living Dead*. Yet it was Faithfull who said she'd had to find out just how far going too far was, a notion that a great many can understand. With the degree of social and individual disruption we see today, it's little wonder that so much pop art is full of disjointed, fragmented imagery expressing chronic horror, confusion, and despair.

Quite a few of us have had to look back and wonder just what the hell we were doing, finally understanding that what the hell we were doing was trying to cobble together an adequate sense of identity because our natural course of development had been so badly undermined. And in wandering out into the world to 'find ourselves' (as the tedious cliché goes), what we were actually looking for were experiences with which to mold ourselves, looking for ways to escape the soft pudding of our lives and find ways for the hardness of the world to work on us.

We hear the overall challenge in an old Joni Mitchell song, the challenge to shine a light on everything—the good, the awful, the wise, the foolish, the noble, the depraved—and it's a seventy- to ninety-year learning curve for most of us. I recall once hearing a music critic saying he disliked hearing Beethoven played by anyone under the age of forty because while they could get the notes right, they were too young to capture the depth of feeling. In much the same way, Hermann Hesse wrote in his preface to a later edition of *Steppenwolf* that while he appreciated that younger readers were drawn to his novel, he felt they were too under-experienced to understand it properly. Of course, we don't want to hear that when we're young, but there's nothing new in that either.

We all start out as children trying to learn how to be in the world, and fumbling around a good deal in the process. It's unfortunate, though, that many of us feel drawn to mold ourselves through extremes, feeling drawn to the seedier nooks and crannies of the human experience (listen, for example, to the lyrics of Tom Waits and John Hiatt), for while some of us seem to develop naturally enough, many of us have had to create our lives out of a combination of trial, error, and sheer tenacity, sometimes through serious mayhem. Yet it can be a fascinating learning experience to have to develop our adult self the hard way, perhaps fighting against our families to do so. The novels of W. Somerset Maugham come to mind. As one cliché goes, our greatest wounds become our greatest teachers and our greatest gifts, but not without effort, for life is a severe taskmaster.

It has been said before that what causes us pain isn't the burden life puts on us—"the burden of excessive sensibility" Lawrence Durrell called it—so much as our resistance to it. But then we all have such wonderful justifications for resisting and putting the blame somewhere else. So, this will involve some difficult confrontations with life, with ourselves and with each other, but anyone who has lived through a tough learning process carries a ultimately positive attitude toward it all: If we can do it, so can you. In this, I have to counter a literary marketplace full of uplifting messages telling us we are beings of light, children of a loving god and so on, for while all that may be true, we still have to do the human dance, still have to grow our way into this stupefying, often frustrating life. While one of those uplifting messages tells us that above every cloudy day is a bright blue sky, the truth is that above that bright blue sky we find the cold, sparkling abyss of deep space, and as Charles Beard once wrote, "When it is dark enough, you can see the stars."

CHAPTER TWO

~THE WAR AGAINST ADULTHOOD~

... oh, it makes me wild,
with thirty years upon my head
to have you call me 'child.'
~Robert Hunter, *Ship of Fools*

I'll never grow up, never grow up, never grow up
~Charlap & Leigh, from *Peter Pan*

As we get older and look back at our lives—our professional lives, our love lives, our spiritual lives—we'll often realize just how utterly foolish we'd been much of the time. Then when we try to tell younger people not to make the same mistakes, they just get angry because, after all, we're trying to tell them things we didn't want to hear either at that age. And when they get older, themselves, they'll also find, probably too late, some harsh truths just like the rest of us did. In general, if we're not at least slightly embarrassed by the person we used to be, we've probably missed something important.

Kids are always a challenge when it comes to teaching, but now we hear of teachers no longer willing to teach because of the arrogant, defiant attitudes, and the vulgar, insulting language they hear from students. While we hear of our schools' failure to teach, some say the attitude of students is a bigger problem, a sarcastic cliché being that for every teacher there are thirty students unwilling to learn, sitting there, thinking, *I ain't doin' nuthin', and you can't make me.* And they'll likely still be saying that twenty years from now when someone will interview them only to find they don't have a clue about important historical events or who Charles Lindbergh was: *Wasn't he president or something?* Or where is Ukraine? *Somewhere in South America, isn't it?* And if you point at a standard clock, the kind with hands (remember them?), and ask what time it is, they'll look at you like you're stupid.

There's a tragedy at work here, for it's natural for children to want to engage in the world around them, yet it seems there's now a strong tendency in far too many kids to retreat into a virtually autistic stubbornness. The standard rebuttal is that kids are only responding to their upbringing, or in the case of minorities that they've been so heavily burdened by prejudice and poverty that their ability and willingness to learn have been stunted, but kids at all socio-economic levels seem to be locking themselves into a self-defeating cycle. Pink Floyd had teenagers chanting, "We don't need no education," but anyone who believed it doomed himself to a life of stagnation until his own misery drove him to reevaluate things.

Still, students from places like Africa and Southeast Asia, kids who never got the message that it's supposed to be effortless, often do extraordinarily well no matter the difficulties, no matter the quality of the teachers. Whatever the problems with our educational system, the greater problem is a motivation gap, an ambition gap that could leave us all in the dust as countries like China, India, and South Korea outpace us.

Part of the problem is that many kids have no way of distinguishing between being taught information and skills they'll need on one hand, and what they see as oppression under adult tyranny on the other, assuming that schooling is simply designed to torture them. But human psyches need a sense of structure, which is why as small children we want to know the rules for the games we play, even if later on we go looking for ways to rebel and tell adults where they can stuff their expletive deleted rules.

In the late nineteenth and early twentieth centuries, John Dewey, C.C. Pierce, and William James, among others, promoted the notion that education should address a child's emotional needs as opposed to the traditional approach of treating children as defective adults and trying to force-feed them information. But while no one wants to be treated like a block of wood being run through the educational mill, the alternative methods are often criticized for producing kids who resist learning anything that isn't immediately gratifying, kids who expect that they don't have to do anything to earn rewards, resulting in adults who get angry when faced with anything that requires intelligent effort.

According to the anti-Dewey forces, if you give a child too many choices, he'll simply take the path of least effort, unaware of the price he'll eventually have to pay, resulting in kids so indoctrinated with unrealistic notions of self-esteem that they have little sense of responsibility, and little concern for the consequences of their behavior. That in turn inhibits a child's overall psychological development so severely that it results in less self-esteem in the long run, ultimately in an inability to deal with adult realities.

Norman Doidge in his *The Brain That Changes Itself* tells us how memorizing things like the Gettysburg Address or the Preamble of the Constitution, challenges kids typically hate, can develop our brains in significant ways. So, the kid who fights his education can be putting himself at a significant disadvantage in more ways than the obvious ones. Taken the other way around, easy tasks result in underdeveloped kids who then grow into angry teenagers and adults unaware of how they create for themselves so many of the things they are angry about.

To be fair, though, there have been improvements on the original Deweyesque thinking, approaches that are neither authoritarian nor overly permissive, and can give a child a much better footing in life. Of course, many kids thrive in any learning environment. Besides, the most important thing we can gain from our early schooling is to learn how to learn, just as the most important thing we gain from household chores is to learn how to work. And if we never gain those basic attitudes, life is likely to run us over like a cattle stampede while we lay there complaining about being victimized.

An August, 2005 report from the National Assessment of Educational Progress concludes that the reason so many test grades in American schools are so low isn't that American kids are stupid or undereducated, but that they're simply lazy. This was followed by a January, 2006 report in which an international study showed kids in the US performing well below their European counterparts, a finding reinforced by yet another study coming out a week later noting that 50% of students graduating from four-year college programs and 75% of those graduating from two-year programs lacked the skills to perform common reading and arithmetical tasks.

One criticism of modern education is that some teachers are so focused on issues of self-esteem that, out of concern that they'll damage his feelings, they fail to correct a student's spelling or grammar, to say nothing of his lack of knowledge or critical thinking. The long-term result is that kids are failing to face challenges that could build personal strength. Instead, adult attempts at generating self-esteem in children too often result in narcissistic imitations of self-esteem such as bragging, bullying, showing off, mouthing off, or anything else that gives a kid a temporary feeling of empowerment, typically at some other kid's expense. It can eventually leave kids believing they don't have to apply themselves, thinking that anything beyond minimal effort is unfair, until they know only to spew obscenities, outraged at challenges most of us consider routine. And, indoctrinated by mass media and by each other in the art of defeating their own maturation, it may be twenty years before they realize how seriously they've shot themselves in the foot, if even then.

But this isn't a book about childhood education or childrearing practices. Rather, it's about the problems we create for ourselves and others when the inadequacies of our early years result in a general dumbing-down of adult culture. Frank McCourt, in his memoir, *Tis*, describes immigrant students clamoring for the education that American kids reject as boring, unfair, or simply too difficult. And writers like Milan Kundera, in contrasting the contemporary American mentality with life behind the Iron Curtain, accuses Westerners of having no idea of what it means to be denied common rights, for those who have lived under true tyranny and deprivation learn early on in life that you have to do what you have to do just to get by, and that anything beyond that is a gift.

Again, the overall sense is that the more technology and ease we have, the more we tend to disengage from life, resenting it for imposing on us; that the more freedom we gain, the more we feel entitled to have, and the more oblivious we tend to be to the burdens we put on others. It starts with the little things, with the ten-year-old bursting out of a convenience store, spilling candy wrappers in his wake, in the teenager tossing what's left of his Big Gulp across the sidewalk, slopping a sugary mess everywhere. Can you remember when it first occurred to you without being told that it wasn't all right to do things like that? Has it occurred to you?

But many kids today, if told to pick up his mess, will respond with the defiance and vulgarity that has become more banal than obscene (*fuck you, you suck, etc., etc.*), that old demon 'Foul Mouth' having him already in its sway. And when assigned a simple household task (*Johnny, did you take out the trash yet?*), he'll slump as if under an enormous burden and crumple in front of the TV where he'll sit and sulk, overwhelmed and immobilized.

And he'll truly feel exhausted! Then he'll leave dirty dishes and snack debris on the floor in front of the TV, or a pile of dirty clothes in the middle of the room, go into a clean bathroom and leave it looking like a hurricane has gone through the place, all as if he's out to prove that none of it is his job, that he can still get Mom to serve him like she did when he was little. And to the dismay of any future relationship partners, he's likely to go on doing that well into middle age. Worse, though, his leaving a mess for others to clean up for him is the same dynamic that will make him a dangerous driver, raging about not getting his way.

Most parents have had the experience of trying to put down a small child only to have the kid, who wants to go on being carried, fold his legs under him, pulling the parent off balance. It's a common enough thing for a child to do, but some of us go on doing the emotional and financial equivalent, becoming adults hardly any more capable than children are of taking account of our own lives.

While a small child has a hard time paying attention to things beyond his immediate wants, needs and impulses because his nervous system hasn't fully developed, in an older person it's more a matter of angry defiance than an inability to take notice. A teenager's nervous system may have developed sufficiently for him to pay attention, but deafened by the hormonal roar, his war against the expectations of the adult world will have him raging that skateboarding isn't a crime, then go about doing incredibly stupid things on those little wheels. And, yes, reckless endangerment, trespassing and property damage *are* crimes. Then he's likely to drive a car or ride a snowboard the same way, seemingly unable to understand why he can't do whatever he wants, then raging at all those assholes telling him to rein himself in. The death toll racked up by reckless teenaged drivers and snowboarders, by the way, is seriously disconcerting.

All in all, the obscenities and resentment say one thing: *All my life I've built up all these fantasies, only to find that life is TOO HARD!* What he wants is for the world to change for his benefit, for someone to shield him from harsh reality just like they did back in pre-school, the idea of changing himself to meet the world being too much to bear. Then he'll take his revenge through petty crime, vandalism, graffiti spraying, and predatory computer hacking, perhaps to serious crime, fraud and high-level political and professional corruption.

It reminds me of a once-famous photo of the protester who, having taken over the administration office at Columbia University back in the 1960s, is sitting in the university president's office with his feet up on the desk; a guy full of radical outrage and not a lick of ability to actually manage anything. It's an old story, and while many of us have felt that way at some point, the greater problem is when we move into our twenties and thirties still holding those attitudes. There's the classic image of the angry young man fuming away in his cold garret, writing bombastic treatises full of political fire, certain he possesses the panacea to all human ills, indignant at the world that fails to fulfill his idealistic notions.

In the same vein, Balzac described young men with nothing better to do than burn the house down around themselves. But the challenge that anyone who seeks to upset the *status quo* needs to confront is whether they truly have workable alternatives. It's one thing to rage against the iniquities of society, quite another to develop alternatives that will actually work. But while the firebrand rages at humanity to wake up, what drives him is his notion that 'waking up' means that everyone should think, feel, and believe the way he does.

Ironically, most revolutionaries tend to be fairly compliant when it comes to ideology. I attended a college where it was chic to be a Marxist-Leninist, and like today's Goth punks, they all tended to look and sound pretty much the same as each other, rejecting the values they'd grown up with while adhering with fawning devotion to a set of values even more rigid. One thing the twentieth century has shown us is the outright failure of modern revolutionary movements, the most successful of them, the Bolshevik, actually having ideologically failed quite early on, surviving as long as it did only through tyranny.

Many of the Baby Boomer generation went out of their way to reject western culture and religion, only to acquire far stricter ones, rejecting one set of authoritative values for another even more demanding. And those radicals, free-thinkers and hippie-style dropouts can be just as prone to preaching and indoctrinating as the authority figures they'd rejected, trading one form of conformity for another that they find more appealing if only because of its being exotic.

When we're young, though, a sense of identity gained through defiance seems better than none at all. In the long run, though, we're all challenged to conform in reasonable ways. We drive at sixty-five miles an hour, narrowly missing cars going the other way, and it only works because we know if we were to violate that fundamental agreement, we would likely die in a sudden and dramatic manner. Yet some of us do some remarkably stupid things behind the wheel of a car as if simply to prove we can get away with it, which we don't always manage to do.

Can we imagine adults pushing and shoving like children, butting in line, shouting at the tops of their lungs, throwing tantrums at anyone challenging them to pay attention? Yet a great many of us act like that when we drive, enraged at a world that expects us to treat others with respect. A local community installed speed limit signs at the approach to a dangerous curve, including a radar display telling drivers how fast they're going, yet the skid marks and scars on the concrete barriers bear testimony to all those drivers who've tried to prove they really don't have to listen.

We sometimes see children pushing the edge, running out of control while watching their parents to see just how far they can get away with it, then throwing tantrums to defeat the parent's attempt to restrain them. That can lead an anxious parent to be reluctant to take action the next time, creating a vicious cycle in which the kid escalates his acting out, learning better ways of defeating adults. That can have us wondering if this isn't what is sometimes diagnosed as ADD or ADHD. Is it simply that the kid has learned that he doesn't have to develop self-restraint, that he can always get away with extreme behavior? Then, as an adult will he really not know how to restrain himself? After all, if we don't learn it as kids, we likely never will, so when we hear researchers saying that college students have a disturbingly Machiavellian attitude, it's little surprise.

Many of us are attracted to films that glorify defiance against the forces of evil when we are simply justifying our defiance against the call to reasonable behavior. The real problem, though, is that if we lack the ability to rein ourselves in, we'll try to defeat the challenge with escalating rage: *How dare you try to make me do something I don't know how to do!*

F. Scott Fitzgerald described youth as a state of chemical madness, while ancient myths reflect how deeply the challenge of moving from childhood to adulthood has affected human culture: Phaeton driving (and crashing) the sun god's chariot, Icarus getting carried away with adolescent enthusiasm and destroying himself. And now we hear adults reacting: *Want your parents to stop harassing you? Get a job, move out, and pay your own bills!*

But for all the teen bashing, every complaining adult carries a past in which he was once singing the opposite of this song, railing against adult oppression: it's a passing phase we all experience to some extent, and each of us was once a young Icarus falling down out of the sky while our fathers looked on helplessly, and one of the things that spur adult resentment toward teens is the recognition of what obnoxious brats we, ourselves, once were. The big question is whether we're still trying to act like that.

We all know how frustrating it can be when someone acts below his age. For instance, driving down a street, we'll give a young kid on a bike a wide berth because we know he's likely to wobble out in front of us. But we don't want to have to cut an adult that much slack, just as we don't want to have to clean up after him or do his job for him or have to listen to his mouthing-off, for what an immature person considers oppressive is actually a matter of adult realities.

We see an example in the film, *The Miracle Worker*, where a young Helen Keller is challenged to learn in spite of her handicaps to interact with the world around her instead of trying to control it with tantrums. Yet while it's normal enough for children to be chaotic at times, splattering themselves all over the place at the tops of their lungs, when an older person acts that way, it's not only offensive, but can look rather bizarre. I once knew a psychotherapist who'd videotaped his teenaged daughter in action in order to have something to torture her with when she got older. But then age has a funny way of getting revenge on us all.

We all start out as infants howling at the world, then go on to become teenagers living in a reality defined by hormones and grandiose notions, convinced we are being so deeply profound only to realize in later years how shallow, oblivious and obnoxious we'd been. Life is full of practical jokes like that.

I recall how when I was about ten years old I was walking to a friend's house and had started to cut across someone's yard only to have the man on the porch snarl, "Hey, why don't you go around on the sidewalk like everyone else?" Maybe it was a bit harsh, but it woke me up with a jolt because I realized he was right. Well, a lot of our important lessons come to us like that, and the angry defiance that has become so common these days even in people well beyond adolescence stands as an attempt to defeat the learning process.

I think of Nietzsche's complaint about the conventional world foisting its *Thou shalt not!* commandment on people, and I can't help but wonder if it's truly about the natural rebellion of creative minds against repression and conformity as Nietzsche claimed, or if it isn't simply the stance of an immature mind resisting *everything*. How much of that original *Thou shalt not* message was simply to keep kids from running out into the street, unable to comprehend what they're doing while stubbornly defying the adults who scream at them to stop? This, in a more adolescent form, is portrayed in the German film, *The Edukators* (*Die Fetten Jahre Sind Vorbei*), where young radicals strive to lash out at social injustice, but can only act like reckless children, or in *The Beach*, about a community of idealistic young adults unable to face some very harsh realities.

The modern-day equivalent of the garret-bound angry young man, though, is more likely to sit at home, sponging off his parents, leaving a debris trail behind him as if to prove he can always get someone else to serve him, refusing to get a job, playing computer games and reading comics, going out now and then to get drunk or stoned or laid, then slumping off in a sullen rage over even the most ordinary demands, refusing to put energy into anything that doesn't feed his self-centered existence.

Yet as much as he complains about depression and defeatism, if he were to put his feet on the ground and put out a little effort, all that would probably lift. As Alfred Adler noted years ago, we all yearn to constructively participate in the world around us, indolence invariably leading to helplessness, anger, depression, and despair.

But indolence and helplessness can be so addictive to the modern day angry young man that the medicine for his ills is often the last thing he'll want. An acquaintance once told me about the time a friend of hers, a New Ager of the Thoreau variety, had sat at her kitchen table telling her about his meditation experiences in the Massachusetts woods, but when she'd mentioned her job, he started making scornful noises about her selfish materialism, which is when she'd exploded: *Now wait a minute! You're sitting under the roof I work and pay for, on the chair I worked and paid for, at the table I worked and paid for, eating the food I pay for and cook for you, and you're being sarcastic?* The spiritual values he'd been leaning on may have been valid in themselves, but childish minds seek spirituality within childish attitudes, and then go drifting off into fantasy, metaphysics, and the self-improvement game when challenged by the realities of life. Besides, begging bowls haven't gained popular acceptance in the West.

We all come from a childhood driven by helplessness and need, then move into a hormone-driven adolescence where we're so enamored with our emotions and impulses that little else has a chance to get into our awareness. Most of us remember what a challenge it was as teens to deal with feeling as if we'd suddenly gone from pedaling a tricycle to driving a Corvette without any idea as to how to manage the thing. That's why it generally takes a person until their late twenties to settle into their lives, everything before that looking like a fit of temporary insanity. Part of the challenge is to recognize that many of the attitudes that made us cool as teenagers are the very things that are likely to undermine us as adults; that the things that make us 'successful' in the eyes of an adolescent will likely cause us to fall flat on our faces later on.

Smoking and chewing gum can both drag out oral fixations normal in infancy, carrying narcissistic childhood expectations into adulthood. We all know the image of the insolent gum-chewing brat and the cigarette-smoking punk, and I can't help but wonder if it isn't because anchoring infantile oral fixations gives some of us a feeling of power.

One of the subtler challenges we all face is that because our psyches are so underdeveloped in childhood, the best we can do is to view the world around us with cartoon-like simplicity. But if we're still like that as adults, we'll try to reduce the complexities of the world to simplistic terms held up against a backdrop of archetypal imagery. Feelings of archetypal glory are highly addictive, and cults and cult-like groups work on a person's hunger for simplistic absolutes, reducing the complexities of life to powerful imagery defined by group thinking rooted in buzz-words and catch-phrases. Moreover, cults and cult-like groups are typically created by immature psyches trying to reclaim the golden throne they'd once ruled from as infants, and the groups they create are attractive to immature psyches looking to structure themselves through grandiose notions, no matter how absurd.

For all our spiritual notions, feelings of glory have lead to some of the most heinous acts ever committed by human beings, and is one of the drivers behind what religious folks call "evil." Because a kid's thinking tends to be simplistic and grandiose, American street gangs, the Red Guards, the Khmer Rouge, Mexican drug cartels, a variety of African rebel groups, Central and South American death squads, and the Taliban have all been horrifically proficient at using teens to carry out extreme tactics—give a kid a gun and the power to use it, and you can expect just about anything. And for far too many of us humans, it's easier to pick up a gun than it is to consider anything constructive, especially since a youngster's ability to realize what he's doing can be so terribly limited. But then some of those inner city and Third World kids grow up enough to look back and recognize the damage they've done.

Aside from the extremes, it's a challenge for each and every one of us to look back and see the foolishness we'd once regarded with glowing idealism and visions of glory. Yet most of us sense during our teen years that there's something missing in us, but we don't know what it is. And most of us try to make up for that missing something with things that don't work—posing, bragging, exaggerating, raging—only to feel worse in the long run because we sense we're still missing the point, and don't even know what the point is. So, for all the posturing we may do as teens (*Quick! Hire a teenager while he still knows everything!*), or even as adults, most of us know we're faking it no matter how we may try to hide it.

What we don't know when we're younger is that we find that missing something by developing it gradually, and it's not easy, not glorious, and not uplifting. But that's part of the challenge of simply being human, the problem being when we try to go on into adulthood having still failed at that gradual development and are trying to imitate maturity instead of living it authentically. And it's a problem exacerbated by all the ways our culture supports people in remaining immature and disconnected from the most basic challenges of life.

This, then, is the focus of this work.

CHAPTER THREE

~NARCISSISM~

The American male doesn't mature
until he has exhausted all other possibilities.
~Wilfred Sheed

Trouble with you is the trouble with me,
got two good eyes, but we still don't see.
~Robert Hunter, *Casey Jones*

Francisco Goya painted a scene in which one boy is riding the shoulders of another, arms thrown wide, head back in ecstasy as he's bathed in golden light, while the boy on whose shoulders he rides appears to be struggling, his face cast down in shadow. It's a disturbing image despite its apparent innocence, for it tells much. The spoiled brat, the loud-mouthed adolescent, the lazy adult, the swaggering bully, the cocky young professional, the arrogant corporate lackey, and the snobbish aristocrat all feel they are in the golden light because they're being carried by someone else. In Goya's day it was the rich riding the shoulders of the poor, the tyrant riding on everyone, yet it's a drama that has been replayed in countless ways throughout history—one race riding on another, one culture on another, playground bullies on the sissies, thugs on the helpless just as children naturally ride on their parents and bask in their golden light as is their right for those few short years.

Years ago, researchers filmed an interaction between two children in which a little boy is sitting alone eating an ice cream cone, at which point a little girl comes to sit next to him, watching with evident longing. Finally the girl asks for a lick at the cone, and the boy meekly lets her have one, then another, and the situation quickly progresses to where she has the cone and won't let him have any.

Of course many men will immediately rail, *Yeah, women are all like that,* while women will say the same of men. The overriding issue, gender aside, is that we all come from an infancy where we expected that everything was for us and about us, and anyone not toeing that line was depriving us of what we deserved. But then we see adults still carrying on this way, insisting that they deserve this, deserve that, and anyone having something for themselves is depriving them unfairly. The point, though, is that deserving is generally not an issue for emotionally sound people—it simply isn't something that comes to their minds very often.

What follows all too often is when a needy person treats another's life as if it's an ice cream cone to be seduced away from them, as if they're simply entitled to it. After all, Mommy didn't have any life of her own or needs of her own, or so it had seemed when we were only a few months old, when Mommy's life seemed defined by our very existence. This is typically called "primary narcissism" or "infantile narcissism," and it's not only normal for an infant, but developmentally necessary, for it's the naked ground from which we start to build our psyches.

As ever, the issue is when our development falters, so that for a narcissist of any age, the battle cry is: *You're not supposed to be you! You're supposed to be an extension of me!* That's what we see in the faces of some kids well beyond their toddler years, a look of victorious possession of their mother, and eventually victorious possession of their girlfriend or wife.

Primate researcher Jane Goodall tells of an older chimpanzee mother who, lacking the strength to wean her infant, was faced with a growing son who'd gone on demanding that she continue nursing and carrying him even when he was nearly as large as she was. Then, when she died, his relentless demands apparently having speeded her end, he fell into such despair that he lay down and died, too.

There's something terribly human in that, for stereotypical 'bloated capitalists', selfish clerics, the pampered rich, and sadistic tyrants have all been a bit like that since earliest history, many of them able to survive only by getting their way, sensing that should their support system give way, they would be doomed. We see it in tyrannical regimes to this day where no one is allowed to do as much as point out the tyrant's behavior, much less object to it. Just failing to give sufficient praise to the child in the president's palace can still lead to the torture room and the firing squad in some countries because telling a monster that he's a monster will turn him even more monstrous.

It brings to mind the old children's tale, *Bartholomew and the 10,000 Hats*, in which a boy has to remove his hat before the king, only to find another hat under that one, then another and another, at which the king is about to have him beheaded for his disrespect. The point is the feeling that we can never do enough to feed the grandiosity of a childish tyrant of any age, and that a tyrant is not only oblivious to the situations of others, but is stubbornly, willfully so.

I recall three people I've encountered who had emanated an unforgettable degree of narcissism, the sort that radiates such an intense glow as to be stunning, and not in a good way. The first was a rock star, the second a manager to another rock star, the feeling in both cases being magnetic and mesmerizing at first, but holding an obviously seedy flip side. The rock star seemed so accustomed to the limelight as to be dependent on it, while the manager came across as an outright thug: *Give me what I want right now, or I'm in your face!* And he probably did get his way most of the time as just standing near him was like getting punched with an invisible fist. The third was the guru of a large cult-like organization, a guy who radiated a raw narcissism that was apparently attractive to people hungry for the charismatic glow he gave off. Not surprisingly, his childish rages were legendary, capable of inducing both awe and contempt in equal measure. But then it was rumored that the only person who could make him cower was his mother, giving rise to a few nervous titters here and there.

Liz Taylor spoke of how her husband, Mike Todd, didn't just walk into a room—he filled it with himself. But while a woman may find that captivating in a man, I'd guess more than a few of his male business associates would have rolled their eyes at the thought. They say Hitler filled a room that way too. Then there's the story of two of Napoleon's officers playing chess when one was asked what he would do if he were playing against the emperor, at which he deliberately made a losing move. You don't dare beat a tyrant, not even in a game.

Most children have a natural glow about them, one that comes in part from the attention and nurturing given them—which they store up like a fuel reserve—and it's obvious when a child doesn't get enough attention and nurturing because they'll seem like a faded photograph in comparison to other kids. In much the same way, while an adult with healthy self-esteem has a natural radiance about them, a narcissistic adult will demand the attention in a way that seems uncomfortably unnatural, as if their charismatic radiance comes from sucking energy out of everyone around them. That's why narcissists will explode in outrage at anyone who fails to feed them enough attention and praise, for it threatens them with going cold turkey, like a drug addict without a fix. It may take a village to raise a child, but it can take an entire world to satisfy the demands of a child in an adult body, and even that might not be enough.

Meryl Streep's character in *The Devil Wears Prada* is an example of someone who carries a good deal of adult competence, even a degree of caring under the right circumstances, yet treats others with the insolence of a bratty child trying to force compliance, obedience, and praise from others. In real life, though, Streep's character would be far more prone to tantrums just as children are when their helplessness surfaces as rage. Mrs. X. in McLaughlin and Kraus' *The Nanny Diaries* is another example—a childish tyrant out to prove she can treat others' needs with disregard if not outright contempt. Oh, how we love to hate them.

As shocking as it is to see it in an adult, the origin of that sort of behavior is obvious enough, for as children we simply don't and can't see our parents as people with feelings and needs of their own any more than we can understand what they have to deal with out there in that scary world beyond the front yard. And the more insecure a child is, the more likely he is to feel threatened and enraged should his parents attend to their own needs instead of to his. In the same way, a childish adult will develop a blind spot into which most of the rest of humanity falls, failing or simply refusing to see others as people in their own right.

Again, when we fail to carry our own weight as adults, we can't help but create a burden for someone else to carry—a burden that, like children, we'll probably fail to notice. But childish narcissism at any age demands the freedom to do whatever it wants without restraint or repercussions, then looks the other way when someone else has to pay for the house, the food, the clothes, the wrecked cars, the vandalism, the court fines, the abortions, the raising of the babies and the general cleaning up of the mess. In short, a childish mind is overtly out to defeat everyone else while covertly defeating the challenge to recognize that everyone else is growing up in ways that they, themselves, are not.

Taking primitive impulses to an extreme, we see some disturbing scenes, such as the mob of fans that trampled eleven people to death outside a Who concert, a Wal-Mart employee trampled to death when he opened the doors to holiday shoppers, videos on the internet of shoppers mobbing stores in an animalistic frenzy, fighting over clothing, gadgets, and toys.

Researchers tell us that under extreme circumstances, whether in fear, excitement, or rage, our forebrain tends to shut down, leaving only our midbrain in charge, an odd little entity not particularly adept at rational thinking. So, when people are accused of animalistic behavior, it's not all that far from the truth, since animals are rather lacking when it comes to forebrains. Nor do we have much of a forebrain functioning as children, and even as teenagers it isn't fully developed, giving rise to the time-worn sarcasm that children are simply candidates for becoming human.

It also brings into question the legal defense of temporary insanity, demanding to know just how accountable we are to be when it comes to maintaining our grip on ourselves. High levels of arousal, be it fear, rage, or excitement, can be highly addictive, and too many of us love regressing to brutish states because they feel so pure, so free of all those nasty impediments that rationality and integrity impose on us.

The challenges confronting us as teenagers can have a profound effect on the rest of our lives, so let's look at a representative scene. A visitor rings the doorbell, and although there's no response, through the screen door he hears a TV playing, so he rings again. Then as his eyes adjust, he sees a teenaged boy slumped in a chair in front of the television not eight feet away, a bottle of pop and bag of potato chips close at hand. Eventually, annoyed by the intrusion, the kid turns to yell toward the back of the house: *Hey Mom! There's someone at the door!* As if to say: *Hey, stupid! Don't expect* me *to do anything about it,* while the guy at the door stands there stifling an urge to kick the door open, grab the punk by the scruff of his neck, and drag him out of that expletive deleted chair.

The adult's outrage has a Darwinian quality, an instinct to protect the survival of the species because fecklessness of that sort can develop into a parasitic attitude that relies on the efforts of others, which a primitive culture couldn't have afforded. Anyone wanting the power of an adult with the lack of responsibility of a child would pose a threat to group survival, and just as a mother cat will kill the weakest of her litter, an adolescent refusing to carry his own weight would be intolerable in a Stone Age culture. These days, though, we're left wanting to whomp the living daylights out of him, although we're more likely to wind up paying his welfare check in years to come while he sits around complaining.

It brings to mind a guy I once saw sitting on a sidewalk in Manhattan with a sign reading something to the effect of: *Don't I just piss you off? Ten bucks to tell me off!* Well, at least he had a sense of humor about it, but then we see people who've lived on the streets since their teens, and we have to ask if it's because of mental illness, harsh circumstances, or if it's simply that they've become adapted to living with their hands out. A twenty-eight-year-old woman who'd been out there since she was sixteen was recently in the news complaining about new anti-panhandling ordinances, raging: *those arrogant rich guys just don't want people like us around.* And it was hard not to think: *Well, yeah! No kidding!*

A term used in social anthropology describes such people as "labor exploiters" because they rely on others' efforts, not their own. It's a term that can apply to thieves and con artists as well as to the indolent rich and others who fit the role of classical royalty. But we're all labor exploiters as children because we're not capable of being any other way. The ongoing issue, though, is when we're still like that as adults.

Yo return to the kid slumped in front of the TV—he'll finally get a job only to have the boss yelling at him, *What are you doing standing around? What is this, daycare for charity? I swear if you went any slower you'd be moving backwards!* So, the kid goes back to slumping in front of the TV, complaining that the boss is an asshole and the job sucks, while the boss is thinking that if he has to pay this kid seven bucks an hour, the kid has do nine or ten dollars worth of work just to break even on his overhead and workers comp, while this kid's barely earning his wage alone, if even that.

And it's not just his parents and the teachers and the cops and the boss who give the kid trouble. It's life itself and the maturing of his own body and nervous system that oppose him, and if he wins the battle at this point in his life, he'll defeat himself in the long run. For all of us, one of the greater challenges in adolescence is to grow beyond the notion that our life is someone else's job. And while a kid may fight against the need to put on a coat on a cold day, making it more important to win a short-term battle than to recognize common sense, if he goes on like that as an adult, he'll hurt a lot more than just himself.

Even if we grew up having to deal with truly destructive parents, our attempts to defeat them can lead us to defeat ourselves in the long run. The challenge quite a few of us face, then, is that of developing a strong sense of identity without engaging in ongoing warfare against everything and everyone around us, for what may have started out as a survival strategy can become self-defeating.

One thing we see in animals, especially among adolescent males sexually frustrated by older, stronger males, is the cruel displays of thwarted power acted out against weaker males and females: *If the big guys beat me up, I'll just go find someone weaker to vent my frustrations on.* Sometimes it seems there's not much difference between a pack of young elephant seals (known for their brutality toward one another) and a junior high school hallway ruled by frustrated adolescent rage. Sometimes those hallways look like a scene out of *Lord of the Flies*.

It's one thing to be like that as teens, but the adult narcissist has never grown beyond that stage, leading to so many of the social problems we see every day, from the bedroom to the boardroom, as the cliché goes.

Another challenge that gets highlighted during our teen years is that as small children we look up to our parents as if they were gods and goddesses, as supreme beings we behold with devotion, awe, and wonder, only to realize at about ten to twelve years of age that they're just a couple of neurotic schlubs like everyone else. For some of us, that realization can be crushing, a fall from the childish fantasy world into one in which people are just people, and we're all neurotic schlubs. But that's a hard fall to take, one we often try to defeat with sarcasm, and some of us want to ride that exuberant high forever, turning all the contempt we can muster on our parents, then on everyone else as we blunder our way into the world with all the faults we blame everyone else for.

A motto we hear from street kids is: *Youth is truth!* But it's only believable as long as we're riding the crest of that adolescent wave, viewing older generations as decadent, depraved, and corrupt. But those idealistic notions will only seem true as long as we don't have to pay a mortgage or raise kids. Eventually, though, we're challenged to reorient to life without that rush of adolescent hormones, which is something we can't see when we're in the middle of that drama. Instead, our teenage tendency is to trash Mom and Dad as idiots for failing to live up to our fantasies: *My Mom is so stupid, and my Dad's such a dork! I'm embarrassed to even be seen with them!*

Yet, this is what happens when the beanstalk to the magical realm fails and our giants come crashing to Earth, but then we go on to expect the ideal lover, the ideal spouse, the ideal boss, the ideal enlightened master, ideal political leaders, and they all disappoint us by turning out to be just neurotic schlubs. Then we're challenged to face our resentment toward the world that has failed us—a world that, except for a few people here and there, doesn't even know we exist.

Another aspect of our early attitudes is found in two important words that crop up in childhood and adolescent vocabulary: *sucks* and *stupid*. A pre-teen boy will typically respond to a difficult challenge by saying with all the indignation he can muster, *That's stupid!* while what he's really saying is that he's being compelled to do something he doesn't want to have to do. He's accustomed to having grown-ups do all the hard stuff for him, so when the hard stuff comes his way, he sulks and calls it stupid. Some stupid teacher has given him another of those stupid assignments that requires him to go down to the stupid library, look things up in the stupid encyclopedia, actually read and understand the stupid thing, then write some stupid essay. *Any*thing that doesn't fit into the little world he knows is just plain dumb.

A teenager, though, tends to be more vulgar about it, having spent his life up to this point fantasizing how life is supposed to be, and when he finds things aren't quite like that, he'll complain: *It sucks, dude; it really sucks!* What he really wants is to remain drunk on his sense of entitlement, for life to change to match his expectations, but short of changing himself to deal with things as they are, he knows only to shrink back into fantasy and throw vulgarities at the unfair demands of that sucky world out there.

But, again, this isn't about teenagers, rather that the struggles of adolescence typify the struggles of humanity at large, for while hints of the worst of human behavior can show up in adolescence, it surfaces in extreme ways in adult narcissism. The narcissist, then, is someone who has failed to gain the tools he needs to move from childhood fantasy into adult competence. Like a wayward teen, the adult narcissist can be childishly selfish, doing or taking whatever they want because it simply doesn't occur to them not to. Yet, that's what lack of psychological development looks like—not so much as deliberate thoughts and intentions, but as a lack of conscious thoughts and intentions—they're simply missing.

Here's another representative scene that many of us carry into adulthood: A fifteen-year-old decides he wants a glass of milk before bed, goes into the kitchen, opens the refrigerator, gets out a carton of milk, gets out a glass, pours the milk and drinks it, then goes to bed. And what's the problem? He left the refrigerator door ajar, left the cabinet open, left the milk on the counter to spoil, left the glass for someone else to deal with, left a puddle of milk for someone else to clean up, then went to bed leaving the kitchen light on.

There's an old notion that awareness ends with puberty, because those teenage hormones tend to make us so self-focused that not much gets into our awareness beyond what we want in the moment. So, we leave a mess in our wake because things like closing the fridge and cleaning up don't fit into the category of things we want, so they simply don't enter our minds.

Or maybe there's a shadow side in that we are unconsciously trying to prove that the things we don't want to do are always someone else's job just like when we were little. In that case, leaving all that mess for someone else to deal with can take on an in-your-face defiance: *Don't you dare expect me to do anything I don't want to!*

Again, the teenage phase is a place we pass through, and it exemplifies, often in exaggerated ways, many of the challenges we have to face as adults. So, while as teenagers we may have trouble paying attention, the adult narcissist will be stubbornly refusing because he's out to prove that his "I want" mantra will run the world, and that he doesn't have to anything that violates his personal reality. Even an insignificant task like cleaning out the lint tray in the clothes dryer can seem as overwhelming as building the pyramids, or as insulting as being made the butt of a joke.

Yet what lies under that indignation is the narcissist's fear that he can only get along by trying to force others into the role of the ideal mother he never had. It starts in infancy when our only way of getting our needs met is to cry until someone does something about it, and some of us seem so fascinated with our ability to get others to jump, that alone becomes one of our greatest motivations.

Sometimes, proving we can compel others to disregard their own needs in order to serve ours becomes our greatest source of comfort and entertainment, eventually hardening into the sneering contempt we see Streep portraying in *The Devil Wears Prada*—the disdain of a dependent person refusing to see others as people with feelings and needs of their own.

One formal term for this is "dependent hostility," and contempt dependent adults feel toward the people they depend on, always trying to bite that hand that feeds them. And what makes people like that all the more frustrating is that, like children, they typically have little or no capacity for seeing their own behavior as anything but justified. And like children, they will demand respect, yet are unable to act in a way that deserves it. Tyrants of any stripe are notoriously incapable of questioning their own behavior as they put others in their service and deprive them of any other choice.

But the face of the tyrant is a mask covering the anxiety that any dependent person feels. We see it in literature and films portraying the aristocracy treating their servants as if they were invisible except when needed, and in older times the serving classes were trained to *be* invisible, to act as if they had no thoughts, feelings or needs of their own, to act as doting parents who exist only to help aristocrats live as perpetually sulking children offended by the slightest inconvenience. Watch the servants in the films like *Gosford Park*, especially when they're in the background, and you'll see it all. Oscar Wilde portrayed this sort of thing with both more humor and a bit more spite, yet like it or not, those nuances have a subtle influence on us all, for they stem from our own early childhoods.

Part of my reason for going on about this is that I've watched some of my peers from the hippie generation deteriorating into tragic, angry old people demanding their way from a world they still don't know how to participate in; carrying on with grand philosophical notions while complaining that someone else isn't doing a good enough job of taking care of their needs for them.

There's a dialogue that starts when we're kids whining: *Do I have to?* To which the adult world says, *Yeah, you do.* To which we whine: *Whhhyyyy?* And the answer is: *Because you're a part of this world, so learn to deal with it, okay?* Then we want to know: *But why can't I just stay a kid?* to which the simple answer is: *Because you can't.* Actually, it's because if you try, you'll have hell to pay, and the rest of us don't want to carry you anymore, so that's why. As an old saying goes, the road to failure follows the path of least resistance. It also follows the path of minimal effort, and that's a habit we can change.

I once watched an acquaintance get halfway through a task, then walk away from it; drop something on the floor and leave it there; cook a meal then leave the mess behind, and when I looked around his house, I saw the same pattern everywhere. Physically, emotionally and financially, everything in his world was a mess of incomplete things. Then I realized I was doing the same thing, although not quite so badly, and when I started to do a better job of completing even the most trivial things, everything else in my life changed. That I found fascinating, that the big things change when we focus on resolving the little ones. Unfortunately, it can take some of us a long time to work that out, but even more unfortunate that many of us never do.

So, you want to change your life? Great! Clean up after yourself and be amazed! Sometimes it really is that simple. Not necessarily easy, but simple.

But technological development since its very beginning has led to a class of people who never have to get their hands dirty, which says a good deal about why so many philosophers, scholars, bankers, and bureaucrats have been so infamously arrogant toward the working class, the very people they depend on to make their clothes, build their shelters, and grow their food, as if their elevated status raises them above such menial things without which they couldn't survive.

In US history, this showed up early on in conflicts between the likes of Thomas Jefferson, a gentleman farmer, and Alexander Hamilton representing the interests of bankers and manufacturers. Jefferson's concern was that bankers and businessmen constituted an aristocracy of wealth and privilege based on the efforts of others, while Hamilton's was that without a class of people who didn't have to get dirt under their fingernails, the economy and the culture itself would stagnate. Even the ancient Greeks and Romans had to deal with those issues, and no one has ever had a good answer, although the likes of Karl Marx have tried and failed.

The underlying dynamic shows in our notions of willpower, for while an adult sees willpower as the ability to persevere despite obstacles and hardships, in the mind of a child, willpower is the ability get his way, the ability to get others to attend to his demands. In the mind of a childish adult, willpower is a matter of manipulating others to do things he refuses to do for himself, and at its pathological extreme, it can result in sadism, slavery, and genocide.

While we love to accuse each other of arrogance, it's more to the point that what we call 'arrogance' is an attempt to hold attitudes and expectations that are normal in a child. But that's just a mask for our fear that we simply don't know how to do anything but pretend to be more capable than we really are.

In the same way, what we call "smugness" is essentially the attitude of a child pretending to understand the adult world when he actually understands very little. It can show up in the smirk of a defiant teenager, masking the struggle between the hormonal tide that has him feeling like a strutting god and the fact that he's incompetent at dealing with his own life: all he knows is to pose and smirk.

By the same token, snobbery is essentially an attempt by the marginally competent to hold onto their childhood stance at the center of the universe, demanding the right to criticize others while seeing itself in heroic terms.

One point Hegel attempted to make is that we can't understand life as seen through the eyes of those more mature than ourselves, that we can only understand people with maturity equal to or lesser than our own. So, kids and teenagers rage at the adult world, while adults say, *Just wait 'til you have kids of your own!* It's also why a relationship between adults of differing degrees of maturity can be such a struggle, for the weaker of the two can never quite understand the behavior of the other, who in turn will feel chronically frustrated at dealing with someone unable to comprehend adult realities.

It's also why so many immature adults feel that the 'system' is trying to keep them down, that there's a faceless power—the corporations, the CIA, the aliens, the gray entities—that's out to oppress them. What they fail to see is that without adult perceptions, the world always seems confusing and hostile. Hegel also said that a slave understands things the master does not, translating here to say that a dependent person, child or adult, has nowhere near the understanding of those they attempt to force into servitude.

It's no surprise that eight-year-olds are likely to think life is designed for them because picking up their mess is the job of grownups. But are self-centered adults any less oblivious, reacting with outrage when challenged to deal with their casually discarded candy wrappers? Corporate polluters stand accused of the same thing, of leaving a trail of debris for others to deal with, their responses to criticism couched in terms of progress and standards of living, but the effect is much the same, that old demon "Selective Self-Deception" having them in its sway.

But we all carry a dose of that. I grew up in a culture based on English values, then had to learn how those ideals had treated the Scots and Welsh and Irish and Africans and Chinese and Indians and a lot of others with cold contempt if not mindless cruelty. What culture has not done that somewhere in its history?

Narcissistic self-centeredness is normal in childhood, and when we are stressed, sick, or overwhelmed as adults, we might slide back there because it's our default position. The process of growing up, then, is not so much one of moving away from that original position as it is one of adding strengths and competence so that we have more to work with. A simplistic analogy is that we don't go through life from A to B to C so much as we grow from A to A plus B, to A plus B plus C, so that even later in life when we've reached X, Y, and Z, we find that A, B and C are still there. That's why the senile and the very ill may regress to infantile attitudes. No matter how much we've grown, we'll always carry at least a ghost image of our old tendencies.

Again, the issue is that far too many of us hold onto childhood narcissism to a degree that was unthinkable in the past, having gotten to somewhere around C, D, and E only to dig in our heels and fight against any further progress. More correctly, though, it's a matter of our having progressed into adulthood with significant gaps in the structure of our psyches, as if we've moved on toward Q, R, and S, only to have H, I, and J missing, while others may lack E, F, and G.

There are many opinions as to why this occurs. One school of thought is that it's a combination of affluence flooding children with consumer products, the effects of television, electronic gadgets and computer games ("techno-narcissism"), social media which lacks any true social value, and the failure of both parents and schools to provide enough constructive challenge.

The general assessment is that this leaves kids heading into adulthood with unrealistic expectations, and that they have a right to absolute control regardless of their inability to make logical decisions or deal with repercussions. Parents distracted and overwhelmed by jobs and financial pressures are a significant part of it, but not as much as the message of expectation driven into kids' minds from an early age by the culture at large, especially through dull-witted television shows written by adolescent minds and music generated by tantrum-throwing children with loud guitars. One thing Jean Twenge emphasizes is that the effect of excessive praise given kids in the hope of building self-esteem is that a child's mind will inflate with ungrounded grandiosity because that's all he knows to do, then he will expect the world at large to keep giving him those feelings. The tragic irony is that in attempting to raise healthy children, we are capable of creating narcissistic monsters instead.

Adding to the mix, consumerism promotes the notion that we can fulfill ourselves with stuff, leaving us with both a hunger for still more junk and a sense of desperation because none of it is ever enough. It's one of the stranger quirks of the human psyche that our pursuit of happiness can make us so miserable, and that we keep trying things that clearly don't work as if driven by a strange compulsion. But then communism, in attempting to right the sins of capitalism and materialism, managed only to create another kind of monster.

Kids try to create a culture of their own at least until adulthood catches up with them, and they have done it with anything from baseball cards in the bicycle spokes, comic books, television shows, and all the rest of the things kids do to define their place in the world. But the trend in the last several generations is to try to build that kid culture even larger and carry it too far, trying to defeat the realities that threaten them. The beatniks of the 1950s, hippies of the 1960s, and their contemporary equivalents have been accused of that and more.

Actually, most of our notions of childhood are modern inventions, creations of a culture that provides little role for children other than schooling, sports, and idleness. Older cultures have understood that planting the seeds of responsibility and decency needs to be done early on, that our most important attitudes and assumptions are set well before puberty. As some of us learn, if we don't learn common manners in childhood, life will generally teach it to us with a whip. Or as the sometimes-curmudgeonly John Le Carre writes, we have to earn our reason for being born.

It's little surprise that traditional cultures worldwide see modern Western culture is seen as a form of madness, and it's with a sense of horror that elders watch their children being sucked into that chaos. In the US, self-styled cowboy poet Baxter Black has commented on the contrast between the lazy, arrogant, foul-mouthed kids he sees in urban and suburban settings, and the hard-working, respectful ones he regularly meets in ranch and farm communities. So, for all the tendencies of city folk to ridicule the lack of sophistication out there, it would seem those country hicks have quite a few things to teach the rest of us city slickers and suburban dwellers.

Is Western civilization is being defeated by its own success, becoming befuddled by wealth, technology, and relative ease? More and more of us are attempting the path of the idle rich, the power monger, and the perpetually dependent child, and it doesn't seem to be serving us very well. It's a base phenomenon that has always been part of the human scene, and as much as we may want the life of the idle rich for ourselves, we'll despise it in others, just as we love to hate people for having what we want.

Again, what we call "arrogance" is a failure to get past the original center-of-the-universe stance we held as infants. And it's a physical experience more than a mental or emotional process, a bodily-felt sense of expectation that has little to do with what or how we think. Few of us, after all, go about *thinking* we're superior to everyone else. Rather, the problem is in what fails to enter our minds: it's not so much a thing in itself as a *lack*; not so much an attitude as a failure to have developed a more mature one.

That's because our primal sense of entitlement was with us as newborns, long before we had a mind with which to think about such things, and the developmental process we go through is essentially a morphing of our physical experience far more than it is one of intellectual or emotional development, for our psyches tend to follow our physically-held sense of what's what rather than the other way around. That's why hard experience teaches us far more than intellectual understanding or emotional expression ever will.

Our most basic challenge in life is the most obvious of all, that we get born as infants, and it doesn't stay that way. Yet, a great unspoken outcry we hear from so many of us is as if to ask, *Why isn't the world the way it was when I was little?* The answer, of course, is that it never really was that way, that it only looked and felt that way when we were little because adults were sheltering us. As Carl Jung wrote, what is true in the morning of life will by evening turn out to be a lie.

I recently passed a teenager in a shopping mall as she was trying to deal with her little brother who had thrown himself on the floor with a stream of shoppers stepping around him. *Please get up*, his sister begged, to which he stubbornly shook his head, *No!* What he was trying to do, of course, was to get his way by acting helpless, apparently frustrated that it wasn't working like it used to.

Adlerian psychologist Rudolph Dreikurs tells us that children are powerful observers, but poor interpreters of what they see. And in saying this, he was following Alfred Adler's assertion that it's often not what we experience that matters, but the meaning we put on our experiences; that it's what we make things mean that drive us.

While that seems obvious enough, virtually all of us have at some point carried a sense of distress and indignation because we're still holding onto some shred of childhood expectation, and it can make even the best of us seem slightly insane at times. After all, we humans have been trying to get even with each other over who deserves what, and over whose job is whose, for at least the last few hundred thousand years. We even see it in primates.

It's part of the human experience that we habitually put the cart before the horse, drawing conclusions about life, love, spirituality and so on before we've had enough life experience to have a broad-enough view of the world around us, and if we fail to develop our psyches any further than those original imprints, our primal sense of entitlement will seem normal and natural. Added to this is the way adolescent hormones can cause us to regress to infantile expectations all over again, leaving us wavering between helplessness and outrage.

As children we're focused on our need for comfort and security at the center of others' attention, and as adolescents we're focused on hormonally-driven power fantasies, but then we are challenged to face the harsh realities that have lain hidden under all that primal self-centeredness. Failing that, anything that has obstructed our development will become a touchy spot, a weak link in our chain, a place where we will over-react to certain situations because they can resurrect all our childhood hurts.

As a result, any relationship, community, organization, or business comprised of emotionally underdeveloped people will tend to become an unstable affair, prone to out-of-control arguments, disagreements degenerating into an inability to compromise. We see seeds of this in a common family scene where Mom and Dad are getting the kids together for a trip, packing and making sure everyone has what they need while the kids are wailing: *Why do I have to carry more than her?* and *You got the window last time!* and *Mommy, he pushed me!* Or we see the older of two children watching his little brother in Mommy's lap and he's thinking, *That was My place. It's supposed to be My place.* So he theatrically falls down and bangs up a knee or two, wails in distress, and soon he's back up there in Mommy's lap, from where he looks down at his dethroned younger brother and, carefully so that Mom can't see, sticks out his tongue. *Gotcha!*

It's not surprising then, to see that sort of thing played out in the upper ranks of multi-national corporations and national governments. A variation on the theme is when a child ignores a toy until some other kid reaches for it, at which he needs *that* toy and *only* that toy as if his very life depends on it. We see this in the opening scene of Thomas Balmes' film, *Babies*, where two kids start fighting over an old plastic bottle that has lain there forgotten until one kid reaches for it, setting the other into combat mode. And it's not just about possessiveness or territoriality, but rather a primitive jealousy that if you want something, I have to deprive you of it even if I don't really need it.

It may make little sense to an adult, but to a small child it makes a great deal of sense because as children we tend to see desired things as "self-objects," as extensions of ourselves through which we gain a sense of identity. This is why Linus in the old *Peanuts* comic strip clings to his security blanket, glomming onto an external representation of the self he's trying to develop, substituting this for what he used to get by bonding to Mommy. In other words, a child clings to a self-object as if to say, *This gives me me!* Some of us do that with our Porsches.

Just as it's important for a child to gain a sense of and individual self, even if in a clumsy, fumbling way at first, the problem is when the need for self-objects ceases to be a stepping stone. This is why it can seem to an insecure person that if you get something for yourself, you must be depriving them. Revenge shall ensue.

It happens every day on the freeway, drivers acting as if having someone changing lanes up ahead of them constitutes a personal insult, and someone getting that parking space I wanted is like being deprived of paradise.

Looking at the pre-World War I history of Europe, we see much the same thing, as if five or six children had been in a playroom with only three or four toys among them, leading to much of the colonization of the rest of the world when they found there wasn't anything left in Europe to grab from each other: The English wanted some little country so the Russians wouldn't get it, the Russians wanted it so the Italians wouldn't get it, the Italians wanted it so the French wouldn't get it, the French wanted it so the Germans wouldn't get it, and the Germans wanted it so the English wouldn't get it. The scars remain in Third World countries to this day.

The underlying dynamic, though, comes straight out of early childhood development, or the lack of it, for as children we all tend to use not just Mommy but the stuff around us to gain a sense of identity, a "self-sense" or "sense-of-self," to use the jargon of developmental psychology, so that when someone takes that precious thing away from us, it's as if they've reached right into us and taken away a piece of our insides. It's little wonder that as kids we scream bloody murder when someone swipes our teddy bear or snatches away that kitchen knife we'd wanted to play with.

Developmental psych tells us that with the development of a stronger self-sense, we have less need for external things to give us a sense of well-being, less need for stuff with which to define ourselves. So, the spiritual discourses we hear tend to miss the point, for materialism and greed aren't so much about egotism and lack of loving kindness as a failure to have developed a self-sense strong enough to stand on our own without all that stuff to make us feel secure. But then, belief systems and scientific theories can become self-objects, too.

In other words, narcissism is an attempt to find substitutes for a sense of loss that goes right back to our earliest childhood.

But most of our battles taking a less direct route. Here's a deliberately simplistic scenario:

A: Let's go out to eat tonight. Is there anywhere you'd like to go?
B: Oh, I really don't care. You decide.
A: Well, we could go to McDonald's or we could try Burger King…

B: No, you decide.

A: Well, okay. Let's go to McDonald's.

B: (Fuming) You always have to have your way, don't you? We went to McDonald's last week and we both hated it.

A: Well, okay. Let's go to Burger King.

B: No, you said McDonald's, and you always have to have your way, don't you?

A: But I *don't* have to have my way. I'm asking you where you want to go.

B: Well, I've always wanted to go to Wendy's.

A: Okay, let's go to Wendy's.

B: Now you're just being a martyr like always. You really want to go to McDonald's, so we'll go to McDonalds, and I'll just have to put up with it.

A: Oh, come on! Let's go get in the car, and we can decide on the way…

B: That stupid car of yours? It's such a piece of junk. When are you ever going to get something decent?

It can go on and on. The point is that A, whatever his or her faults, is trying to come to a mutual decision while B is struggling to feel like a real person, but knows only to try to out-control the other person in an attempt to achieve a feeling that somehow eludes them. And in the process, B is out to yank A's chain any way possible, which would drive most of us straight round the bend. Yet that's something we often resort to when we feel powerless. Kids do it all the time:

"Johnny, did you take out the trash yet?"

"The dashyet? What's that?"

"I said, did you…"

"*Huh?*"

"The trash. Did you…"

"Dash? What dash?"

"No, the trash."

"No the trash? What are you talking about?"

"The trash! The trash!"

"Trash what?"

"Did you…"

"Huh?"

It can make you a little crazy, but then it's meant to, for a person lacking inner strength knows only to lead others in circular arguments and meaningless debates as a way of deflecting the challenge and feeling in control. But underneath that meaningless argument, a person with a poor self-sense is like a soap bubble always just a little afraid of bursting, so that even the slightest conflict can feel like a matter of survival. And when things break down, rage usually rears its ugly head, for if losing an argument amounts to feeling annihilated, mediation and compromise are virtually impossible.

Again, it's one thing for kids to act that way, quite another for adults, which goes a long way toward explaining why history is full of wars fought over things like issues of politics and dogma that now seem meaningless.

Really, though, we generally do the annoying things we do, even as adults, because we don't realize there are other choices available. But those choices are likely to take us outside our comfort zone, which is exactly the challenge we need to face. And a great many of us as adults seem out to prove that we don't have to step outside our comfort zones, preferring to remain stubbornly oblivious to any other possibilities available. Yet, even as small children we have choices, although it's hard for us to realize it at the time, much less act on them. The perpetual question before us as adults, then, is what can we do about it now?

CHAPTER FOUR

~HUMAN INCARNATION 101:
A DEVELOPMENTAL PRIMER~

And now the infant with its cord is hauled in like a kite
One eye filled with blueprints, one eye filled with night.
~Leonard Cohen, *Stories of the Street*

I have nothing against children.
I just wouldn't trust one of them not to giggle
if I accidentally stepped on a land mine.
~Maartin Troost, *The Sex Lives of Cannibals*

Well, yes, this is a harsh way of viewing humanity, but there are times we need to take a ruthlessly honest look at things, and to parody a line from Jim Morrison, no one here gets out unscathed. For all that we may yearn for stable, predictable lives, we generally learn important lessons only when serious difficulties force us to. So, there comes a point when we're challenged to stop and take a hard look at the ground we've been standing on all along, otherwise we'll go on taking for granted attitudes that not only undermine our own lives, but create a general nuisance for everyone around us, especially for our children.

Life is a generally disorganized affair, what novelist Douglas Adams calls a WSOGMM: a Whole Sort Of General Mish-Mash. Or as Salman Rushdie refers to it, a P2C2E: A Problem Too Complex To Explain. Whatever we call it, we're all confronted with the challenge I like to call "Human Incarnation 101," a required course that, at best, has to be repeated a few times over because it's just too much to take in all at once, especially since the first time through we're usually too busy just trying to get by.

The overall question right from early infancy is, *What's going on here, anyway?* But then we're all subject to the human psyche's resistance to seeing itself too clearly, for there's a psyche-phobia (literally: fear of the psyche) that runs throughout humanity, yet generally eludes notice. At the heart of it is a dread of facing primitive tendencies that probably date back to the Australopithecines of a few million years ago, things so deeply-ingrained that we take them for granted. But it can be scary to see how automatic so much of our behavior is, how out of control our own actions are much of the time, for it can shatter our self-image in a serious way.

We're all reality-challenged to some extent, for it's comforting to carry a sense of certainty as to what's what in this world. We're all born into a potentially desperate situation, helpless and dependent with under-developed brains and bodies, and the way that situation works out will go as long way toward generating our sense of reality. As adults, though, we're required to look back and assemble an overall sense of what life has been for us, for as the Roman orator Cicero once said, if we don't know where we came from, we'll always be children. In psychological terms, that means that if we don't come to terms with the things that have affected us, we'll go on acting on habitual compulsions without ever questioning ourselves.

Moreover, none of our history goes away. There's a line in the Disney animated film, *The Lion King*, where the Yoda-like sage whacks the young lion over the head, then says, *It doesn't matter. It's in the past!* We all laughed, but well, that's wrong—very, very wrong, tragically and absurdly so, because for all those fine notions about leaving the past behind, the harsh reality is that our past experiences are imprinted into us like fingerprints in clay, and that impact is always operating in present time. So, while an event may have happened decades ago, the feelings associated with it are always right now, sometimes driving us to our knees with pain we thought we'd left behind ages ago, perhaps driving us to mindless violence.

In dealing with our past, what we're challenged to deal with is very much in the here-and-now. And while we may be able to release much of the pent-up emotional charge around difficult memories, in a sense there is no past, and amnesia is not therapy. The extreme case is post-traumatic stress disorder where an emotional imprint is too much for a person's psyche to bear, and the feelings and imagery overwhelm them. Yet we all carry that dynamic in lesser ways. To quote a line from a documentary about the Jonestown mass murder/suicide, whoever said that time heals all wounds didn't know what he was talking about.

What we can do, though, is to grow enough to carry those wounds. But none of it is easy, and none of it really quite goes away.

The intention here is to take a hard look at things we've taken for granted, and that's a process that is certain to be a bit brutal at times. A cautionary note, though, is that some of us go to pieces when pushed too hard, and some of us are inclined to think that human psyches should bear one of those labels like they have on the back of a TV: *Don't go prying this thing open, because there's nothing in here you can fix, and you'll only give yourself the shock of your life if you try.* Then again, what is the unexamined life worth?

In our teens and twenties, we're likely to be on a search to find our true selves, yet later find ourselves wondering just what is it that makes a self in the first place. Our challenge is to take a hard look at what it is that gives us a sense of identity, how this Me thing gets put together, and that's what this section is about.

Psychologically speaking, what we call a "self" is a compilation of chemical processes and biological impulses mixed with emotional and mental patterns, many of which were imprinted into us at birth and in early childhood, others of which may have been determined by our genes. The jury is still out on that one.

We all are also subject to a process in which our minds create metaphorical representations of the life we find ourselves in, those curious little adventures we call dreams and fantasies. Then there's the added twist that many of us are prone to believing in our imaginary worlds more than we believe in the solid world around us, some of us going to great lengths to prove that the tangible world out there isn't real at all. Consider, for example, the Matrix films as well as many of the teachings of Eastern religions. At the very least, we're all prone to some extent to believing our nervous systems more than we believe the world 'out there,' driving some of us to try to prove that our inner worlds define reality. Well, they do define our immediate experience to some extent, but that's not quite the same thing.

In simplistic terms, our most basic emotional dynamics are a bit like a balloon hooked up to a tire pump. If something pumps us up we feel grand, but if we do nothing else, we'll sooner or later feel blasé as we gradually deflate. And if we deflate too far, we'll become depressed, while if we get pumped up too far, we'll become grandiose, perhaps manic to the point of becoming delusional. We see it in sports fans going wild at a game, in kids playing air guitar, even in the couch potato raging at the evening news. Some politicians seem chronically like that, at least when they're in front of the microphones. Just look at the way they go at each other on CNN and Fox News, making political commentary look like the Jerry Springer Show. And what about the guys who advertise gizmos on TV? *But wait! This amazing offer just got better!* For some of us, religion works like that, hyper-inflating us into a manic state we identify as being spiritually-elevated. Others of us go to such extremes as to commit murder and rape because it pumps up our balloon, then sit on death row still determined that we'd been right, our over-inflated balloons having given us such a convincing sense of reality.

Going back to the kids fighting while their parents try to pack the car, the adults are trying to get things done while the kids are attending to the size of their balloons, following the notion that the best way to pump up my balloon is to burst yours.

Or we'll try to out-inflate another kid, fighting over things that seem silly to adults: One kid brags, *I've been to Disneyland seventy times!* and the other answers, *Yeah, well I've been there seventy hundred times!* when neither has been there at all.

This is something teachers are often faced with, for no one, child or adult, can learn very well while focusing on their balloon, as if pumping up our grandiosity plugs our ears and blinds our eyes to everything else. The bully in full battle cry, the seducer at his game, the tantrum thrower lost in the glory of his rage, the dreamer wandering in alternate universes are all like that, and so we all are when we obsess too much on inflating ourselves.

As silly as much of it can be, the drive to inflate our balloons by bursting someone else's is one of the things that can drive genocide, reducing others to subhuman anonymity and justifying appalling violence and depravity.

Developmental psychology describes this as "grandiose inflation" or "ego inflation," and while the connotations are generally negative, we all need at least some measure of that inflation in order to function. We see its beginnings in infants where if you put on a big, wide smile and coo at an infant, he'll expand like a balloon, giggle and flap his arms and legs like he's swimming, but if you turn your attention away, he'll start to deflate as if you've pulled the plug on him.

That's fair enough for an infant, but some of us as adults are still so dependent on someone or something to keep us pumped up that we're forever trying to compensate, often in destructive ways. We all start out lying there helpless in our diapers with adults crooning: *Oh, look at the cute little baby! Oh, he's sooo sweeeet!* And it doesn't stay that way, potentially leaving us with a sense of loss that might drive us the rest of our lives.

Drugs like methamphetamine and cocaine are compelling in part because they provide that expansive feeling, as in the song verse: *Everybody knows that you live forever when you've done a line or two.* But while Freud had initially considered cocaine capable of resolving mankind's problems because it seemed to rid people of their insecurities, now we see bloody mayhem worldwide, folks throwing away their life savings for a few moments of fool's paradise.

Even without drugs, people in positions of authority have historically felt godlike, which is why power corrupts, for it tempts us with a return to infantile glory. As far back as the Egyptian pharaohs and the god-kings of Babylon, rulers have assumed the role of incarnated deities and have tried to rule with god-like authority, and the notion of divine right flaunted by French and English kings well into the eighteenth century was only a little short of claiming divine status. Consider Louis XIV's famous dictum, *"Le etat c'est moi"*— *I am the state.* In more recent history, we heard Moammar Gadhafi, the self-styled King of Kings, shaking his fist at protestors, declaring, "This is my country!", like a furious little boy raging, *This is my toy truck!*

A question confronting leaders at all levels asks what is public service versus what is personal narcissism in which the public is required to play parent to an infantile monarch. It's fortunate that not many rulers have been as mad as Caligula or Idi Amin. Still, the basic trait has caused untold misery throughout history, from international politics to the boardroom, the kitchen and the bedroom.

All in all, the feeling of inflation is the greatest addiction of all, and it's one of the things that hits us when that flood of hormones sweeps us up in our teens, imbuing us with a naïve sense of splendor as if we have become living gods before whom all are to bow. Sex, drugs, rock and roll, power and control, outrage, and indignation are all fairly effective at providing that addictive rush, but the core addiction is to inflation itself, and history is full of people, even entire nations, killing each other for its sake.

But while terms like "grandiosity" connote self-importance,

following the balloon-and-tire-pump analogy, it comes down a matter of degree. We all need to be able to inflate ourselves to a reasonable degree, for if we lack that ability, we'll resort to anything from glorious fantasy to fits of rage as a way of pumping ourselves up, trying to stay ahead of the leaks that are constantly deflating us.

As children, we need the presence and attention of adults to fill us and surround us, cocoon-like, until we're strong enough to hold ourselves together without depending on others to do it for us. This is why children can be so clingy, and it's why leaving them alone is abusive, for it traumatizes small children to be without an adult to help keep them intact. It becomes a problem, though, when adults, like perpetual larvae without a cocoon, still can't hold themselves together and take to compulsively clinging to others out of sheer desperation.

The other thing about balloons is that they burst, which is what happens when someone goes into hysterics, withdraws into a shell, or flies into out-of-control rage, their sense of identity and integrity having gone to pieces for a moment. Those three responses to the feelings of falling apart—panicky hysterics, autistic-like withdrawal, and rage—are fairly typical, for they say something basic about the way our psyches are structured.

Our most basic stress response as children is to cry and cling to our mother as if to immerse ourselves in her, surrounding ourselves with her presence in order to pull ourselves back together. Rage is also a common response, not just because it can be so grandly compelling, but because a large emotional charge can give us the illusion of pulling our fractured pieces back together, of having an intact balloon again. The other response is to go a bit catatonic, withdrawing into ourselves in order to regain a sense of 'okay-ness' by shutting out our environment.

But our attempts to inflate and hold ourselves together can create so much of the misery and madness that have marked human history. For all our capacity for rational thought, we humans have at times shown the sensibility of a horse running into a burning barn, and the tenderness we see in a nursing infant can all too easily turn demonic when that dynamic is driving the life of an adult.

Yet we are drawn to movies, books and magazines that reinforce our grandiose fantasies, supporting the hope that our strategies will lead us to some sort of fulfillment. Some of us love adventure films that portray the defeat of evil enemies, some of us love the ones that promise ultimate romantic fulfillment, while others crave magical powers and magical realms.

But life has a way of demonstrating how those impulses generally fail. Obviously, the rage tactic is the most immediately problematic, having driven the likes of Saddam Hussein, Josef Stalin, and Slobodan Milosevic. In its extreme, some will turn to outright sadism as if the ability to inflict pain and death on others at will makes them the masters of life, like the Nazi SS with their skull and crossbones insignia, inflicting violence with the resolve of little boys torturing ants.

It's a common understanding, though, that a rageful person is really just a needy child, and as any playground bully knows, the best way to ensure my balloon's invulnerability is to bust yours. That's why some kids right from an early age will impulsively look for another kid's weakest point. We may wonder about the cruelty of the Nazis, Khmer Rouge, or the Red Guards, yet we can often see its seeds on the playground and in the high school hallway.

The underlying insecurity is reflected in the old Roman symbol of the *fascisti* (hence: fascism), a bundle of sticks lashed together symbolizing strength through unity, a notion that attracts anyone looking to feel superior through group cohesiveness. But it's not only physical abuse that matters, and it's not only boys who are prone to it, for girls are notorious for much the same thing, although they're more likely to be emotionally abusive. Either gender will attack another child's vulnerability, trying to fill their own sense of weakness and emptiness through vindictiveness. Maarten Troost, for instance, speaks of the thrill children get from watching a fight, describing it as "human nature undiluted by age and experience... mankind fresh out of the box."

Just as girls do it with high school pettiness, the geekier of us find ways to do it intellectually—consider the bombastic professor. Whatever the method, the underlying drive results in the shame-based culture we see in so many schools. Then we see movie characters like Rambo, a host of martial arts stars, and the comic book-based super heroes that are so popular, no matter how childishly unrealistic: *If I can take on ten bad guys at once, jump off a five story building as it explodes, bounce off the roof of a car and walk away without a scratch, then my balloon will never fail me again.*

There are some in the self-help game who equate rage with personal power, but throwing a tantrum doesn't make us a strong person, no matter how much the two-year-old in us wants to prove otherwise. Rage, in other words, is desperation in disguise. The blueprint is with us from an early age, for when a child realizes his life-as-infant no longer works the way it used to, he'll try to get the world to behave itself by raging at it. And some of us, it seems, never quite get over it.

It's not a great stretch to say that religious outrage can be similar to sexual jealousy in that both involve a dynamic in which a person bases his personal security on something outside himself—dogma in one case, attachment to a love object in the other. Anything that intrudes—a competing belief system in one case, a competing lover in the other—threatens to emotionally annihilate him, and that threat can spin some of us into such desperation that we'll turn violent in the blink of an eye.

To an unstable person, anything that threatens to burst his balloon can be so profoundly terrifying as to seem profoundly evil. So, he will see good and evil in terms of his fragile grandiosity, and to some of us, the world is just teeming with things that threaten to burst our soap bubble, just as it used to teem with monsters under the bed and boogey men in the closet.

So, we have a handful of basic dynamics right from birth and through our early years: a need to emotionally connect and feel nurtured, a tendency to wail in despair when that need isn't met, a tendency to turn to rage in order to push down that despair should our needs still not be met, and an overall instinct to develop an inner representation of the world we experience around us. And while normal in themselves, any of those dynamics can become so obsessive that they dominate our lives, so much so that we'll use them to try to dominate others.

To follow the developmental model, the most important emotional process from childhood through adolescence is the development of our energetic envelope, our self-sense as a reasonably sound individual, growing from infantile dependency to individuality with a reasonable degree of autonomy. In this, we are moving from that primordial place where we need to have others living their lives centered around our well-being to an adulthood where we can carry that responsibility for ourselves, and with a sense of well-being that has become a natural part of us. It's only then that we can have authentic relationships, for the person dependent on others to hold them together and keep them pumped up can only relate to other people the same way they'd done as children—treating others partly as gods, partly as objects, partly as food sources, partly as slaves, partly as victims to be tortured. That's why it's a byword in the Twelve-Step community that dysfunctional people don't really form relationships: rather, they take prisoners. It's also, by the way, why cults and cult-like groups focus first on breaking down both a person's self-sense and ability to judge reality for themselves, reducing them to naïve children easily led and manipulated.

Overall, it's all about how we develop relationships and how that ability changes as we grow up. The overarching question is how different our way of relating to others can be once we've learned to behave as responsible adults capable of making conscious, creative choices in life.

Our first experience of relationship is one where we're helpless and in need of nurturing—being fed, being kept comfortable, having our diapers changed, and most importantly, feeling cocooned by someone else's energy, feeling held together by another's presence. And as long as we're in that place, we'll associate love with being nurtured, not an expectation that can maintain healthy adult relationships. That's because as we move out of that primal experience, we're challenged with finding more resourceful ways of relating to the world around us as our sense of ourselves morphs in ways that are generally invisible to us. We may feel that the world itself is changing when it's really ourselves that are changing.

There's a point at which even the most spoiled child starts to realize that the golden throne he's held for so long is getting shaky, at which point he's likely to turn on other kids, trying to lord it over them and get them to fulfill the role the adult world is no longer providing. Still, some of us go on to expect royal treatment as adults, expecting others to cower in submission: Considering how the attitudes of royalty and infancy are similar, in the original "Marriage of Figaro" an aristocrat is told, *In all your life you have taken the trouble to do nothing except to be born, as if that were enough*. That's why so many aristocrats have historically relied on their bloodlines to merit respect, because many of them haven't have the strength of character to deserve it.

That, though, is the challenge before us all, the task of developing the true strength of character to get beyond our original notions of royal grandiosity.

The Tyrant in the Highchair

So, we start out as babes in arms dependent on the nurturing attention we get from adults, especially from the great goddess we call Mommy. Then we hold onto that experience any way we can as we move into toddlerhood only to discover that she no longer focuses on us as intently as she once had. Some of us at that point learn to control Mom's attention with complaints, maybe with tantrums, while others of us learn an early form of seduction, using cute vocal sounds and the set of our eyes and facial muscles to win attention.

By the time we've reached nine months or so, we find ourselves perched in our highchair while Mom is doing all sorts of other things instead of focusing entirely on us. Instead, she's over there washing those stupid dishes, sweeping that stupid floor, and talking on the stupid telephone until we can get her to stop and make us the center of her attention again. So, we'll whimper and cry, scream and yell, throw our applesauce across the kitchen, make cute sounds, whatever it takes until she stops all that other stuff.

That language, by the way—stupid this, stupid that—is what we hear from seven-year-olds, anything that doesn't fit into their seven-year-old world being simply stupid. But the template is in the toddler's sense that something's wrong here, that things have changed in ways we don't like, and we're going to do something about it.

And as we gain speech, we're likely to start trying to turn Mom into a short-order cook: *I want that. No, I want this. No, I changed my mind, and now I want...* Then we're likely to grow into adults who compulsively change their minds just to exercise control over someone else, trying to trump others' needs and make them subservient to our own. The core of that compulsion, though, isn't control in itself, but rather that we associate manipulation with being nurtured, which is what we'd been trying to get from Mom back when we were in that highchair.

As kids we feel a balloon-inflating thrill at receiving a gift, but it can get to be such a deeply-set expectation that any time a kid doesn't get something he wants it can result in a tantrum. That's what we see in supermarkets and department stores where a parent is wheeling a shopping cart through the aisles with their kid screaming for some toy he'd just seen on a rack. More to the point, though, he's screaming not only because disappointment is so painful, but because the world isn't working right according to his expectations.

Some of us develop a dynamic at an early age where we feel loved and nurtured whenever we can get Mom to stop whatever she's doing and cater to whatever demand we send in her direction. Well, it's one thing for a child, but some of us become so fixated on that attitude that even as adults we'll carry on as if to say: *You don't have the right to not give me what I want!* Or, more to the point: *You don't have the right to not pump up my balloon for me.*

We often see adults carrying on with fundamental highchair dynamics: To go about as if they have a bank of spotlights shining on them, and treating others as if they are entitled to impose demands— Do this for me, do that—as if desperate to reassure themselves that they can always get that feeling of being nurtured. In some adult relationships, it can seem as if one person has a dog collar and leash on the other, and will give that leash a yank now and then just to prove they have control, and just to remind their partner that it's there. Yet, a person trying to control others is really just trying to reassure themselves the way a small child would, by trying to give themselves a feeling of nurturing out of a sense that they've never had enough.

This is a classic case of the toddler's dilemma, one we see all too often in adults demanding independence from anyone else's authority while demanding authority over anyone he sees as responsible for his needs: *Your life is mine to control, but don't you dare try to control me!* When men do it to women, they get called male chauvinistic pigs or patriarchal louts, while when women do it to men, they get called bitches or worse.

Because it represents an important early developmental step away from infancy, the highchair scenario can be one in which an essential blueprint for future behavior is established. One behavior we are likely to carry out of this moment in childhood is rooted in the sense that being able to stop others from doing whatever they're up to and do something for us instead can give us a powerful sense of wellbeing, a sense of security, even of love. This is why we see adults who will walk into any given situation and try to take over, dancing everyone else around like marionettes on strings even when it's none of their business, even when they really don't understand what the business is.

On the other side of that experience, many of us who grew up with a parent like that develop a speech habit where we ask permission for simple things: *Wait, let me get the phone, let me change my shirt, let me...* as if asking permission to move our arms and legs under our own volition. And while it may seem silly on the face of it, the source of that habit is a serious one. But that's the way a needy person can affect others, as if they are always requiring others to get permission to have any control over their personal lives. It's one of the dynamics that can drive a tyrant to control his nation, equating the population's acquiescence with the nurturing he yearned for all those years ago.

We see it in people everywhere who yearn for positions of authority, even in yoga or tai chi instructors, for directing others can take them right back to the highchair where they felt loved by ordering Mommy around the kitchen. It's more common, though, to see it in relationships where one person tries chronically to order the other around with petty demands, assigning them tasks they could just as well do themselves, and generally trying to manage the other person's life the same way they'd tried to manage Mother's. It can be another of those things that some of us just seem to never quite get over.

So, one of the challenges of emotional maturity is to interrupt some of our most coveted dynamics, even when we think we have the best of intentions at heart, for claiming a position of directing others can be so compelling that some of us don't stop to consider whether our intervention is wanted, or even appropriate.

The Wicked Stepmother Syndrome

Having infancy and childhood fall behind typically leaves us with at least some lingering sense of loss, and for some of us it can become one of the strongest factors in our lives. It may seem strange that life can break our hearts right from the starting post: We lose the womb, Mother's breast, the oceanic bliss of infancy, the innocence of childhood, the naïve godliness of adolescence, and eventually our vitality and strength as paradise is lost over and over again.

Yes, good parenting can soften that original sense of loss, yet the theme remains, for we all get born into a scenario in which we reign at the center of everyone else's attention, with others doting on us, feeding us, loving and nurturing us, carrying us, and cleaning up our mess, and it doesn't stay that way no matter how much we want it to.

A feature we find in many archaic creation myths is one in which the sky and earth deities are so tightly pressed together that there's no space for people to live until a new god arrives to push the two apart. At this, humans, who had always been spontaneously fed and nurtured, had to learn to feed and shelter themselves. The metaphor is obvious, yet it's easy to miss the enormous impact that transition from the blurry infantile bond to individuality can have on us. And although some kids yearn for that step toward separation when the time comes, our theme here regards what happens when we either fail to take that step forward or actively rebel against it. Following these lines, one interpretation of the wicked stepmother theme as it's found in many of the Grimm fairy tales goes like this:

I'm three years old, and somehow I remember that things were once very, very different, although my sense of the past is a bit vague. So, to use those famous words, once upon a time I had a Mommy who attended to my every need, responding to my every little twitch and whimper as if it were a lover's call. I was in paradise, at the absolute center of the universe, and there, at the Center of All, Mommy held me and loved me, fussed and cooed over me all day long, worshipping my very existence, feeding me with the blessed milk of her sacred breast, the precious warmth of her divine body filling me with holy glory. Whenever I made even the slightest sound, she would be there, her face inches from mine, her beautiful voice singing: *What was that, baby? My beautiful baby! Is Mommy's baby alright? Are you hungry? Do you need your diaper changed?* But now she's gone away, and in her place I have this mean Mommy who wants me to pick up my toys and be quiet while the baby's sleeping. Hey! Wait a minute! I'm supposed to be the baby around here! I'm supposed to be the center of everything! Now she wants me to pick up my toys and learn to tie my own shoes so she doesn't have to. I know her game, and she's not going to get away with it! Worst of all, now she expects me to poop in the potty! It's an outrage! My real Mommy has died and gone away, and now I have this mean, bad Mommy instead, and I HATE her.

Of course, at three years old it seems that Mommy has changed in some terrible way when it is actually we, ourselves, who have changed. But in our toddler's self-absorption we have no way of seeing that, and can only assume that others have become mean when they are simply expecting us to grow up at a pace with our bodies. In our confusion, though, we can only throw tantrums at the world for being so bewilderingly obstinate.

Then, as we edge our way into mid-childhood with fantasies of growing up to be a NASCAR driver or astronaut or rock star, we also have a tendency to resist out of a sense that it's all going too fast. And in resisting, we'll hate anyone, especially that mean Mommy, who expects too much of us. Still worse, that mean Mommy will too often speak that evil word, "No!", for which she deserves the most dire revenge of all.

The punishment dealt to the wicked stepmother in the Grimm Brothers tales (in the parts left out by Disney) is a reflection of the vengeful rage a child feels at being put upon so unfairly, which is why one of the more significant parenting skills is the ability to withstand the firestorm of outrage a child can throw in your face.

It's only in later years that a growing child can come to realize how necessary the impositions put on him—the need to learn to use the toilet, to tie his own shoes, to have dessert after dinner, to sit down and be quiet when needed, to learn to share—were all along. Lacking that awareness, he'll go on feeling anxious and bewildered, occasionally lashing out in petulant rage at a world he doesn't and can't understand.

And if we go on like that we'll see a world full of wicked stepmothers, all of them betraying us by making us do things we don't want to. We hear about a high school girl attacking her art teacher, pinning her to the floor, and laying on a flurry of punches; a group of third graders (third graders?!) caught planning to knock their teacher unconscious, tie her up with duct tape, and stab her in revenge for her having scolded one of them; a kid shooting his parents and the local minister because they'd tried to curb his video game addiction. Those are extreme cases, but we see lesser shades of it in the casual vandalism, stealing, and bullying that so many kids engage in, some of whom go on to far more pathological things as adults.

And every mother of a tantrum-throwing child knows the message: *You're not the boss of me, but I'm the boss of you, and don't you forget it!* Then, many mothers of teenagers get the message: *I have all the power, you're supposed to give me everything I want, and you're responsible for everything I don't like.* A bit of a mixed message, that. And any mention of the word "No" means you deserve to be hated for all eternity. But while it's not unusual for us as children to feel resentful at being reprimanded or denied, acting out their resentment in such drastic ways leaves us wondering why so many kids are becoming out-of-control monsters?

The deeper issue is the underlying desperation so many kids feel, shows up in their dependency on electronic stimulation and their fits of rage when faced with the fact that Mom and Dad can't give them everything they want.

Some of us as adults have a hard time being any more reasonable, and go through life looking for someone to blame for anything that upsets us, seeing wicked stepmothers everywhere. While many of the hurt feelings we bring out of childhood are valid, we are challenged to ask if things had really happened that way, or if it wasn't simply that we had interpreted them that way because we'd been unable at the time to see things any other way. Kids truly are poor interpreters of what they experience, which is why reviewing our past can be an eye-opening exercise. A good many adults, though, are still incapable of seeing their current situations other than as victims, while other people are likely to see them as willfully pigheaded.

We are also faced as kids with the surprising notion that our likes and dislikes aren't universal, as in the four-year-old feeding the adults' favorite snacks to the dog because it isn't even remotely possible for anyone to like something he thinks are yucky. This can be one of the more significant realizations to hit us in childhood, for it represents an early step in recognizing our separateness from others, yet it can play a major role in adult problems. One example is the notion that if something isn't important to us, then it shouldn't be important to anyone else, and that others should abdicate their own needs and personal motivations in favor of our own. It starts with the shocking realization that some people actually like chopped liver or tofu, and goes on to the challenge of facing a world full of people who devote their lives to things that make no sense to us at all.

Another thing we confront as teenagers, even as adults, is that much of our experience of love can be terribly one-sided. A highschooler may feel awash with passion for some girl only to have her dismiss him as a creep, at which she becomes a detestable bitch. After all, while an infant expects that Mommy has no choice but to love him, the girl of his dreams will probably feel no such obligation.

In general, the wicked stepmother syndrome represents an attempt to defeat the natural forward momentum from infancy to adulthood. Yet it's a dynamic that can take elegant forms at times, even high-minded philosophies sometimes being little more than disguised attempts by immature minds to tell the adult world how wrong it is for being the way it is. At its heart, though, it's a failure to accept the gradual loss of dependency and loss of freedom from responsibility, and any failure on our part to meet that challenge leaves us blaming anyone who fails to help us remain forever infantile. It starts with Mom, and in time is transferred onto teachers, bosses, the police, the landlord, and the government.

It's in the nature of the immature mind to blame the adult world for being adult, holding to a child's notion that freedom means freedom from repercussions and natural consequences. I recall a piece in the Harvard Lampoon in the early 1970s in which a writer tells parents, *If your kids knew what you're really like, they would kill you in your sleep.* Well, a good deal of the hippie movement was about wicked stepmothers, and if that writer is still breathing, we would hope he's learned a thing or two since then.

Overall, the wicked stepmother theme reflects a normal period in a child's life when he feels unfairly put upon by those who had once doted on him as an infant. As ever, though, while it's a period children generally move through, the issues at hand result from a general failure to do so. Emotional maturity can be gauged to a large extent by our ability to deal with the ordinary rigors of life, while immaturity can be gauged by our continuing expectation that others are supposed to do things for us.

To an immature psyche, matters of comfort, pleasure, and safety always come first, turning the world "out there" into a bewildering, threatening wilderness that fails to nurture us like it once did, and why should I have to go to that stupid job when I want to party all night, sleep in, and watch TV? So, let's reframe Freud's pleasure versus reality principle as a clash between our need for nurturing versus the challenge to constructively engage with life, for failing that challenge will leave us seeing a world full of wicked stepmothers wishing us nothing but ill.

In the vocabulary of developmental psychology, any interference with our trajectory from infancy to adulthood is termed "narcissistic wounding," an injury to our developing self-sense. That is, anything obstructing the development of our psyches can hold us prisoner to a childish stance, because that's our default position. So, the bully, the geek, and the spoiled brat are all narcissistically wounded, each seeking to bandage themselves in ways that generally fail, and we all carry at least some variety of that wound.

Concert pianist Arthur Rubenstein once said we can truly live our lives only once we've learned to face life on its own terms, something he surely learned that the hard way. Said a bit differently, there is no grand path to wisdom, only a dropping in and landing as deeply as we can on the ground under our feet, and that comes only through outgrowing all those behaviors that are both normal and necessary in infancy and childhood. Contrary to our early impulses, our need as adults is not to get what we want, but to become emotionally strong enough to deal creatively with our lives instead of expecting the world to meet our demands. Failing at that will leave us struggling to over-inflate ourselves with excessive grandiosity, and for all our grand philosophies, one of the more painful ironies we face is that we are rarely so hurtful to one another, and rarely so oblivious to the harm we inflict as when we are filled with grand notions, be they romantic, spiritual or political.

The Drama of Conception

Actually, we can consider things that happened a good deal earlier than childhood. It goes like this:

Half of your first experience as a human being is as an egg floating down your mother's fallopian tubes, and for whatever else may be going on, you have one big concern: Where are all the guys? But you're helpless, unable to do more than bob along like a cork on the stream, the underlying feeling being that if no one shows up, you're going to die an empty, hopeless, futile death. Which, by the way, is true.

This, also by the way, goes off in a woman's body about once every four weeks, and it's little surprise that some women report that menopause ends, or at least greatly diminishes, their anxiety over relationships.

Now you're a sperm swimming amidst a raging horde of guys just like you, all seeking some great and glorious goal that's out there somewhere. It has to be out there *some*where! But when you do find it, you find that it (she) is stunningly huge compared to yourself, overwhelming and utterly spectacular, and your deepest motivation is to be the best, the chosen one, the most special of all, or you'll die an empty, hopeless, futile death. Which, again, is absolutely true, for there is no second place here—either you win, or you're dead. Looo-zer!

But when you *are* chosen, your reward is to be engulfed, to disintegrate and be absorbed into her. Your tail breaks off, your head splits open, and all that you are spills out until you are no more. In effect, you sacrifice your entire being to her so she can go on to her greater glory. On the other hand, if you *don't* sacrifice yourself, it's all over for you anyway, so what choice do you have? Yet, in this sacrifice you sense you are going on to become a part of something completely beyond your comprehension, which again is true.

We can ask, by the way, if this is why ancient matriarchal religions seemed so fascinated with human sacrifice, the king sacrificed each year to become fodder for the Great Goddess's fertility. After all, sperm are everywhere while the egg is of supreme importance. And are the traditional wedding gown and the altar-like lacy four-poster bed that thrill so many young girls an attempt to replicate the feelings of the egg as the recipient of this grand sacrifice? It may also say something about the male notion of self-sacrifice for the higher good.

We can also ask if the act of the egg falling from the ovary into the fallopian void isn't replicated in the notion of virgins tossed into volcanoes: *Oh dear! There she goes!*

Back to the egg's journey, your waiting is over and all these panting, lusting guys surround you. There's a scene in the film Moulin Rouge in which Nicole Kidman is performing a song and dance routine on a swing as men swarm in on her from all sides. At this, she looks around, spreads her arms wide to the swarm and gushes something to the effect of, *"Oh, just look at you all!"* She's been saved, surrounded and enfolded, penetrated and filled with another's very essence without which she would have come to a horrible end and been washed out into the abyss on the next menstrual tide. Yet, when the one she chooses penetrates her, erupts within her and loses himself there, he changes her forever into something grand, something magnificent, and something so far beyond her experience as to be utterly incomprehensible.

Great stuff, isn't it? Sperm and egg cells with delusions of grandeur is how one theorist has described us, and do you get the mystical imagery? And we can ask if the fear of failure surrounding this dance is a source of our childhood fears of monsters under the bed, the boogey man in the closet, that sense of a lurking abyss that threatens to swallow us should we let down our guard?

Of course there's no real evidence that any of this actually influences us, but it's too rich a notion to ignore, if not outright funny. The obvious stereotype is that women tend to act like eggs and men like sperm—as the old saying goes, he chases her until she catches him. And we are left with an unsettling question as to how much that we call "love" is actually a release from desperation, a salvation from that awful abyss that threatens us the moment the object of our affection fails to come up to snuff.

And failing to achieve that relief can throw us either into despair or fury. She rages at him, *You're fifteen minutes late! Don't you realize I'm going to die here?* He threatens other men, *You think you're gonna get in front of ME? Take THAT you sonuvabitch!* She wants to sit around acting helpless, expecting him to take charge while he feels like he has to keep going because he'll die if he stops. She dresses to attract sperm as if to say, *Don't you want me? Won't you stop dead in your tracks for me?* while he struts around saying, *See how choose-able I am? See how tough, how cool, how fast, how suave, how smart, how special, how gentle and loving I am?*

So, there he is, the frantic sperm always trying to be 'The One,' then complaining that she acts like she'll die if he has any life other than her, that he has to sacrifice everything of himself to her needs: *How dare you have attention for anything but me!* And what Lola wants, Lola gets.

Then we look at things like the trench warfare of World War I, and it looks like a flood of spermatozoa throwing themselves into it, filled with the power and the glory, expecting that they will all die, all but for the special one who will make it all the way to paradise. Then again, s it can look like American football, a rugby scrum or a NASCAR race. *Boogity, boogity, boogity!*

Infancy

Let's move the clock up nine months and a few days. You're now flat on your back, unable to do much more than twitch your arms and legs, suck at a nipple, and mess your diapers, and no matter how good the mothering you receive, there's an anxiety that lurks somewhere in the background, a thing that's hard-wired into your psyche that realizes: *I'm helpless here, and if I don't get loved and nurtured, I'll die!* Which, of course, is really quite true.

Even if we get our physical needs met, we potentially face the "failure to thrive" syndrome, which can amount to a psychological death if not a physical one. The mess that came out of Romanian orphanages after the fall of the Iron Curtain is a case in point, resulting in some horrifically pathological kids. The woman who notoriously sent her adopted son back to Russia said that this is what she'd been facing, and for all the uproar against her, she may well have been right.

But then most of us of Baby Boomers spent our first few days abandoned in sterile metal boxes in hospital nurseries along with a lot of other screaming abandoned babies, then were raised by parents who'd read Dr. Spock telling them that hugging us too much would ruin us, which is maybe why so many of us insist all we need is love.

Yet, we did get loved and cared for, at least enough for us to get along, and we did get at least some sense of living at the center of all existence. The positive side of the general dynamic is termed "infantile narcissism" or "primary narcissism," a sense of being at the center of the universe where others feed us, clothe us, carry us, dote on us, and nurture us. "Narcissism" in this sense is an attitude that puts us not so much at the center of our own universe as at the center of someone else's, usually Mom's. In the Greek myth, Narcissus was obsessed with himself to the exclusion of everything else, which is the way we all are to some extent as small children, and need to be, able to see the world around us only in terms of our own dependency.

This, though, is what drove Augustine to conclude that children are born sinful, failing to understand that narcissism is normal at that age. However unsavory it may be in an adult, it's necessary for us as infants to sense ourselves at the center of other's concern, for we develop the foundation of our psyches, our self-awareness and emotional security by internalizing the feelings of love and nurturing we get from others, cementing in place the fundamental building blocks upon which we develop our emotional selves.

We were apparently doomed to this extended period of infantile dependency and helplessness the moment our forebears came down from the trees to go about on all twos, because walking upright necessitated a re-ordering of women's hips, forcing them to give birth to infants that are, relative to other animal species, drastically premature. So, does this mean that walking upright, having opposable thumbs, and thinking brains condemn us to a whole slew of emotional problems? Perhaps. But then we also lost the ability to graze off the landscape and go without protective clothing, not evolutionary moves that have done much to promote our survival as a species.

It's not as if there's anything we can do about these interesting handicaps, but for all the dependency we experience as infants, an adult who demands what an child naturally needs can become something of a monster. There are, by the way, some interesting comparisons to royal traditions, for when we look at the classical images of royalty, especially the truly incompetent ones, we see many of the same dynamics we see in infants. In some traditions, members of royalty didn't dress themselves, didn't even wipe their own backsides at the toilet, or were considered too divine to allow their feet to touch the ground. So, the king as a helpless infant? Some have certainly acted that way. And maybe this has something to do with those coy references to the genitalia of the man of the house as the 'family jewels,' as if everyone in the home is to worship his crotch. After all, when he was an infant, the state of his diapers truly was a matter of practical concern to others, and some men seem to never get over it.

To an infant, the whole world is an extension of himself, and more than a few tyrants throughout history have shown little more maturity. As that ultimate toady, Niccolo Machiavelli, so forthrightly asserted, the word of the prince is to carry the force of law if only because he's the prince, the source of all law and subject to none. Not a few politicians have been accused of the same thing, no matter that *Le etat c'est moi* isn't a very workable political stance these days. But then poor Niccolo, having chosen the wrong side in a war, had been kissing up unsuccessfully to the victor by telling him things he wanted to hear.

This may also say something about our concepts of paradise, a place where, to borrow an old line, all is peace and harmony, and notions of "mine" and "thine" don't exist. By the time we've reached the age of two, though, our expectation is that everything is mine, and the notion of their even being a thine will seem utterly wrong. And we've all known adults who act like enraged dogs snarling through the fence as if everything out there is his domain.

I once caught a brief scene from a TV film about the life of William Randolph Hearst in which he and his young trophy bride are sitting in the Hearst Mansion, bemoaning the fact that they're going bankrupt and losing the place. Hearst's wife gestures at all the expensive artwork and complains that he really hadn't needed all that stuff. "But I wanted it!" he whines, to which she argues, "But you didn't *need* any of it!" And his response is classical: "If I *want* something," he says, "I *need* it!"

I don't know if Hearst actually said that, or if some screenwriter didn't simply make it up, but it's interesting because the first thing we need and want at birth after we've taken those first few breaths is to root around for a nipple to suck on, without which we'll die. Yet even years later, we're likely to find ourselves saying, "If I don't get… (fill in the blank)… I'll just die!" And if we're driven by that impulse as adults, we're likely to run up insurmountable debt, be driven to obesity, addiction, crime, and all manner of scenes we'll have a hard time getting out of. And when we get behind the wheel of a car full of indignation at not having everything we insist we need and deserve, we're likely to get someone killed—perhaps ourselves.

All this starts with the tyrant in a highchair, and Hollywood scriptwriters know that if they want their audience to absolutely hate a character, they simply have to give him the dynamics of a self-centered child. But there's a dilemma for the infantile tyrant, for while he may glory in his power, at the back of his mind lies the recognition that the only power he truly has is to bully and threaten people, without whom he can't even get his own shoelaces tied. Our first servants, after all, our first slaves, were our mothers, and failing to hold them imprisoned to our needs can leave us feeling a betrayal of cataclysmic proportions. This is the desperation that drives a tyrant's rage at any age. If he doesn't have control, he's lost; if no one obeys his will and inflates his flimsy ego, he just might fall into the helplessness and despair that underlie every human psyche.

So, he pumps himself up with the wrath of the gods, hoping to threaten everyone into obedience. And as it says in the Bible, woe to the land whose king is a child. Not a few tyrants, though, have fallen when their subjects finally got fed up with them—Mussolini, Robespierre, Ceausescu, Savonarola, Nero, and Caligula to name a few. Speaking of the wrath of the gods, the gods of chaos in world mythology are typically presented as childlike; as incapable of rule, exerting power without purpose, disrupting creation itself, which is pretty much the way a childlike ruler is. Well, we were all once kids trying to get away with acting that way, weren't we? And the challenge of growing up is to stop being like that.

There are two important notions regarding infantile experience. One says that as newborns we can't tell the difference between our mothers and ourselves, that we experience her as part of our selves, and that it's only with time that we start to realize she's a separate person who can get up and walk away from us, a realization that can be somewhat startling. The other notion is that we actually do realize she's a separate person, but expect her to always respond to our will, that just as our finger moves at our command, Mom will too; and when she fails to do so, which is bound to happen sooner or later, it can frighten, then enrage us.

I think the second theory holds up better, and shows up in what I call the "Captain Bligh Syndrome." This is what happens when an ordinarily mild-mannered soul takes friends and family out for a day on the sailboat, only to turn into a screaming lunatic the moment they clear land: *Pull the goddamned halyard! Not that one, stupid! The halyard! Right there in front of you, you idiot!* Quite seriously, I've known men to get rid of their boats in order to save their marriages, but the same thing happens on construction jobs, camping trips, and any other situation in which one person expects everyone else to respond as extensions of his will just like Mommy once had. At the very least, the syndrome implies: *If I know something and you don't, then you're stupid!* More generally, though, it's a matter of wanting to move another person according to our own impulses and needs, and if you won't respond the way you're 'supposed to,' you're a moron.

Yet, that's a fairly natural attitude for children. I remember a six year-old escalating his whining until his mother asked why he was being such a pest, at which he wailed, "Don't you know I'm HUNGRY?" To which she said that, no, she hadn't known that because he hadn't told her, a notion that simply hadn't occurred to him. And it's no surprise that ten years later his favorite name for her was: *Hey, Stupid!*

In some traditional cultures, mothers carry their infants on their backs, swinging the kid off to the side whenever he has to relieve himself, the woman who gets soiled by her baby being thought of as a bad mother because she's not adequately attuned to her child. But assuming that others will always intuit our needs as we move toward adulthood will lead to chronic outrage, which is what drives a Captain Bligh, the expectation that you're supposed to know what I need without my having to tell you, *Stupid!* That's a compellingly addictive feeling for some of us, to the extent that some Captain Bligh types will deliberately give minimal information or insufficient instruction to others because it gives the Captain an excuse to rage at someone and show him how inadequate he is. But just as Dostoyevsky tells us how some of us long to sleep "on the withered breast of their mother" in order to escape the horrors that confront them in life, there lives in every Captain Bligh a child desperate to badger the world into working the way it had back when he was in diapers.

On Being Terribly Two

Moving the clock forward another couple of years, our attitude now is that when I want something, you give it to me; when I want to do something, you let me do it; when I want you to do something, you do it or I'll scream and yell until you do. Of course we don't all become so terrible when we're two years old, just that we're too young to understand when our intentions are unreasonable or even self-destructive because thwarted intention, thwarted will, feels cataclysmic, even when it's to save our lives: *But I WANT to run out into the street!* But.

The underlying dynamic is that we're trying to gain a sense of personal autonomy while still being dependent, still being far more helpless than we like to accept. And we generally do it in a fumbling way because it's all a bit confusing. I once heard someone give an interesting description of what it had been like to learn to walk as a child, that it was as if she would project an arc of energy out in front of herself, then follow it with her body. Whether taken literally or simply as poetic license hardly matters, for we all know the frustration of projecting our intention out in front of us only to have someone block it, and whether it's a parent stopping us from sticking our finger in the baby's eye or a car changing lanes in front of us, we're all challenged by the frustration we feel. In the same way, we are prone to confusing liberty with license, expecting that "justice" means getting our way, while injustice is any time some wicked stepmother tells us "No!"

A mother once told me how her two-year-old would hold his breath and pass out when he didn't get his way (mostly when it came to chocolate), which she'd assumed was his way of trying to manipulate her. It seemed more accurate, though, to say that he was trying to escape the feelings that were erupting within him, feelings so overwhelming that he would escape them any way he could. Most kids, though, simply resort to tantrums, because at two years of age we get so charged up with expectations that having them frustrated blows us apart, and rage is the only way we know to respond. Isn't the Incredible Hulk a personification of the raging little boy bellowing in the face of a world full of wicked stepmothers? *Don't get him mad, 'cause you don't want to see what'll happen!* Act like that behind the wheel of an SUV, though, and someone might wind up getting killed.

Yet even as toddlers we're faced with the challenge to bear up to things that can't be changed. I was recently in an airliner coming in to land when a child a few rows up started wailing from the pressure in his ears to say nothing of the tedium of being imprisoned with Mom in a narrow seat for an hour and a half, and all the way down he howled at his mother who, to his frustration, couldn't do a thing about it. There's something important for all of us in a simple scene like that, because as children it's natural for us to assume that the way to change our experience is to compel someone else to change the way things are, perhaps by screaming at them.

At any age, the feelings that hit us when our balloon bursts can replicate those of an infant when no one is there to comfort us, or those of a two-year-old when the world refuses to obey us. One aspect of emotional maturity, then, is the ability to maintain the integrity of our psyches in the face of life's difficulties. Otherwise we're left facing primal desperation.

A War of Needs

The picture so far is that our most troubling behaviors are rooted in emotional blueprints dating back to infancy, a blueprint that in adulthood can never truly be fulfilled. Moreover, attempting to fulfill that blueprint can be like running on a treadmill, sometimes putting others on a treadmill and running them to exhaustion. That's why the Buddhist writer, Pema Chodrin, comments how curious it is that we're born wanting something that is essentially impossible.

When it comes to gender issues, each side has a standard litany of complaints against the other. Women stereotypically complain to men: *You expect me to cook for you, feed you and pick up your dirty underwear from the middle of the floor, then give you sex whenever you want as if I'm your mother, a maid, and a whore for charity all in one.* And feminists remind us how even those male radicals who took over Columbia University back in the 1960s had expected the women to do the cooking and cleaning, inspiring a protest movement within a protest movement. Even radical thinkers tend to be conformists when it comes to the basics.

Then, men stereotypically complain to women: *You expect me to sacrifice my life for your sake, you blame me every time you don't feel the way you want to feel, you want to be equal yet demand preferential treatment, and you stand there looking helpless, trying to manipulate me into doing all this stuff for you so you won't have to suffer the indignity of doing things for yourselves.*

She complains that he can't learn to put the toilet seat down, that he won't listen, that he's just an oversized little boy, that if you want to grow dope, plant a man. He in turn wonders if he has to raise the toilet seat all the time, why can't she exert half the effort and put the damned thing down once in a while? And when she responds that he doesn't appreciate what it's like to get up in the night to pee only to sit down on a cold ceramic bowl, he wonders: *My God! Why in the world didn't you check first?* Would he go in there and pee in the dark without checking the seat? And people who prefer the toilet lid left down as well as the seat (to keep the dog from drinking out the bowl, or to keep the toddler from throwing Barbie in there) will find that she'll always leave it up. Instead, she simply gets up and walks away without a second thought, doing her version of what she blames him for.

It's a little thing, but it represents quite a lot. We find men assuming that women, even business executives, are expected to make the coffee and clean up the mess men leave behind, and the guy who grows up never having to cook for himself or do his own laundry will tend to live in a bachelor pad mess, and when confronted about it will likely feel helpless, at least for a second or two before he gets angry and looks for someone to blame. I've seen this in the restrooms of high-end office buildings where highly-paid employees will dry their hands then drop their paper towels on the floor next to the trash can as they head for the door, as if to prove they can always get someone else to serve them. Pity their wives and kids. I recently watched a group of guys from a well-known security company, belligerent bully types, not only throwing their paper towels on the floor, but leaving the water running in the sinks with a "Fuck You" attitude, as if to prove what powerful men they are by acting like angry little boys.

The reason, by the way, that a man wouldn't go in there in the dark and pee without checking the toilet seat is that he's been trained since early boyhood not to, while she has not been trained to pay attention to the seat, so she sees no reason to. So, as trivial as the business of toilet seats may be, the underlying issue isn't trivial at all, for it demonstrates how any failure to be challenged and shaped early on can result in a refusal to move beyond our early childhood experience, and we're likely to defend our stance with outrage. Underlying it all, though, being challenged to pay attention in ways we never learned in childhood can leave us feeling bewildered and anxious, a bit like putting on skis for the first time and taken to the top of a double black diamond slope.

One way this gets played out that's all too familiar to many of us is where one person tries to control a relationship by raging: *It's supposed to be my way! My way!* while the other person responds, *Oh, alright, alright!*, and caves in, and that becomes the basic dynamic of the relationship.

Our initial sense of entitlement is both a simple expectation that the way things are is the way they'll always be, and a survival sense that if we don't get our needs met, it may well be the end of us. But then a fundamental human desire is to attune ourselves to hard reality, though as children and immature adults we'll want the world to attune itself to us instead, then judge it as wrong when doesn't cooperate. The classic snob, the strutting Mussolini, the bully stomping around in heavy boots, the mincing high-heeled dandies of Versailles, the tough punks seen on street corners as far back as ancient Athens and Rome, and wheeler-dealers and robber barons seen all across Europe and the Americas over the last two centuries are all examples.

A primary psychological approach to human development is Object Relations Theory, a somewhat unsettling term as it describes how people relate to one another, yet as infants and small children, we do relate to others as objects to a large extent, and as an object, you don't have needs—I do. In fact, a parent's need can feel threatening to a child because it takes attention away from the child's own, which is why many kids, on hearing that Mommy is sick, will escalate their demands, trying to get her back where she belongs. Or as one of the daughters in the old 70s sitcom, *One Day at a Time*, whines, "Mom! Mothers aren't people!" Neither is anyone else we project our needs onto, which is why the ability to acknowledge others as people in their own right is such an important aspect of emotional maturity.

As an example, a man describes staying with friends while building his own house nearby, during which he developed a close friendship with the wife that in some ways provided her with emotional support her standoffish husband did not. Then one day he came back after a hard day on the jobsite, so stunned with exhaustion that he was unable to do more than slump in a heap, at which the wife became upset, insisting he'd gone crazy! But then her husband apparently never worked hard enough to get all that tired, and perhaps her father hadn't either, so apparently she hadn't had any experience with exhausted men. More to the point, though, she'd reacted with the emotional stance of a child, the only reason she could give for his exhaustion being that he must have gone crazy because she simply didn't have any other explanation.

Odd as it may seem in an adult, we can describe the underlying desperation in two ways. One is that it's a child's fear that if someone doesn't meet his needs, he'll be in deep trouble, which may be quite true. That's why kids often become more demanding when Mommy's sick or busy, trying to reassure themselves that she's still there for them. Mom answers the phone, only to have the kid wrap himself around her leg, whining miserably; she goes to the toilet only to come out and find the kid spread-eagled across the bathroom door.

There's a classic example early on in the otherwise rather questionable film, *The Blair Witch Project*, in which a mother carrying a child is being interviewed, and after a few moments the kid starts clamping her hands over Mom's mouth. Then there's the three-year-old daughter of a woman I was recently speaking with, who spent the entire conversation clinging to Mom's leg and glaring up at me, the intruder, with a look that could kill.

The second way of describing the underlying desperation is that when a child finds that his source of nurturing isn't providing for him the way it used to, he'll sense that the blueprint he's working from has gone all wrong, as if the world itself has gone mad, and even at forty-five and otherwise reasonably competent, that fear can overwhelm some of us: *If you're not the way I want you to be, you must be crazy!*

Either way, many insecure people will take an attitude that's tantamount to saying: *You don't have a right to be sick or tired or sad or busy or distracted or depressed or interested in anything but me!* This is what I once nick-named the "You're-Not-Allowed Syndrome," in that you're not allowed to have attention for anything but me, not allowed to violate my version of reality, and not allowed to confront me because if I ever see how loopy my behavior is, I'll go to pieces, and we all know whose fault that is.

We typically face a hint of this when we're only a few months old, and Mom starts leaving us to ourselves from time to time to wash the dishes, talk on the phone, or any other of her ordinary daily routine. That's when we're struck with the realization that things aren't quite the way they once were, and one way we have of getting Mom back is to start acting up and trying to order her around the kitchen.

This is the tyrant-in-a-highchair scenario where the kid tries to control Mommy. We see aspects of it in a child's play-acting, a little girl playing tea party with her dolls, a little boy acting out scenes with his action toys: *You do this, you do that, say this, say that* . . . creating a world that's under their personal direction.

But when an adult tries to operate that way, seeking a sense of well-being by issuing demands, they'll drive others to resent them. Worse, the moment that other person turns to attend to some task we've assigned them, they have to turn their attention away from us, at which we'll have to assign them another task, give them another direction, then yet another, for none of it gives us what we really want. What we want, of course, is for them to play the role of a mother always at our beck and call, only to find that no one likes being danced around like a marionette by someone else's needs. What we actually need, though, is to develop mentally and emotionally to where we don't feel driven to control others in order to feel secure in ourselves.

So a man rages at his partner as she goes to work that she's making him feel abandoned and unloved, while she responds, *Hey, I'm just doing what I always do, and you're making me angry with all this nonsense.* Then he launches into a pop-psychology lecture on how only she can make herself angry, and needs to take responsibility for her feelings. And what's sadly yet laughably obvious is that in his version of reality she's responsible for her feelings while he's not responsible for his own.

Or there's the couple walking down a street, she regaling him with a stream of criticism and blame, which he silently absorbs until, embarrassed by the public spectacle he finds himself in, he makes one brief grumbling reply, at which she sneers, *Oh, you're such a whiner!*

It's an attitude that implies: *You don't get to complain! I do! You don't get to criticize! I do! You don't get to have needs! I do! You don't get to have feelings! I do! You don't even get to have a voice!* Ultimately, what it comes down to is: *You don't get to be a person! I do!* All of which would be fairly normal for a three-year-old, yet this was someone in her late forties.

Although these may be fairly extreme examples, the underlying traits are common, surfacing even in high-level businesses and international politics. And we see it in psychotherapy circles where there's a trend for people to develop psychotherapeutic treatment modalities that justify what they've been doing since childhood, as if to say, *The way for the rest of you to be emotionally healthy is to be just like me.* Skinner, Ellis, Rogers, Freud, Jung, and Perls have all done that in their own way. Fritz Perl's Gestalt therapy, for example, lead in part to Tom Wolfe's labeling 1970s attitudes as the "Me Decade," a criticism directed in part at the encounter group scene for giving license to some fairly outrageous behavior under the guise of healthy self-expression.

A major factor in that culture is the notion of catharsis, that screaming and punching pillows, or thrashing about in a padded room will lead us to emotional health by discharging pent-up emotions. The results, though, have been questionable, for while intense emoting can provide temporary feelings of exaltation, decades of that sort of therapy have not produced greater emotional maturity. In fact, it seems to have kept people at the same level of immaturity while priding themselves in how in touch with their feelings they are.

Gestalt was in some ways a reaction against the emotional rigidity of the 1950s and early 1960s where we had Sergeant Joe Friday in the TV show *Dragnet* constantly telling hysterical woman, "Just stay with the facts, ma'am. Just stay with the facts." But, of course, reactions against an earlier trend tend to be overreactions, and when hyper-emotional people started dominating the psychotherapy arena, a certain degree of mayhem was bound to result.

There's an old adage that people go into therapy to improve their neuroses rather than getting over them, but the same can be true for people becoming therapists, for we typically adopt therapeutic notions that reinforce our own habits. So, when we see a therapist insisting that people in his therapy groups expose each and every one of their innermost feelings, we have to question whether that's really a therapeutic thing to do, or if it isn't simply that the therapist feels anxious when he can't pry into others' personal space. In much the same way, we see group leaders putting themselves on pedestals while telling others how arrogant they are, therapists who can't understand why others don't want to think and feel the way they do. And discussing it can be like arguing over religion, which, in a sense, it is.

Then there are gender stereotypes, for it's common to say that men tend to define themselves through isolation while women tend to do it through attachment. Yet while it may be that women's yearning for closeness mimics the infant's need to merge into Mother, it's also an important aspect of mothering and community cohesiveness, for the person who yearns for too much distance will make a poor nurturer and a poor community builder. An argument that gained momentum in the early 1970s was that male attitudes dominating the field of psychology had wrongly judged women's attachment orientation to be neurotic, leading feminists to create more a specifically female-oriented theoretical basis. It's important work, yet there's a counter-counter argument that women can't adequately understand maleness and the needs of a growing boy, and wind up committing many of the same gender-based errors in reverse.

In a popular book of letters written by women at the end of relationships (Anna Holmes' *Hell Hath No Fury*), we read that women fall in love in the hope of finding someone they can lean on to keep themselves from falling down. Well, men do that too, although the tendency seems more generally hardwired into the female psyche, and yes, we all lean on each other to some extent. More to the point, though, we all have both a need to be close to others and a need for personal space, that it's just that men and women stereotypically have different tolerance levels in either direction. It also brings to mind Garrison Keillor's comment that marriage is all about seeing another person at their dumbest.

Women's instincts are an important part of every culture, which they quite rightly complain has been downplayed by men. Depictions of places like Somalia describe women struggling to keep things going while the men make plans for killing each other, and it's a sad truth that many men have as little tolerance for group cooperation as they do for the sound of a baby's crying, or for holding an infant for hours at a time. And while that lack of tolerance can drive him to shake a crying infant, trying to make that screeching thing stop, it can also drive him to pick up a gun rather than trying to work out how to get along.

But men typically yearn not so much for isolation as for a sense of inner space, a place within themselves where they can find solace. That's why Ed Abbey said that without wilderness there can be no civilization, and it's why lack of contact with nature makes city and suburban kids prone to being a bit crazy. Ever think what it would really be like to live on the Starship Enterprise? It also recalls Harold Bloom's comment that you can't teach irony any more than you can teach solitude, for we have to take our focus off our sense of need in order to appreciate the odd incongruities of life.

So, while a little boy feels a need to be close to his mother, he also feels a need to separate from her—not to reject her, but to find a sense of his own maleness distinct from her femaleness. In doing this, he's starting to find that silent place within himself which he finds difficult to do in her presence, for to some boys it feels like Mom is right there inside his body with him, allowing no space for himself.

And it isn't limited by culture. An acquaintance traveling in North Africa once told me how he'd asked the men he'd met why they didn't spend more time with their women, at which they all laughed and, with thumb and fingers, made gestures of mouths endlessly talking. It's a classic issue, and from a male point of view women talk simply to have their mouths going, filling their leaky balloons with the sound of their voices filling the air, while the female point of view is that men seek silence only in order to avoid closeness.

But we're all more complicated than that. From a male point of view, women will get together not so much to share ideas or experiences as to be awash in each other, like the emotional equivalent of a mud bath. Men, on the other hand, have little tolerance for that sort of thing, our trash talk being a kind of verbal sparring for its own sake, a bit like throwing medicine balls at each other. Or as a racecar engineer fondly expressed his brotherly love for a famous driver, "He's like a kid brother. You want to grab him and punch him in the face two or three times."

In the same way, men tend to share through joint effort, whether through adventuring, working and sweating alongside each other, or through play-fighting like football, and when a man overworks himself it's partially a way of exercising his instinct to challenge himself, partially a way of escaping that suffocating female mud bath.

This isn't to dismiss female tendencies any more than we like to hear women dismissing ours. It's just that a man tends to feel gripped by a strange desperation when forced to spend too much time eyeball-to-eyeball with another person of any gender. From his point of view, a woman will talk a steady stream until all his inner spaces are so filled with the drone of her voice that he can't think clearly, and starts dropping things and bumping into walls. Then, when she senses him shutting her out, she becomes angry, becoming even angrier when she realizes he can't remember a single word she's said. From his side, it just doesn't seem to occur to her that he might be in the middle of something important, for to her nothing's more important than blurring herself into him, and if he distances from her in order to reclaim himself or simply to get on with whatever else he may have been doing, she feels that she's losing her connection with him. To her, his distancing is uncaring, cold, and strange, his tiredness meaning that he doesn't care, while he's starting to feel she's not content until she's filled every nook and cranny of himself with herself, that he has to compete with her even for the space inside his own head, and sooner or later he'll simply snap: *My God! Do you ever SHUT UP?*

Which tends to put a damper on things.

But while he accuses her of running her mouth like a spigot, of using her constant stream of talk as a substitute for sucking her thumb, that she can't drive a car without yammering away on the cell phone, she accuses him of being a workaholic to avoid intimacy, of hiding within his isolation and silence to avoid the relationship. She sees him as a cold, callous beast while he sees her as a clingy, obsessively needy manipulator. Each is running on their own habits, each dealing with their own lack of personal strength, one trying to escape a chronic sense of emptiness, the other trying to escape feeling cannibalized and paralyzed.

It's really not a matter of posing men against women, rather one of contrasting stereotypical dynamics. So, while it may seem tediously cliché, it's better to think of this as a contrast between yin and yang, for some women yearn for solitude while some men feel that spending time with other men traps them in a tormenting hell of silence.

Still, there are important gender issues. For a young boy, the gender difference between himself and his mother has repercussions that most women, even female psychologists, don't understand very well. It's common for a boy to grow up with a sense that women control everything in and around him, and it's often reflected in the marital home where he feels he barely has a place of his own—the furniture and décor are hers while he maybe gets the garage and the tool shed. And anything male showing up in her space, such as the toilet seat in the up position or traces of his shaving around the bathroom sink, is an intrusion into her domain.

So, many men feel that they'd grown up in women's space with women telling them what to do and how to be, and they just don't know how to get past it. As the famously misogynistic lyric from *My Fair Lady* says, "She'll redecorate your home from the cellar to the dome, then go on to the enthralling fun of overhauling you!" Misogyny generally stems from a fear of being overpowered by women's demands, yet the "she" in the lyric can apply to anyone who tries to gain a self-sense by obsessively fiddling with their environment, trying to gain the feelings of nurture and security they'd longed for in infancy by micromanaging anyone close to them. That can make a person a compulsive nag, running on the relentless demands of a child that can never be fulfilled, as in the title of the old Off-Broadway show, *I Love You, You're Perfect, Now Change.*

On the other hand, as feminists have quite rightly complained, men have traditionally tried to mold women into servants just like Mommy once was, discounting women's natural instincts in the process. But then a typical woman's viewpoint is that if she doesn't take charge around the home, the place will deteriorate into a bachelor pad mess. It's not that she *wants* to control everything, but that she feels forced to while men sit about basking in their own glory. It's little wonder that women have been angry about it for a few millennia. Then men complain that women misuse notions of chivalry, playing at being helpless and incompetent to the point that it sometimes seems their greatest competence is in getting their way through manipulation.

So, there are stereotypical ways that men are selfish toward women, and stereotypical ways women are selfish toward men, and finding a way to meet each other in a healthy way is rarely a simple matter. And this is to say nothing of the ways men are cruel to other men, women to other women. Either way, our yearning for fulfillment tends to have a carrot-on-a-stick quality, leading us to endlessly badger and blame others for things we really need to take responsibility for, ourselves.

Building Blocks:
Developmental Issues Throughout Childhood

*The American male doesn't mature
until he has exhausted all other possibilities.*
~Wilfred Sheed

The building of a human psyche from infancy to adulthood is a complex and drawn-out process, one theme being that our self is a thing to be created, not something to be discovered as implied in the personal growth subculture. The early stages involve "introjects," the feelings, emotional and mental dynamics that we take in as children from the people around us, absorbing them as if by osmosis. Throughout childhood we absorb the world around us like a dry sponge, the quality of the nurturing and attention we receive contributing to our sense of who and what we are, and of what we are to expect from life, and in that process we take on other people's strengths and weaknesses, competence, insecurities and neuroses.

As newborns we are programmed right from our first breath toward such basic things as bonding, skin-to-skin contact, eye-to-eye contact, and sucking at a nipple, and as we grow, we want a continuing mirroring from others to give us a sense of ourselves. This is what a mother is doing when she meets her baby's eyes and babbles baby talk, giving out feelings that validate the infant's existence.

Researchers once filmed interactions between mothers and infants in which the mothers were directed to act out the extremes of a spectrum. In one case, a mother was to sit looking at her child with a blank expression, at which the infant would try to engage her, only to eventually break down and cry in distress, while in the other the mother was to playfully poke and tickle her infant and failing to stop when it was clearly too much, at which the baby would try to squirm away and wail in despair until going slack, glazed-eyed and drooling. This shows the range of emotional injury an infant might experience, from the emotionally distant parent to the relentlessly invasive one who overrides the child's fragile psyche.

In each extreme, the mother had been instructed not to respond to the infant's needs, and it's hardly surprising that the mothers eventually refused to go on with the experiment because it violated their natural instincts. But not all parents are all that aware of how they affect their children, some tending to be overly-invasive while others tend to be chronically distant.

Either way, as we develop a this-is-me sense of ourselves, it's typically somewhere around one and a half to two years that we encounter a tug-of-war between wanting to maintain the bond we'd developed in infancy on one hand, and a need to separate not just from Mother but from our infantile origins on the other. This is when a child starts toddling away from Mommy and out into the wide world until anxiety sends him scampering back, the first exploration going five or six feet, the next twenty, until he packs up and moves to Montana. And as we grow, the mirroring we need changes—a little boy runs into the kitchen babbling, *Mommy! Mommy! I saw this BIG TRUCK! And it was all RED and it went rrrRRRRrrrr and it had all these flashing lights and...* He wants her to validate what he's seen and felt, but if Mom responds with the same exaggerated mirroring she'd given him when he was an infant, he'll feel diminished and discounted, while if she ignores him, he's likely to feel that his experience, perhaps even his very existence, counts for little.

What a child needs is a reflection that validates what he has experienced, because it's from these building blocks that his sense of who he is will be constructed. That's because as children we internalize all the responses, feelings, looks, and voice tones that we get from adults in order to create an inner experience that defines us.

But then we develop ways of defining ourselves without needing to lean on others for it, for as Alfred Adler emphasized, one of our most important challenges is to live as unique individuals in relationship with a larger social environment. So, as infants we need to bond to a parental figure, while starting around age two our greater need is to experience ourselves as separate individuals, and the way we handle those conflicting needs will color the rest of our lives. We can also become stuck in an ongoing dilemma around the time we start to walk where we feel a conflict between our curiosity about the world around us and our need for Mom, and that's a conflict some of us have a hard time resolving.

Patterns

We all find ourselves at times lost in self-undermining patterns without realizing how we ever got there. Most of those patterns are impressions we took on early in life, and such they were probably once useful, but can become habitual ways of responding to other people and to life in general. As children we spend a lot of time trying to figure out how things work, and it's natural to assume that the way life works at one point is the way it will always be. That's why acting on a pattern gives us a sense of security, a reassurance that we know what to expect.

But as kids we are poor interpreters of what we experience, and our early inability to understand what's going on with the adults around us can lead us to distort things in serious ways. So, most of the patterns that cause us problems later in life were originally defenses against something that had been frightening, painful, stressful, frustrating, or simply too much to handle when we were little. They then developed into rigid defense mechanisms in anticipation that what had happened before will happen again. Not only is it natural to do that, but it's resourceful and brilliant in many ways.

However, if we fail to take in new experiences, gain additional resources, and develop better choices over time, our initial responses can become rigid assumptions about other people and about life in general. After all, the protective choices we'd made as a seven-year-old, or even a seventeen-year-old may not be especially useful at twenty-seven.

Our most basic patterns are bodily-felt dynamics that tell us, *This is who I am, this is the way I am,* and our conscious thinking will justify hose dynamics with what we call "logic," although others may not think them very logical at all. That's because our deepest patterns have a lot to say about what we call "reality," which is why changing a pattern can require us to experience life at least a little differently.

As adults, we are challenged to be more deliberate and choiceful in our lives, and that typically requires an act of willpower, an intentional choice to have a different response rather than an automatic one. And one of our greater challenges is to learn to distinguish between the hard reality around us and the perceived reality we carry within ourselves. Ultimately, the question comes down to whether we want to be living out of habit or in the present, able to make intentional choices and be responsive to the present moment. Predictably, the greatest issues arise when one person's pattern touches off patterns in another, resulting in two people reacting to old triggers and patterns. Yet, when we act on our habitual patterns against another person, it can feel powerful, convincing ourselves that we are right and the other person has something wrong with them.

What's required is that we find choice points and be willing to make use of them. That means changing how we experience not only ourselves but life at large, yet even a small degree of change can have major results in the long run.

When all's said and done, though, it all means one simple thing—that what we are convinced is reality isn't necessarily very real at all, not when it comes to our emotional reactions to the world around us.

Ego Needs and the Need for Ego

So, we're confronted with the challenge and the opportunity to understand as best we can this thing that calls itself 'me,' and see what makes it tick. Our most fundamental challenge starting from infancy is to develop what can be described as an invisible muscle with which we hold ourselves together, a glue of sorts that binds our psyche together. It's the skin of our balloon, the thing that contains and defines us, giving us the ability to stand on our own two feet. Developmental psychology describes this muscle as "ego strength," and its development is what takes us from the helplessness of infancy to the individuality and autonomy necessary to be reasonably self-reliant adults inter-related with each other. It establishes our sense of reality, defining not only our selves but our experience of the world around us. Conversely, a serious threat to our invisible muscle can plunge us into desperation, which is why those of us with an inherently weak self-sense feel driven to create an over-inflated balloon, trying to fake being stronger than we are.

There tends to be confusion regarding vocabulary at this point. Spiritual teachings and our most common social attitudes see ego as the thing we have to rid ourselves of or "rise above," because it's seen as arrogant, manipulative, selfish, power-hungry, and so on. In other words, ego is commonly seen as being all about narcissism, vanity, entitlement, and grandiosity—terms that describe lack of ego strength in the parlance of developmental psych. The problem is that the word, "ego," is used to mean opposite things, in that what we commonly call ego is seen as lack of ego strength from a developmental point of view.

So, while the term "ego strength" may be an unfortunate one, it's the commonly used term, and whatever we may choose to call it, it's what gives us the ability to carry ourselves in the world, the ability to tolerate difficulties and stress, pain, frustration, delayed gratification, loneliness, loss, failure, differences, disagreements, and everything else life throws at us. It's the driver, the "get'r done" ability that moves us out of indolence, helplessness, and dependency. It's also the thing that defines us so we can have authentic relationships rather than simply trying to reenact the dynamic we'd had with our mothers.

Lack of ego strength, on the other hand, is the reason children cry at the smallest frustration, fear the dark, throw tantrums, and cling to adults, and it's the reason adults attack each other with selfishness, violence and blame. In other words, what we think of as egotism represents a failure at having gained the ability to act any way other than what was normal in childhood. Conversely, ego strength is the basis of individuation, self-actualization, self-esteem and emotional intelligence, for without ego strength, emotional maturity and healthy autonomy aren't possible.

This is what we see in the Three Little Pigs tale children love, for it shows a child the need to develop an inner structure strong enough to manage the winds of the world instead of falling down at the slightest provocation. Yet most of the Baby Boomer generation who joined the hippie movement in the 1960s had psyches built of sticks and straw, and had to realize that grand philosophical notions in themselves were insufficient to the basic tasks of living. Many neo-hippies today still haven't learned that lesson.

One of the challenges in childhood and often in our teen years is an inner conflict between forming our self-sense by conforming to the expectations given us versus trying to gain a sense of identity by rebelling against anything that implies authority. But neither way really works in the long run, for a person with sufficient ego strength is free to choose to conform or to depart from norms, for his self-sense isn't deeply affected by either.

So, some of us start in elementary school to become the classic "Goodie-Two Shoes" while others of us fight everything, becoming every teacher's nightmare. But then a lot of the trouble kids eventually realize it's not working out so well for them, so the learn to behave more reasonably, while the Goodie Two Shoes kids start to realize that's not working out for them, either, and start breaking bad.

Either way, our ability to be at choice is determined by our ego strength, for it's the basis upon which our experience of ourselves stands. Conversely, selfishness, cruelty, criminal behavior, as well as many of the loonier things we do, demonstrate a lack of it.

Above all, our self-sense isn't based on anything we think. Rather, it's a thing we feel, a physically-felt sense of integrity, a "bodily-felt sense of well-being" (as a therapy cliché goes), a bodyset rather than a mindset, something generally we take for granted about ourselves and about life in general. More importantly for this conversation, without ego strength we act on the default dynamics of a child because we can't not, and that's where most of our problems arise.

As an invisible muscle, ego strength works three basic ways. First, it holds us upright, which is what basic military training tries to instill in slouching adolescents, although it tends to overcompensate with a ramrod posture. Otherwise, lack of that particular muscle shows up in the slouching, sulking teenager, unable to hold himself up straight except with contempt and defiance.

The second way our invisible muscle works is that it holds us in. We were all once kids living at the tops of our lungs, giving vent to any feeling that happened to run through us. And if we lack the ability to contain ourselves as adults, we'll still feel entitled to splatter ourselves everywhere, imposing on others as if it's our right.

The third way this invisible muscle works is to establish our personal space, and the person lacking this will have a hard time holding their own ground and standing up for themselves. This is the doormat, the space cadet, the absent-minded professor, and the geeky intellectual going through life in a bit of a daze as if having recently taken a blow to the head.

One thing this implies is that we can be terribly predictable, that while we like to think of ourselves as unique individuals, we all tend to act on predictable impulses, and that's something that can get us wondering just what this thing that I call my "self" really is, anyway? So, if you were to talk about someone on the other side of the world with dynamics like my own, I would likely respond unconsciously as if you were talking about me, and you would be to some extent, just as if we talked about someone with dynamics like yours, you would likely respond as if we were talking about you, and we would be.

There's something quite primitive about it, for there are three primal ways most life forms react to another life form: to mate with it, to attack it and maybe eat it, or to flee. And it shows up in three basic ways we all have of reacting to each other, impulses that drive us in ways our "conscious" minds typically don't recognize: to push at others, to grab hold and cling to them, or to run away.

The famous hypnotherapist, Milton Erickson, related how, when confined to an iron lung as a teenager and with little to do but observe people, he'd realized it was as if there were two individuals in everyone he watched: one in control of their conscious actions, the other driving everything else. That's why he devised a form of therapy to address the part of the psyche that's actually running things. It's a bit like the sign we might see on a secretary's desk: *Do you want to talk to the boss, or to the person who knows what's going on?*

We're all prone to being oblivious to our own behavior at times, which is why I refer so often to behaviors we see on the highway, for much of the time a driver's conscious mind isn't the one with its hands on the wheel, its foot on the gas. Many of our most common behaviors can look quite odd when viewed under a strong light, yet we take our behavior for granted and justify it even when the effects we have on others range from the simply annoying to the outright dangerous. No matter how dignified and sophisticated we may be, we're all confronted from time to time with the primitive creature that emerges as if from nowhere.

It says something about why we are capable of doing certain things while insisting we're not, as if unable to stop ourselves. It also explains why we'll repeat the same things over and over even after it's become clear that they don't work. I once heard a taxi driver comment on how many times he would see a dent in someone's car right where he'd just almost hit them, and it makes me wonder what our Martian anthropologist would think watching us stumble about, convinced we know what we're doing.

This also shows why personality styles become so polarized, for we react subconsciously to other people's behaviors, wanting to match in agreement, oppose them, or protect ourselves from them, setting up most of the strife we've seen throughout history. It's because our sense of propriety, even our basic sense of reality is based not on the world around us so much as on how we internalize things, and how we internalize things is rooted in dynamics developed early in childhood. And, yes, we all have our ways of distorting reality.

This three-aspect dynamic was defined over ninety years ago by Alfred Adler as the "getting" (although "taking" often seems a better translation) personality, the "ruling" or "dominance" personality, and the "avoiding" personality. Karen Horney in turn described them as "moving toward," "moving against" and "moving away" styles. Either way, these three essential motivations represent in their extremes three basic ways of having failed to develop sufficient ego strength.

Said a little differently, we all have a tendency to push, to pull, and to retreat. That is, we're motivated to go up against the world and apply ourselves to it; to move close others, to relate and share; and to distance ourselves from others to be within our inner space, to contemplate and imagine. Each motivation is based on an odd collection of healthy motivations and dire weaknesses, and each can be taken to extremes. Moreover, each represents a way we react to stress: with anger if not outright rage, with anxiety and hysterics, or by going inward—perhaps going slightly catatonic. When pushed to it, though, rage is the last resort for most of us, for whenever we sense ourselves starting to fall apart, we all have the capacity to regress into hysterics and fury in order to pull ourselves back together, for rage can imitate a feeling of having an intact balloon, an intact ego structure, at least for a short time.

Borrowing the classic Taoist jargon, the moving toward, getting, clinging tendency is yin; the moving against, dominating tendency is yang; while the avoidant, moving away tendency is generally neutral. Of course these distinctions are artificial, and we break things down into distinct categories simply for the sake of describing largely unconscious motivations we all have. When it comes to those of us who are more extreme, however, the distinctions become clearer, and we are all, for better or worse, subject to extremes at times.

Adler, though, went on to describe a fourth style he dubbed "socially useful," meaning someone who is healthy enough to participate in society without being dominated by immature impulses. But while he was looking at these styles as pathology my intention is to use them to describe three basic tendencies we all have, although we generally tend toward one more than others. The socially useful style, then, describes someone who can moderate their impulses enough to act in a reasonably mature manner.

Again, our bodily-felt dynamics are so deeply-set as to color not only our sense of who we are and how others are supposed to be, but they color our sense of reality as well, so much so that unless we carry sufficiently mature ego strength, we can only assume that there is something defective about anyone too different from ourselves.

Others, on the other hand, may think at times that we have a piece of our brain missing. What's true is that there's a piece of our developmental process missing, although we generally don't have the means for recognizing it. After all, our basic bodyset was in place before we developed an intellect, and as our thinking mind took shape, it learned to explain and justify our pre-existing dynamics. It makes me think of those Renaissance paintings of European peasants wandering among Roman ruins without a clue as to where these things had come from—they'd just always been there. That's how our mind sees our early bodyset—we don't know what it is; it's just always been that way.

There's a basic notion in the Adlerian coaching world that while animals generally respond to a stimulus in blunt, primitive ways, as humans we're challenged to have choice before we respond, that instead of stimulus-response, we're challenged to a stimulus-choice-response way of living. And that takes ego strength, for without it we're limited to childishly simplistic ways of responding to life in general. So, if we lack the ego strength to have other choices available, our experience will be limited to whatever validates us. We're all challenged, then, to confront what happens if we don't act on our most basic impulses. Many of us become disoriented, even vaguely frightened when challenged to take our attention off our feelings, others of us become disoriented when compelled to take our attention off our interior mental worlds, while still others of us become anxious when compelled to stop trying to take charge of everything.

While much of the following discussion can be taken as mother-bashing, it's really just a matter of seeing what shapes us, and much of what shapes us early on is Mom, or at least someone in a mothering role. Mothers, though, are in a difficult position, an impossible one in many ways because any weakness on their part can have such a powerful effect on their children. As small children, we build our self-sense largely by taking in feelings from our mothers, absorbing their personalities so that both their strengths and their neuroses become our own. As a novelist (sadly, I've forgotten who) comments, seeing our parents clearly can be like trying to see our own eyeballs or taste our own tongue. That's why our family's effect on us can be much like hypnosis, for implied messages carry far more weight than ones spoken outright—the voices may be silent, but the impact is powerful. And because that curious hypnosis can define our reality, one of the keys to solving the question marks of our own personality lies in comprehending our parents' lives in a matter-of-fact way.

F. Scott Fitzgerald comments (in *Tender is the Night*) that we all carry the egos of people "early met and early loved," and that we tend to feel only as complete as those people were themselves. This is why our greatest obstructions are typically the ones we hold most dear. But our sense of ourselves and our ways of seeing others is challenged to morph as we go through life. And one of our most basic challenges is to face the general messiness of life: the mess in our own lives, the mess in others' lives, and the mess we can make in each others' lives.

Three Personality Styles: Dissecting Our Habits

Reality is not about the way you feel
~ Chris Smither

The main point of all this discussion is that we generally undermine ourselves by holding onto dynamics that had served us in childhood, many of which are derived from a blueprint we took on at birth. While many of our earlier dynamics were not only normal but necessary in infancy and early childhood, they can become problems as we grow up, and as adults, we're challenged to take a ruthlessly honest look at our lives and recognize how many of our attitudes and behaviors are things we're challenged to stop doing.

And that can hurt. It can also seem impossibly wrong because we're challenged to change the very ways we see and feel ourselves to be us. If I stop doing something I've done all my life, will I still be me? Isn't it easier to simply go on telling everyone else how wrong they are, and how wrong the world is?

It's important to be clear as to what we're about, for we're all in it together, and we all have habits that obstruct our lives. Otherwise, this material can become an excuse to attack each other without taking the responsibility to address our own lives. This takes courage, yet there's no right way of doing this life although there are a lot of ways of making problems for ourselves while blaming others.

Right from earliest childhood we start constructing an interior version of the world we experience around us, and one of the greater challenges in maturing is to face the fact that most of the rest of the human race doesn't even know we exist much less care about our interior world. After all, they're busy dealing with their own.

One offshoot of this is a notion popular with politicians and religious fundamentalists that the angrier we get, the longer and louder we shout, the more right we are. But those angry rants are often coming from the fear that we might not be right, that our interior world might have no hard reality behind it. On the other hand, some of us try to use a seductive tone or an intellectual stance to the same effect, trying to break down other people's integrity in an effort to get others' lives to work our way.

Following Alfred Adler's stance that our experiences carry the meanings we give them, we're challenged to reevaluate the conflicts between our interior versions of the world and the hard edges of our exterior world, and face the feelings that conflict brings. And one of the sharpest edges of that conflict is that the exterior world has no obligation to meet the expectations of our interior world. Without getting that, we can remain stuck trying to prove ourselves right in the face of some serious realities.

As someone who lived through the hippie period of the 1960s, I'm struck by the journalist's later comment that the hippie movement failed as all utopian movements fail because it couldn't deal with the fundamental realities of the human condition. My response is that it failed because we were all too screwed up; screwed up by drugs and alcohol, by inadequate parenting, and by a culture that not only didn't encourage us to grow up, but actually gave us messages that we didn't have to.

The overall challenge of life can be said many ways, one of which is that before we start waxing eloquent about love, philosophy and metaphysical notions, we have to get here, to become grounded in this life. Otherwise we live with our heads in the clouds, full of grand notions without the ability to bring them about, or even know if they can be brought about. This is what Human Incarnation 101 is all about, and the hippie movement from 1967 until today has generally failed at it. For any of us, though, the challenge is that while we want it all to be easy, we're forced to face the fact that it's not.

Developmental challenges are with us right from an early age, taking us through the "terrible two-year-old" phase where we try to control a world we don't understand with tantrums, then through those angry teenage moments when we rage at a world we still don't understand anywhere near as much as we like to think. It's common for us as kids to expect that people around us will adapt themselves to our needs, but the adult need is to learn to adapt ourselves to the life going on around us, and that's where so many of us fail.

This was apparently what inspired classical pianist Arthur Rubenstein to say that we can fully live our lives only when we learn to meet life on its own terms. Life itself has a way of confronting us with our assumptions despite our stubbornness, and so many of our life issues evolve out of challenges we have still not dealt with well enough.

And with the uprising of conspiracy theories over the last few decades, we're seeing a blurring of the line between science and superstition, and stubborn irrationality and outrage that mirrors the witch hangings and burnings of past centuries, the madness that took over Germany in the 1930s, and the demented religious movements that have scarred human history over the centuries.

With this in mind. we'll go through three basic personality dynamics that Alfred Adler laid out a century ago, and see what use we can make of it.

Moving Toward: the Getter, the Clinger, the Other-Oriented

One difficulty that looms over this discussion is to work out how to develop something that's intangible. How do we develop ego strength and an adequate self-sense when we don't have much to begin with, and don't really understand what it is we need? It's a basic conundrum, for as an old adage says, good judgment comes from experience, and experience comes from bad judgment. Or, to put it more bluntly, we often gain intelligence by acting like fools at times, then pulling clear of it enough to gain some mature sensibility. That's why we wake up at three in the morning to lie there staring at the ceiling until dawn thinking of the foolish things we'd done when we were young and thought we had life by the horns. And as F. Scott Fitzgerald said, in the dark night of the soul it's always three in the morning.

So, we'll start with the default position of the human psyche, that of longing for closeness, for being the focus of other people's energy and attention. And it's an underlying trait that will show up in the other two tendencies as well, although in different forms.

The move-toward style is the way virtually all of us were as children, but without gaining more depth and range along the way, it won't make sense to us that others don't act the way we expect. And it will make no sense for anyone to criticize us, although we'll feel entitled to criticize them for violating what seems natural to us. Then write self-help books and spiritual literature, even show up on TV dictating how everyone else is supposed to live according to the blueprint we've been running on, failing to understand that we've missed a few developmental steps along the way.

I recall a friend describing when his daughter was learning to ride a bike she would habitually veer toward pedestrians as if unable to stop herself from acting on her need for closeness. But then some adults walk down a sidewalk that way, even drive a car that way as if drawn by the magnetic pull of flesh and blood, trying to find comfort by snuggling up close, even at 60 miles an hour. We even see dogs acting that way, ambling out in front of an oncoming car with a big doggie grin as if to say, *Oh! You're coming to see me, aren't you?* So, will that girl on the bike grow up to be someone who habitually crowds in on other people because it gives her a sense of comfort? And will she drive a car that way?

I was once reading to a child who, when I leaned to reach for something, impulsively grabbed my arm, as if to say, *Don't leave!* In the same way, if you try to end a conversation with a clingy person, telling them you're going to be late for something important, they'll say, *Oh, just one more thing!* But it'll be just one more thing after that, and then another, as if to prevent you from leaving them alone in a frighteningly empty universe.

It's an impulse that can compel us to tailgate other drivers on the highway as if our need for closeness overrides all common sense. And it can drive others to see us as incapable of understanding dangers they see as obvious, and it can cause others to back away from us—the opposite of what we want. The feeling behind it is a bit like being a house with three walls, looking for someone to provide a fourth, treating others as extensions of ourselves rather than as people in their own right. That in turn can subject us to criticism we'd really rather avoid because we have such a hard time understanding it.

This has been referred to as an "other-oriented" personality dynamic, and while it's the basis of our most basic relationship and community-building instincts, when taken to obsessive extremes it becomes a problem. We see the bare bones of those extremes right from an early age when kids will put themselves in the middle of adult activities, often in obstructive ways. They simply want to be engaged with the adults in their lives, but they'll have forgotten by the age of eight or nine that they were doing it on purpose, hesitating and dawdling at critical places so as to control as many people as possible. I recently encountered a man in Costco standing at the intersection of three aisles with four or five shoppers and their carts waiting for him to get out of the way, and there he was where his sense of need wanted him to be, at the point of maximum attention. Then there was a driver at the gas pump outside, chatting on her cell phone while other drivers lined up behind her.

The basic impulse is to claim a feeling of being nurtured by demanding others' attention and making them subservient to our needs. It's a basic impulse in childhood, yet it becomes a problem when kids try to control adult situations they don't understand. Worse, of course, is when an adult does those things, then uses anger to defeat others and control things that aren't their business.

We all have a clingy, needy child inside us, and we're all capable of acting on it at times, often in the way we drive a car. The highway, after all, is one of those microcosms where we are subjected to others' best and worst traits, a place where our more primitive instincts can easily take over, yet it's a place where we are challenged to be each other's keepers.

So, when someone has to change lanes, a clingy person might pull up alongside and match their speed, speeding up when the other driver tries to get ahead as if to say: *Oh, wait for me!,* slowing when the other driver tries to drop in behind: *Hey, where'd you go now?,* not noticing the sign that says, This Lane Ends, not seeing the brake lights or the turn signals because their attention on their feelings obscures everything else. And when a sign says Slower Traffic Keep Right, it doesn't seem to occur to them, *Yo, dude! That means you!* Or when a line of cars stuck behind a slow-moving truck finally gets to a passing lane, a clinger will pull up alongside that slow-mover and glom on with a dozen other drivers back there shouting at them through their windshields. In much the same way they'll hang in the blind spot just off another driver's left rear fender, replicating the position of a child toddling along just behind Mom's left knee, which is where they would likely be with a right-handed parent. And if they sense someone waiting for them, they'll slow down and dawdle for no apparent reason other than to hold the other person' attention.

I remember one time I was riding with my mother, a classic uber-clinger, watching her speed up when a motorcycle tried to pass, hearing her giggle nervously as she accelerated faster and faster while the guy on the bike frantically yelled at her. And it struck me that her giggle was because her rational mind had suddenly recognized what she was doing, yet didn't have the power to get her foot off the gas pedal. I saw the same sort of thing when a mother burned herself at the kitchen stove and dashed for the sink to cool her hand under the tap only to have her three year-old lunge into her path only to get knocked flat and lay there wailing.

It's a child's impulse to cling to Mother, but when an adult does that at random, it leaves others wondering, *What the hell are you DOING?* And that question—*What are you doing?*—is one a clingy person dreads, for they really don't know what they're doing because they're in a "glommer trance," a state we can fall into when our sense of need overrides common sense.

Overall, the problem clingers pose is that even as reasonably intelligent and competent adults we can act in ways that can make us look stubbornly oblivious. The reason for calling it a trance state is that as clingers we can be so taken by our latent sense of need that our conscious thought processes will be shunted aside. What we are doing, though, is trying to rid ourselves of uncomfortable body memories of what were once authentic needs but have become fixed imprints lodged in our psyches as if branded there. Falling in love can make it seem like those needy feelings have gone away forever, yet they return the moment our beloved turns out to be just another schlub. And we're all just schlubs when you get right down to it.

All of this makes for a high-maintenance relationship partner, a label generally applied to women, although there are plenty of men who fit the bill no matter how we may try to hide it. And it's not just that no one can ever be good enough to alleviate those deep-set feelings, but that we have difficulty seeing how we can drive people away, ruining one relationship after another. And those in relationship with a clingy person quickly learn to protect their partner from feeling anything they don't want to feel out of fear of setting off a storm.

That brings up the issue of deservedness, for people with sufficient ego strength don't go through life thinking about what they deserve. Instead, they simply work competently toward whatever they want to achieve. The notion of deservedness, though, stands out in the personal growth arena, although it misses the point, for we don't find fulfillment by getting anything, but rather by developing authentic personal strength so that we don't need so much in order to feel secure in ourselves.

These things may be trivial everyday annoyances, yet they demonstrate behaviors that can affect every relationship. Kids are more obvious about it, dumping their schoolbooks and coats on the floor right in everyone else's path, raising their voices to a shout when someone is on the phone, or doing calisthenics in front of the TV, trying to make themselves the center of attention: *Look at me, damn it!* But will we be driving a car like that and trying to run our relationships like that at the age of seventeen, and when we're forty-seven will we flare with outrage should anyone dare to object?

Extreme clingers seem to have a sixth sense for tracking others' energy, for just as someone may turn around if you stare at their back, clingers will sense where you are about to step, and there they'll be, just as children often are. That leaves others zigging and zagging around a clinger while the clinger is zagging and zigging to be in the other's energy field. And if someone starts speaking, a clinger takes it as their cue to start talking over them. Or they'll hold a shouting conversation on their cell phone when there are other people about, as if trying to fill the very air with themselves.

The origins can be seen in the toddler hovering at knee level while Mom's bustling about the kitchen, and it can readily evolve into the driver who speeds up when you pass them, the person who feels good when keeping others from doing things, the parent who obstructs their child's development, or the man who can't stand for his wife to have any life of her own.

It's important to realize, though, that these are almost completely unconscious impulses, and we all carry some measure of them. And no matter how these behaviors may look on the surface, they stem from infancy where our feelings and needs are potentially a matter of life and death.

Yet it leaves us asking a double question that hangs over so many human behaviors: Is it that obsessive clingers simply can't see what they're doing, or are they are stubbornly refusing to see what they're doing while insisting on making it someone else's problem? Either way, extreme clingers can look at times as if their rational minds have simply switched off as they habitually stand in doorways, stop at the end of escalators or in any place where there's a narrowed flow of traffic, veering into others when they try to get past. We see it in one of the last scenes in the old film *K-Pax* in which a character is running down a hallway only to have the person coming the other way throw herself, with a bewildered look, straight into his path. Yes, it's just a movie, but I would bet the scriptwriter who wrote that scene did so out of accumulated frustration.

In any case, clingers instinctually sense the presence of another person and lean into it. While fairly normal for a child, that compulsion can drive an adult to impose on others anyway he can, for while our instinct for contact with others is one of our most basic needs, it can drive us to paralyze other people's lives just as children often try to paralyze their parents, trying to make the adult world obey a child's reality. And for all our criticism of things too mental, as clingers we'll obsess on words, trying to adjust our feelings with vocabulary, often by trying to adjust other people's vocabulary: *Don't say it that way, say it this way!* For all our explanations, though, it's really just another way of trying to control our environment in order to feel safe inside our own skins. We were all once infants able only to see others as extensions of our needs, and if we don't develop beyond that stance, we'll wind up treating friends, spouses and children, even strangers on the highway as non-persons meant to give us what we want.

The basic clinging tendency in an adult may be the result of inadequate bonding at birth, which can drive a newborn into adrenal stress, and that feeling of incompleteness can run us for the rest of our lives. More commonly, though, it seems to result from feeling starved by emotionally distant parents, leaving us forever longing for more. On the other hand, it can just as well result from growing up in a highly-enmeshed family where it's difficult to gain a sense of individuality, so when we venture out into the world, we'll go looking for someone to moosh ourselves into because we haven't learned anything else. Then again, it may be that we had plenty of nurturing as children, but became so overly fond of it that we simply refused to move on any further. Either way, we're left feeling that others having personal space is strange and wrong, that others' privacy constitutes a vague threat.

One way or another, obsessive clinging is one way an incomplete psyche acts, and a parent with that dynamic may attempt to defeat their child's developing psyche in order to not feel left behind by their child growing up and away from them. As Hegel suggests, anyone more psychologically-developed than themselves must have something wrong with them. That results in immature people trying to control those more mature than themselves, just as children often do.

The heart of the matter is that no matter how romantic the other-oriented may seem at times, adults chronically out to use others to prop themselves up are trying to escape facing how frightened they are of standing on their own. They may declare how in touch with their feelings they are while actually they are in touch only with those feelings that fill their balloons with warm, nurturing sensations while desperately avoiding a wider swath of feelings they'd rather not have to deal with.

Moreover, when we're in that mode we'll refuse to hear anything that conflicts with our sense of the way things are, for we'll have learned at an early age both to adjust our own minds so we won't recognize what we're doing, and to manipulate others so that they won't confront us about it. If that strategy fails, we'll resort to blackmail: *If you want me to love you, if you want sex with me, if you want closeness with me, then you'll just have to put up with me.* And although we'll freely complain about others, we will become enraged should anyone complain about us: *Don't you dare try to make me look at what I'm doing or I'll make damned sure you never make that mistake again!* This is how an extreme clinger will train their family, creating a family dynamic where everyone is trying to avoid the landmines laid by the clinger.

This dynamic has driven things like the Gestalt Therapy/Encounter Group movement popular since the 1960's where everyone is to fit a clinger's expectations. Yet, facing their own expectations can be frightening to a clinger, for they expect to hold a superior stance, dictating how life is supposed to work their way. This, by the way, we'll see in the other two styles, and beneath it lay the terrible sense of emptiness that underlies any narcissistic stance.

Whatever its origins, the obsessively other-oriented dynamic represents a failure to attain the healthy degree of individuation that was our challenge starting at around two years of age. One result is that, as outright clingers, we come out of childhood with two primary feelings: A feeling like a bottomless pit, a black hole in the middle of our chest, a feeling constellated from years of disappointment, loss, despair and longing dating back to our earliest infancy where we fear we might shrivel up and die if our needs aren't met. That in turn is tied with an expectation that this bottomless pit is someone else's responsibility. After all, when we were little it really was someone else's responsibility.

This is why many of us chronically complain and criticize, seeking an explanation for our sense that things are somehow wrong, that something's missing from our lives. And while we're looking for someone else to supply what's missing, the notion that no one can truly provide it for us can send us into anything from despair to rage. What we generally miss is that getting someone else to provide us those feelings isn't what we need. What we actually need is to gain a feeling of wholeness by developing better ego strength, a fuller self-sense.

But none of that makes sense when we're younger and don't have much of a self-sense, and are trying to fulfill ourselves by being right, by manipulating and raging at a world that doesn't suit us. We first start feeling that despair-rage in our terrible-two phase, then again in our angry teenage phase where we're upset that the world doesn't match our hormone-driven idealism, above all upset that the wonderful dependency of childhood is slipping away from us.

One thing that can frighten us so badly is that, as in particle physics, the nature of a black hole is that no matter how much is stuffed into it, it will always seem empty. It's hardly surprising, then, to see a popular magazine called *More*, and it's why those in relationship with other-oriented people often feel they're being cannibalized.

For all their talk of emotional openness, and for all their criticism of others for being closed-up and defended, the other-oriented among us are highly defended against that bottomless pit we all carry in the middle of our chests. And it can be a serious matter, as those feelings we pretend we don't have are capable of tipping a clinger into a panic attack if not a psychotic break, requiring hospitalization and medication.

This is what drives a clinger's manipulation, yet that narcissism can be devastatingly attractive to some of us. We see it in the works of F. Scott Fitzgerald with his mixed fascination with and contempt for haughty young women, and we see it in young women throwing themselves at attractive young rock stars. Yet, avoiding that horrifying void is drives a clinger more than anything else, meaning that an ardent clinger has to disguise their most basic motivation. In extreme cases, this is where people with borderline and narcissistic personality disorders live, yet those of us who are nowhere near as unstable can get caught in endless loops of attraction, hurt, resentment, and revenge.

So, extreme clingers live with a sense of hyper-vigilance, always looking for someone to feed them, always on the lookout for anyone who may confront their behavior, always ready to let loose the hounds on others should the need arise. A great many other-oriented people bank on the power of that unspoken threat, and while the stereotypes are aimed at women, there are a great many men who rely on the power of a hissy fit, trying to get others to cave in and abdicate any sense of personal volition so as to avoid triggering a clinger's fear and outrage.

At the heart of it, though, lives a child trying to rule a world he doesn't understand and is afraid of, and when a child gains a sense of satisfaction by making Mom stop everything else and attend to his demands, he may grow up trying to do that to everyone. In short, clingers love to put others in servitude.

We all start out in life with an assumption that we are entitled to take advantage of others, that that's simply the way the world works, and anyone depriving us warrants our revenge. In *Love in the Time of Cholera*, Garcia-Marquez has a young girl habitually turning to whoever is closest whenever something goes wrong, telling them it's their fault, and when, after decades of putting up with it, her husband finally challenges her over a trivial oversight, it nearly ends their marriage.

This is why an extreme other-oriented person will badger lovers, children and friends with a litany of demands, while anyone expressing a need of their own is just a whiner. Yet while men may complain about female helplessness, when another guy acts that way, they're likely to be far more sarcastic: *Come on, man! Figure your shit out, okay?*

So, much of what clingers call "love" is desperation in disguise, which is a bit jarring to anyone familiar with *A Course in Miracles*, which preaches that the opposite of love is fear. Yet it's easy to take the clinger impulse for granted. A friend refers to her life before she had kids as "back when my body still belonged to me"—a sentiment most mothers can relate to. So, it was a moment of deep honesty when an other-oriented person admitted that she'd had to ask herself, *What are people for?*, because no matter her intellectual understanding, her emotional expectation was that other people existed to meet her needs, and if they weren't doing that, well, why were they even there? That's a normal-enough expectation for a child, yet it says something quite serious when it's coming from an adult. Consider, for instance, Martin Luther's comment that it doesn't matter that women die in childbirth. That's what they're for, isn't it?

This explains an attitude we often hear from the other-oriented, that no matter how busy you may be, if you're not doing something for them, in their minds you're just not doing anything at all. Actually, seeing someone doing things for themselves can make an extreme clinger anxious because it can trigger the feeling that their needs don't matter. Then read (if you can bear it), Proust's opening passages in *Swann's Way*, describing a child's maneuvering for attention as the desperate stratagems of a condemned prisoner. Or listen to Josh Groban's "When You Say You Love Me," and you'll be in the world of an ardent clinger. At our worst, as clingers we'll use hysterics and tantrums as weapons, using blame, guilt, even suicide threats to defeat other's personal boundaries and keep them focused on our needs.

It's common for children to try to get their way by breaking down adults' boundaries, but as needy adults we won't want others to have private feelings, thoughts, or personal space of their own. As Faulkner comments (in *The Reivers*), traditional Southern manners dictated that a closed door was regarded as a locked one, but an adult operating with the notions of a child is likely to respond to others' personal space as if it were their own to do with as they please.

Most of us start learning boundaries in a rudimentary way: *Eew! You have cooties!* Sure, it's silly, yet it's our first step in an important process. Still, it's a surprise to many kids to have Mom telling us not to go rummaging through her closet or dresser drawers because it's her space, not ours. But that's how we learn about boundaries, by

117

having someone force theirs on us.

Personal boundaries are an aspect of ego strength, and we can't have authentic boundaries without it, but can only imitate them with anger and defiance. As young children, though, we'll often try to defeat any boundaries imposed on us because our sense of need tells us other people's boundaries are wrong, that we belong in others' space. Yet one thing that develops ego strength is being compelled to restrain ourselves, and if we fail or refuse to accept that challenge, we are likely to grow into adulthood with a sense of entitlement that implies: *The business I need to be involved in is YOUR business!* Then, as parents, we're likely to see our children's developmental process as a threat to our own security, as something to be defeated.

Because of their sense of need, we'll see children orbiting their mother, chanting their mantra as she pushes a shopping cart through the supermarket: *Hey Mom! Hey Mom! Mom! Hey Mom!,* their attention so fixed on her that they'll run into other customers and into store displays—soup cans rolling all over the place. It's as if their center of gravity is inside Mom's body, which is why we see small children, especially when they're tired, squirming against Mom as if trying to burrow into her like a gopher. And there's a character in *The Great Gatsby* (likely based on someone Fitzgerald knew) who would speak in a murmur so as to force others to lean in close to her.

This can mean more than what is obvious, for not only do we bond to our parents, but to their version of the world at large, and without gaining at least some individuation, we'll never develop our own sense of things. And it's often seen as a gender issue, for while the other-oriented tendency is often considered a female trait, I prefer to think of it as a yin characteristic, as both genders carry it. But then some (mainly feminist) theorists feel that the notion of autonomy is a male neurosis opposing the female attachment orientation.

But autonomy doesn't imply distance or alienation; rather it's a matter of gaining personal identity through individual experience, which many of us have difficulty developing. On the female side, Nancy Friday's *My Mother, My Self* explores this theme, as does Deborah Tannen's, *You're Wearing That?*, both describing women's struggles to gain a sense of identity separate from their mothers—an especially tense issue because women are the same gender as her mother. According to Tannen, for instance, a mother may look at their adult daughter as if looking at herself in a mirror, thinking: *But I don't want my hair to look like that!* While the fact that she's looking at her daughter's hair may be obvious on a rational level, emotionally it's not obvious at all. Moreover, a person locked into that bodyset will treat another's emotional dynamics the same way: *But I shouldn't be feeling that way!,* then set about trying to change the other person's feelings in order to secure their own.

It's not just between mothers and daughters. Girls in my junior high school class used to pass a wad of chewing gum from one mouth to another as a way of feeling enmeshed with each another, and recent authors have spoken out about how inhumane girls and even adult women can be to one another when it comes to personal differences, how high schoolers tend to be hyper-vigilant toward any one of them failing to fit in to everyone else's satisfaction, be it in clothing, hairstyle, or choice of friends, creating a tyranny of conformity. And only a few years later those girls in my class were passing around gonorrhea during the Summer of Love when having personal boundaries meant that you were hung-up about sex; that the more diffuse your boundaries, the more enlightened you were. What it led to instead was the frayed exhibitionism and dissipated promiscuity that characterized much of the hippie scene.

What those hippie notions missed, and what young adults often continue to miss, is that it's not about prudery so much as it's about personal integrity. The same thing can be said about popular themes that emerged during the hippie period of all humanity being one, of rising above our individual egos to gain a sense of oneness. Despite what may be true in a spiritual sense, it led to a drugged-out haze of promiscuity and the sense of diffuse fuzziness that characterizes much of the personal growth and spiritual scene today where the "come from the heart" dictum becomes a directive: *You come from your heart so I don't have to feel empty and insecure!* And when that underlying fear surfaces, a come from the heart person can turn vindictive, making "love" one of the most abused words in any language.

There's a contrast I find between two versions of the song "I Had A Dream" from *Les Miserable,* Susan Boyle thrilling audiences by singing from her heart while Anne Hathaway shook us to the core by singing from her pain. That shines a light on a serious issue, for the come from the heart attitude is so often used to avoid many of the core experiences life demands that we face.

Just as we go through an adolescent phase where the grandiosity induced by our hormones tells us we know everything when we actually understand very little, we're capable of believing that our inflated grandiosity at any age informs us of the ways of the world when it's simply holding us to an under-developed state. When Tom Wolfe dubbed the 1970s the "Me Decade," it was in response to a scene in which self-improvement, emotional well-being, honest self-expression, and love were being defined by adults acting like self-absorbed children. Moreover, many became therapists and group facilitators in order to claim the voice of authority and tell all those non-clingers out there how wrong their lives were.

Much of our behavior as clingers, then, is not so much about love, connectedness or relationships as to avoid disturbing feelings and keep ourselves together the same way we had as children. This is why the other-oriented among us are notorious for taking prisoners and calling it love, and it's why our obsession with eye contact and closeness can feel a bit creepy. Worse, our tendency to distort not only our own reality so as to avoid all those horrible feelings, but also that of everyone else in order to get away with it constitutes a sort of Orwellian double-speak, crudely referred to as "mind-fucking." So, the other-oriented can be ardent mind-fuck artists—not because they're out to deliberately deceive others, but because they're trying to feel secure the only way they know how, and can't see how they look while doing it.

But it can exact a high cost others dearly to keep a clinger immersed in loving feelings, a cost a clinger will typically refuse to recognize. This is how clingers can become emotional tyrants, always set to assault another person's deepest emotional wounds, attacking them for being shy and withdrawn, for being depressed, for being sick, for being tired, for being busy, for having needs of their own, for doing anything that doesn't meet a clinger's demands. Then there's the passage in *Catcher in the Rye* where Holden Caulfield complains about girls accusing a shy boy of being arrogant. "Even smart girls do that," he says. But that's true of any clinger looking to tell others how arrogant they are for not making a clinger feel special. I've even seen highly-respected therapists do that sort of thing, people who knew better, yet were unable to restrain their primal impulses.

The overall theme is that it takes ego strength to handle the pain and loss that life inevitably throws our way. As a personal example, I remember the surprising insight I had the first time I fell down, scraped my knee, and didn't cry. The insight was that I wasn't scared, and it dawned on me that I'd cried before not because it had hurt, but because I'd been upset that something bad had happened.

This is an important characteristic of Human Incarnation 101 for it typifies the gradual development of ego strength, the gradually-gained ability to handle painful experiences without going to pieces. It also puts a different spin on the notion that boys shouldn't cry, for it's not that we have to numb our feelings, but that we need to gain enough inner strength to not be overwhelmed by every little thing that goes wrong.

It also says something about the adult who bristles with indignity at the slightest provocation, for while we may call them spoiled, arrogant or egotistical, it's more to the point that they lack the ability to be any other way, that it's the only thing they've ever known.

As outright clingers, one of our greatest challenges is to gain the ego strength to deal with the chronic dissatisfaction, disappointment, and loss we all face instead of badgering others to adjust their lives so we don't have to deal with our own. In relationship terms, it takes ego strength to not cling and manipulate, for while romantic ideals tell us that two people in love become as one (remember that scene in *Children of a Lesser God* where she links her fingers?), it's more realistic to say that two become three: the two individuals and the relationship itself. That, however, takes work. Or as pilot and author Antoine de Saint Exupery once said, love isn't about two people gazing into each others' eyes so much as it's about two people looking outward together. Love, he said after being forced down in the desert with a friend, is sharing the last of your food when there's no more.

Well, it's all of that and more. I once watched a mother elk and calf crossing a road in Colorado, the little one trying to nurse on the run, oblivious that it was in the middle of a four-lane highway. It was a touching scene, but it's quite another matter when humans act that way, so obsessed with need as to be oblivious. And as novelist Scott Spencer says, our culture has become so obsessed with love that a virtual religion of narcissism has developed, a religion in which people worship their own emotions, driven by an almost religious fervor to pursue, especially sexually, whatever they want regardless of others' feelings.

This is Freud's pleasure versus reality principle all over again, or more correctly a nurture versus reality principle, for we can all get caught between our yearning for comfort and our need to get things done. It also conjures up terms like "ditsy," implying someone so self-focused as to seem bewildered by the demands of everyday life, and while it's a label typically aimed at women, there are a significant number of ditsy men about.

For either gender, excessive self-focus can make even competent adults deeply irresponsible at times. Consider Leona Helmsley's infamous comment that only little people pay taxes. But then clingers may walk four abreast down the sidewalk, not noticing as they force others off into the gutter; hold a long conversation with a cashier, oblivious to the line of people behind them; blunder straight into strangers as if to force them to step aside; and manipulate others into opening doors for them so they don't have to do anything that would require undue effort.

Yet those of us who go through life this way do it because we don't know how not to, because it pumps up our balloons to claim all the space, attention, and energy as if it belongs to us, and because it thrills us to be served as if we're helpless. After all, that's the way was back when we were in diapers.

We all have to face a great many basic challenges, and we all try at times to block out anything that fails to fit into our world. But are we doing these things because we've never learned to pay attention beyond what we want for ourselves, because as children we'd fought against any attempt to get us to pay attention, because we want things to go on being the way they'd always been? And have we been proving ever since that we don't have to feel anything we don't want to? Are we still trying to prove that we can get away with forcing others to do things for us? Do we park our cars so as to take up two or three spaces, deliberately leave our things in other people's way, push our way in front of others as if to prove no one else's needs matter?

While Adler referred to this style as "getting," what we want to get is something that will finally fill that awful hole in the middle of our chests, dreading the notion that nothing ever will. And when getting turns to taking, we may become compulsive shoplifters, although we're more likely to resort to becoming emotional pickpockets, always out to take whatever we can.

Our challenge as other-oriented people, then, is to interrupt our habits, which means not doing all the things noted above. And in doing that we're challenged to face our chronic sense of emptiness and loss, and the entitlement and lingering dependency that are driven by those feelings. That in turn requires us to challenge our assumptions about our motives, for what we consider loving may feel anything but that to others. Overall, we are challenged to deal with feelings of disappointment and loss that may date back to our earliest infancy, confronting feelings of hopelessness and despair that we've likely been avoiding for decades. Then we're challenged to face all the things we'd done when we didn't have enough ego strength to do anything else, perhaps damaging some of our most prized relationships. And that requires us to gradually grow strong enough in ourselves to carry those feelings for ourselves, a process that is rarely simple or easy.

If it seems I've gone into excessive detail here, it's because we all have a clinger in us, and the clinger dynamic describes challenges we all face in moving from infancy to adulthood. And while clingers may refuse to look at their own behavior, those of us who grew up on the receiving end of that behavior need to understand it well because it was likely the driver that created many of our own personal dynamics.

Moreover, the following two dynamics have clinger tendencies of their own, although they are acted out in different ways.

Moving Against: the Pusher, the Bully

While our sense of need draws us into relationship and community, we've been looking at what happens when that most natural of impulses runs to extremes and becomes distorted. This takes us to the second of our three basic tendencies, that of moving against the world around us. While it can be said to some degree to be an extension of a two-year-old's drive to impose himself on a world he can't yet understand, it's also a basic instinct to apply ourselves, to motivate ourselves and accomplish things, to apply ourselves in constructive ways. As before, though, the problem is when that impulse goes to extremes.

Even for the best of us it's easy to become so taken with our impulse to push ourselves at the world around us that everything else falls out of focus. And that puts us at odds with the clinger stance, for the other-oriented instinct is not to act, but to settle into a comfortable nest. Generally, ardent clingers have a hard time understanding work "out there" in the world—work around the home, perhaps, but out there, no. So, one of a pusher's great concerns is that a clinger's demands for nurturing will undermine everything, that their compulsion for immediate gratification and comfort will lead to disaster, which it does at times. That can drive a male pusher to attack male clingers, instinctively sensing someone who might make a mess of things. But pushers also have an instinct to dominate simply for the sake of dominating, and that's where our discussion leads.

In many ways the pushy move-against impulse seems an extension of a demanding two year-old's attempt to prove to himself and everyone else that he's no longer a vulnerable, dependent child even though he obviously is, and he does it by demanding dominance over his world, starting with Mommy. And when we do that again as teenagers, our behavior gets labeled as "hostile dependency"—hating those we depend on. What that doesn't say, though, is when we're in that phase we're actually feelings lost and helpless, although we'll rarely admit it.

While the Beatles song "She's Leaving Home" describes a teenager breaking away from the oppressiveness of her parent's home, it was inspired by the news story of a young teen running away only to come home months later, sick, emaciated, hooked on drugs and pregnant. And that's what parents fear—that angry kids will get themselves in over their heads before they realize what they're dealing with, then need to be rescued.

Fair or not, a great many of us felt as small boys that our female caretakers wanted us to stop being adventurous, to stop exploring and learning, to not go out into the world, and that they were trying to impose their needs on us and prevent us from being ourselves. So, we became defiant, pushing away anyone we saw as trying to hold us back, even though they may have been trying to keep us from running off a cliff or out into traffic. As adults, then, we'll be prone to imagining a faceless opponent who has to be defeated before they can defeat us.

While this can drive us to achieve, it also can make us overachievers and workaholics, or turn us into outright bullies dead set on beating into submission anyone and anything in front of us. Even at our best we can be like a dog straining at the leash, as if we just won't know ourselves unless we're pushing against some kind of restraint, real or imagined.

As kids we're drawn to power fantasies, which is why superheroes are so popular, but our long-term learning process is to gain the experience and competence to deal with our world in realistic ways rather than expecting the superpowers of comic book heroes. But that process is mysterious to young boys, which is why we're so taken with images like King Arthur's sword in the stone, which only the chosen one can claim. In a little boy's world, only he gets to have that power.

In its extreme, it can show up as a chronic drive for dominance in a person too underdeveloped to have concern for others' feelings or needs. One way of viewing the bullying tendency, then, is as a child's attempt to overcome feelings of helplessness and dependency by trying to take charge—first with Mommy, then with everybody— potentially turning him into a dangerous little boy in an adult-sized body. Abraham Lincoln once said that the true test of a man is in what he does when he gains power, yet we're all challenged to act with regard for others rather than brute instincts.

When adolescent hormones kick in, most of us feel driven to push ourselves at the world around us, and learning to modulate ourselves is one of our most important teenage challenges. However, researchers tell us that far too many contemporary children demonstrate less ability to feel empathy toward others that in earlier generations, a trait that some relate to the distance kids feel from their working parents, while others relate it to kids' obsession with computer game violence and video addiction in general because it lacks any true human element. Whatever its source, the increase in overt bullying among children is alarming, especially when it happens online where there's no direct contact with their victims.

Oddly enough, bullies and clingers share many of the same tendencies, one feeling entitled to use physical force (or at least the threat of it), the other using seduction and manipulation, complaining and tantrums. Both are out to impose themselves on others and defeat their boundaries, and both are driven by fears they pretend they don't have. Bullies, like clingers, regard the world as if to say:

Everything's for me, although with a different style, seeing emotional rigidity as strength, compulsively pushing their way through life with an elbow-in-your-face attitude. Ironically, both are yearning for nurturing, the primary difference being that bullies learned early on to distrust needy feelings: *Don't give me all that sissy stuff, just gimme what I want.* Yet the drive behind it is one of helplessness, need and entitlement, and it's nothing new to say that bullies are little more than frightened children bellowing at their world with infantile rage.

Yet, the primal nature of the pusher dynamic can be captivating. Novelists like Ken Follett and Tom Clancy glorify it in more or less socially acceptable terms while Bernard Cornwell creates raw bullies raging with the "battle joy" that, at least in fiction, fascinates even those of us bullies regard as hopeless wimps. One basic bully impulse is to reduce the complexities of life to a simple matter of dominance, trying to claim a god-like sense of authority. This is what we see in ancient mythology where the hero is half-divine, or in superheroes endowed with alien powers that surpass mere humanity.

That impulse dominates some of us so thoroughly that being pumped up with rage can feel like walking on holy ground among ancient gods. So, we see the seven-year-old stalking the playground looking for someone to pound on, the classic image of the fifteen-year-old smoking in the boy's room with the other hoodlums, the twenty-something hanging out in bars and looking for fights, the forty-year-old obsessively charging rear bumpers on the highway, looking to turn even the most trivial situations into an excuse for getting high on the aggression drug. Or he may work his way into a corporate position where he'll trash a community's environment, abuse customers and take advantage of his employees while shoving one skeleton after another into his already crowded closet. While the other-oriented may have a predatory nature when it comes to others' attention, bullies are predatory in a frankly aggressive if not outright violent way, and even in an Armani suit he can come across as a thug.

Because they learn early in life that bad behavior can get them what they want, they keep doing it, and unfortunately childish selfishness often wins. That's why we need lawyers, guns and military forces, for the homicidal maniacs we've seen throughout history prove a need to have a ready store of bullies of our own at hand should the need arise.

A bully sees every encounter as potential warfare, even a simple thing like a car on the freeway changing into his lane up ahead. And his urge to feel more powerful than everyone else has him driving a 4x4 with the suspension jacked-up to loom over every other vehicle on the road. It recalls what Gregory David Roberts tells us is called in the Australian prison system a "stand-over man"—a predatory thug who hovers over weaker prisoners, bullying and stealing from them, which is probably why he's in jail in the first place.

At worst, a bully is the psychopath who puts a gun to the head of a young girl and forces her father to have sex with her, for it's not enough to simply defeat someone, but he has to prove he can get them to violate their own integrity in the most extreme ways. Playground bullies act out lesser versions of the same thing, watching other kids, sensing which ones are easy pickings, then defeating any attempt to stand up for themselves.

Even as children they'll sense how willing others are to resort to force, for only those willing to be violent deserve respect. And even at that age you can't tell a monster that he's a monster, or he'll become even more monstrous and start looking for ways to get revenge. That's what we see in tyrants dependent on their political cults to stay in power, scanning the populace for even the slightest signs of resentment, the gibbet or the firing squad being the fate of any who fail the test. In the same way, the everyday household bully will live as if on guard against impending threats, daring anyone— their spouse, their child, the driver in the next car—to show the slightest frustration.

Even for those of us who fit the average overachieving workaholic mold, the predominant feeling is that if we stop pushing, things will fall apart, which is sometimes true. This is why the other-oriented person can trigger us so strongly, for we'll feel as if we're bailing out a sinking boat while clingers want us to stop and gaze lovingly into their eyes. As workaholics, though, we tend to push whether it's needed or not, and we're capable of driving ourselves to heart attacks in the process.

To those of us with a pushy temperament, the world seems out to render us as helpless as the children we once were unless we can get the upper hand, and we can become so obsessed with that struggle as to become irrational, seeing aggression is its own justification. But it's just that we're out to prove that we're not vulnerable, that we don't have to feel anything that might imply sensitivity, or else we might slide back into the infantile abyss we've been trying to escape since we were two years old. This is why bullies love things like hazing, for the meek inherit the earth only in the silly philosophies of all those wimps out there, and if we take the novels of writers like Bernard Cornwell to heart, it would seem that much of human history has been created by guys who were part pro football linemen, part Hells Angels on meth.

This has also shown up in things like the killing off of the dodo bird and carrier pigeon where people were driven to a bloody frenzy for no apparent reason other than an impulse to destroy, as if nature itself were an enemy to be defeated. It's not all that different from the vandal bent on destroying whatever he can get his hands on just for the sake of destroying something, seeing art and culture as things to be despised.

There's a rigid bodyset that goes with the dynamic, one we see in the military posture, the goosestep and the Nazi salute, for in attempting to force ourselves into a high state of alertness, we'll rigidify our bodies as well as our minds and emotions, unaware of how much we cut off our intellectual and emotional depth in the process. Thus, the stereotypes of the dumb jock, the moronic thug.

Moreover, as necessary as the pusher dynamic is in its own right, there's an inherent dilemma in it, for it tends to become so invested in itself that it will keep pushing in one direction despite all evidence and reason to the contrary, often in the hope that if we just keep going it'll somehow all work out. Mountain climbers have died that way, for it's an attitude that discounts care and caution, treating awareness and understanding as the marks of a fool. We've seen this in employees of highly toxic facilities who've shown flippant disregard for hazards that could easily kill them, and those still living are now faced with health problems they'd once shrugged off.

So, we've seen situations like the infamous Love Canal where polluters concealed their actions, then used armies of lawyers in an attempt to defeat their critics; rainforests cut down for the sake of short-term gains despite concerns over long-term consequences; blatantly toxic products hitting the world market; the US military using depleted U238 in projectiles regardless of its effects on its own personnel; and sweatshops, child labor, and human trafficking that treat human beings as cattle. And all this with a *So what?* attitude by people who, like children hiding the vase they've broken, do their best to avoid responsibility. Then they'll try using absurdities to get their way, such as how workers cleaning up the mess at Chernobyl were convinced by their bosses that drinking vodka would make them immune to radiation. So what if they all die? And their kids, too.

We've seen the extremes in the likes of Josef Stalin and Saddam Hussein, in the rule of the Khmer Rouge, in the banana republics of South and Central America, in China's Cultural Revolution, and we see it in countries like North Korea that exemplify government by insanity, as well as in areas of Africa run by warlords—places that make even North Korea look relatively sane.

Like any personality dynamic, bullies yearn for the freedom to act out their impulses without restraint or consequence, because it's such a joy to not have to rein themselves in. But while old power families like the Medici used armies to control their power bases, now we see it done with armies of lawyers, those with the most money winning simply because they can. History, though, is littered with leaders capable of great accomplishments only to fall because they'd done it with reckless disregard, and it eventually caught up with them.

It takes ego strength to disagree in a healthy way, to cooperate without feeling a battle has been lost, to let others be themselves without trying to dominate them. But as children we often can't tell the difference between cooperating and being controlled, and the person who never learns that difference will go through life assuming that any request for cooperation implies tyranny, something to be defeated. So, while a schoolteacher may have good reason for disciplining a child, the kid may spend the rest of the day, if not the rest of the school year, sitting there fantasizing revenge. Harper Lee's *To Kill a Mockingbird* gives a portrayal of the notion: *Ain't no snot-nosed slut of a teacher ever born can make me do nuthin'.*

And he'll prove himself right, but what he doesn't understand, what he can't understand, is that he can undermine his own life that way, defying the education he'll need in later years, chasing his ball out into the street with that you-can't-make-me attitude, then go on to drive a car as if he's out to defeat the Federation.

A bully at any age tries to see things in simplistic terms, and that sense of simplistic purity is one pushers crave, and they'll use it to justify themselves with lofty idealism and do-or-die ambition, holding themselves above all those sloppy emotions that clingers crave. That leads us to question whether the rebel and the anarchist aren't simply rebellious children with heads full of rhetoric.

Yet we all have a tendency to push ourselves in ways that exceed usefulness, sometimes because we're afraid of failure if we ease off, sometimes simply because that feeling of determination renders us oblivious to everything else.

All things said, the pusher style is the most straightforward, the least complex of all, yet without it we stagnate. A popular saying tells us we are human beings, not human doings, and while that may have its appeal, it glosses over the nebbish-ness we're prone to when we lack motivation. It also brings to mind a movie line from that archetypal uber-pusher, John Wayne: "Life's hard, but it's a lot harder if you're stupid." The problem, though, is that few agree as to what "stupid" really means.

Still, for all their grand self-concepts, bullies can be like children lacking the intellectual equivalent of fine motor skills, believing that the simplest solution to any problem is to use force. But then they're eventually challenged to face the damage they've done, and that can be a shattering self-confrontation.

Ironically, pushers are in many ways clingers in disguise, living as if it's everyone else's responsibility to give them their way, enraged by others having wants and needs of their own, all while being driven by insecurities they'll never admit to. Both can be so self-absorbed as to seem oblivious to anything beyond their own immediate wants, the opposite-gender equivalent of the pouting, manipulative woman being the male chauvinistic pig, each operating on the same underlying instincts, just in different ways.

But while clingers are generally appalled by any confrontation with their own behavior, bullies generally don't care what others think or say about them. Yet the pushy personality has eventually to face the same drowning waters of loss, disappointment, hopelessness and despair that clingers have to face. Beyond that is our fear of not being in a dominant position, our fear of defeat, our fear of being overwhelmed if we're not constantly in charge. Of course, this is in direct conflict with the move-against person's self-image, for he's been trying to avoid his underlying feelings of helplessness and dependency since he was somewhere around two years old, not realizing how they've been running him all along anyway.

Moving Away: the Avoider, the Fantasy-Prone

Because the aggressive and the other-oriented both feeling entitled to impose on others in order to get a sense of well-being, they go a long way toward creating the third dynamic, that of holding others at a distance. And because it's a dynamic that's invented on the fly by each of us, it tends to be more complex than the other two.

One of the great challenges of childhood comes as we emerge from the infantile morass of instinctual feelings to wonder just what is this world we find ourselves in anyway? What's this, what's that, and above all, what's going on here?! One dilemma, then, is that while our developing intellect wants to figure it all out, we can get stuck there like Brer Rabbit with the Tar Baby—while our feeling side tends to glom onto a world of emotions, our mental side tends to glom onto a world of descriptions and explanations.

And it gets more convoluted with time. The greatest of all those convolutions is that while avoiders are criticized in the clinger-driven self-development scene, those of us who grew up to be avoidant adults typically started out as normally dependent children only to learn by the age of four or five that we had to protect ourselves from a needy parent who was meant to nurture us. So, like pushers, we learned early on to distrust nurturing, for it too often felt like a candy bar with a razor blade inside. That's the result of an adult's emotional demands being too much for us to stand up to, driving us to protect ourselves by backing away, perhaps by dissociating altogether. And since it's common for that razor blade to have gotten at us through seduction, avoiders see seduction as a form of attack, one that's designed to make the victim feel good as he's being wounded. But anyone who gives in to seduction, be it sexual, financial (as in the sleazy salesman), or emotional, knows that once the seductive glow wears off, they're left with a sick feeling telling them they've been had. That's a feeling avoiders commonly live with along with a chronic sense of horror that there's something terribly wrong without quite knowing what it is, a sense that will likely become a background drone in their lives.

That feeds an avoider's distrust of the world they find themselves in, and for some, the results can be a bit odd. If, for example, you could climb inside the psyches of many conspiracy theorists, you would likely find they'd had a clingy parent they couldn't trust, giving them a sense that something is out to get them, which may have been quite true in childhood. But it wasn't the government or the evil corporations or the aliens or grey entities. It was probably just Mom. And conspiracy theories can take on the dimensions of spirituality for some of us—hence, Conspirituality. Even mainstream literature can take on that tone—note, for example, how the *Celestine Prophecy* books and Dan Brown's *DaVinci Code* series have a paranoid trend running through them, as if there's a faceless enemy out there bent on depriving us of divine wisdom.

We all tend to create our own versions of reality: Drunks live in a world defined by alcohol, potheads live in a world defined by THC, teenagers live in a world defined by hormones. So, while the fantasy-prone try to create a world based on whatever they've created inside their heads, the other-oriented try to create a world out of infantile longing, while move-against people try to create (unfortunately rather successfully) a world based on conflict and conquest.

The avoider's part in this has resulted in anything from the Inquisition and Salem witch hangings to the Jonestown and Heaven's Gate suicide tragedies, each an attempt to justify a self-created reality with outrage and violence, even self-destruction. Galileo and Copernicus were faced with that mindset when even the earliest attempts at science were met with dangerous paranoia. More commonly, though, it results in people whose minds are like a car that keeps jumping out of gear, leaving them to coast in aimless fantasy.

Avoiders are likely to sense early in life that to be a good person is to be a non-person. One underlying reason is that by the time a needy, invasive parent is old enough to have children, quite a long list of people will have backed away from them until all they have left is the kids, the youngest usually getting the worst of it as the parent realizes that this is their last chance to get someone to fill that distressing hole in the middle of their chest. At least, that is, until they have grandchildren, at which point it's again the youngest who typically gets the worst of it. That's one source of the chronic paralysis so many avoiders feel, the reason they can feel so emotionally numb, especially as they're trained to never let a clingy parent see their honest feelings.

Moreover, that parent will have been acting this out since his or her own early childhood, habitually projecting the message, *It's your fault!* at others whenever they'd felt their chronic sense of emptiness and loss. Then they'd gone on to project that message onto their children, who then grow up with a sense that something is their fault, without a clue as to why. The parent doesn't have a clue either, because they've been projecting that feeling at everyone since childhood.

This becomes an invisible dynamic between avoiders and other-oriented people, for as the other-oriented sweep their secret feelings of desperation and fear under the rug, they also sweep avoidant people under the rug, for avoiders represent the clinger's fear of having to see the consequences of their own behavior. This is why so many avoiders grow up feeling invisible, for in many ways they've been treated that way, or at least treated as not worthy of having their integrity respected, which is the same thing.

A common avoider feeling is that life is a constant Catch-22 with some unknowable force always out to make things impossible and irresolvable no matter how hard he tries. It's reflected in Lewis Carroll's Red Queen declaring how it takes all the running you can do just to stay in the same place, for that's what it feels like to have a clinger parent as Carroll had. At its worse, it's the emotional equivalent of having a clinger parent fire a shotgun at him five or six times a day, blowing big holes in his psyche—invisible holes he'll spend the rest of his life trying to deal with.

So, an avoider feels an invisible wound, invisible for two reasons: because it was inflicted consistently throughout childhood, often in doses too small to be recognized at the time as a serious injury; and because parents who deliver that wound refuse to see the repercussions of their own behavior, and refuse to let their children express anything about it. And feelings we can't express tend to sink into our unconscious depths, yet continue to run our lives.

Because they grow up as the target of so many selfish demands, it's common for children of needy parents to grow up with a sense that they need to keep others immersed in good feelings while dreading being attacked should they fail. As a result, they're likely to carry a chronic sense of urgency, always on edge against someone assailing them with needs impossible to meet.

One way or another, those of us who are avoiders typically grow up sensing that our psyches are full of holes like Swiss cheese, a thing so disturbing and embarrassing that we know only to hide it and try to fake our way through life, pretending to be real people when we feel like nothing of the sort. Above all, one of our primary motives is not so much to avoid other people as to avoid that awful feeling of having been gutted before we'd even had a chance to develop a self-sense.

That leaves us floating like a balloon on a string so that life seems a fuzzy blur exaggerated now and then with numinous meaning. And that can make us look silly to everyone else, setting up a dynamic where clingers and pushers get to ridicule and blame avoiders for being avoidant, oblivious to the fact that they are attacking a wound that they, themselves, inflict. So, the people who blame us for being stuck in our heads are the same as the ones who drove us there in the first place.

Oddly, one of the more obscure reasons we get stuck in our heads is growing up with a parent who projects a ditsy persona seemingly incapable of intellectual thought, giving their child the sense he's obligated to put out the intellectual effort for someone who either can't or simply won't do it for themselves. That can give us a feeling that having answers and explanations is a way to feel nurtured, or at least safe. And it's why the typical avoider sees clingers as lunatics unable or unwilling to understand what should be obvious, and he can get stuck in explaining things, sometimes in tedious detail (*Good God! Am I doing that right now?*) because that's what he feels he has to do. After all, he assumes he's talking to someone so stubbornly oblivious that they won't ever listen—which is sometimes true—and it's why he may speak in a whining voice, the tone of some who expects to fail no matter how hard he tries.

But what that avoider couldn't understand as a child was that he was up against a parent's habitual way of manipulating other people, and that's a battle he was guaranteed to lose. In many ways the parent who indulges in obsessive mind games will leave their child torn between the words he hears and his intuitive sense of what's happening. And when we can't tell anyone about it, the only person we can tell it to is ourselves—over and over inside our heads because telling ourselves is never enough. So, given the stereotype that clingers are women and avoiders are men, we see a joke posted at a local business: "*My wife and I had words, but I didn't say mine.*"

Despite what the other-oriented say, those of us who are avoiders aren't so much afraid of our feelings as we're afraid of the repercussions of our feelings, having learned the hard way that expressing the wrong thing to a clinger could draw an attack. We understood early in life that we couldn't afford to be honest, especially with a person ten times our size and age. This is why so many avoiders live with feelings of guilt over having failed to fulfill the impossible task they've been saddled with, along with a chronic fear of attack.

One of the most insidious forms of child abuse is when an adult projects onto a child an expectation that implies: *You exist to meet my needs, and don't you dare try to protect yourself from me.* It's particularly insidious because it inflicts an invisible wound to the child's ability to develop a sense of himself, and by the time he's reached adulthood he'll be left wondering why he's the way he is. It's hardly a surprise, then, that in many archaic creation myths humanity is created to serve and feed the hungry gods.

So, when an adult insists on smooching a little boy while he struggles to get away, it can feel to him like she's trying to suck the life right out of him. But if she's too self-focused to see his reaction, she'll tease him for struggling, which an avoidant child will feel obligated to go along with it. What he feels inside, though, is not humorous, for what to her is playful can feel to him like the emotional equivalent of rape, and she's incapable of recognizing it.

As a result, a great many of us grow up with emotional dynamics disturbingly similar to those of incest victims, even though we were never touched sexually, for while some people are raped with a penis, others feel raped by another's obsessive neediness. And just as incest perpetrators live in fear of being exposed, the needy adult will intuitively react with outrage and indignation. Then they'll blame their target for showing symptoms of the abuse perpetrated on them—*What's the matter with you, anyway?*—when that's a question they never want answered. And so avoiders learn by five years of age to lie about their feelings and endure it all, bringing to mind John Le Carre's comment (in *Our Kind of Traitor*) about children who are always quiet, always good, won't look you in the eye, don't know they are victims, and blame themselves for things done to them by adults.

Biologically speaking, what any of us experiences when someone imposes on us is that our prefrontal cortex starts to become overloaded, leading to the forgetfulness, confusion, and mental disruption most of us are familiar with. As any parent learns, an infant's cries will take over our prefrontal cortex in an instant, driving us to drop everything and run to attend to the baby's needs. But while that's normal between parent and infant, many adult clingers will try to insert themselves into others' mental space as if it belonged to themselves, and some of us know only to respond by withdrawing because we'd had the same thing done to us when we were kids.

If we are overloaded on an ongoing basis in childhood, we'll become habituated to a constant muddled state of confusion. This is why multi-tasking is so prevalent in the avoidant personality style, for a child constantly intruded upon is forced to split his focus in multiple directions. Then, because we repeat what was done to us, we'll have a hard time keeping our minds on any one thing for very long.

By the way, an avoidant person is likely to speed up when someone passes them on the highway because they'd been too distracted and hadn't realized how slow they'd been going until someone blew past them in frustration.

Tragically, their low threshold for overwhelm can drive an avoidant adult to shake an infant in a desperate attempt to reclaim their mental space by stopping all that awful screeching any way they can. More generally, though, avoiders have a hard time telling the difference between the normal needs of a child and the abnormal neediness of an adult with the psyche of a child. That's why avoiders commonly react to a child by withdrawing, pushing the kid away just as they do everything else. That's why avoidant parents tend to raise clingy children just as clingy parents tend to raise avoiders.

In any event, the avoidant child learns to be careful and indirect. This results in the classic space cadet, the absent-minded professor, the geeky intellectual, someone who has a difficult time in the hardscrabble world. So, while one kid hits homeruns, another fantasizes about hitting homeruns while imaginary crowds cheer. And he knows all too well that were he to step up to the plate, that strange paralysis would make him look a fool.

So, those of us who are avoiders are apt to embrace the world of the intellect because that's where we're far more likely to succeed. Yet intellect is essentially an elegant form of fantasy. After all, landing men on the moon requires a highly evolved fantasy life, and this is the avoider's power. Bullies can beat us up, clingers can beat us down, but we can out-think them all.

Extreme avoiders, though, can become recluses, spending their lives watching TV, playing computer games, doing anything they can to create a life detached from the harsh world outside as they search for glorious fantasies. That's why they'll love surrealism, for not only does it reinforce their notions of alternate realities, but it tells them they aren't alone in having all that weird stuff inside their heads.

Tangentially, we have to ask if modern technology doesn't in itself dissociate us too far from a life that skins our knuckles and works dirt under our fingernails. Picasso and Dali showed up as the technological age was getting up a full head of steam, leading eventually to movies like the *Matrix* series where reality is untrustworthy and dangerous.

In both religious and scientific terms, we define ourselves in terms of what we believe, often defining others by whether the stuff inside their heads agrees with the stuff inside our own. Hence, the Spanish Inquisition and the vindictive paranoia associated with religious zealotry, for one shadow element an avoider carries is the dread that his profound notions may have no reality at all outside his own skull. A disturbing example is Marshall Applewhite, leader of the suicidal Heaven's Gate cult, a man with the staring eyes and head-on-a-stick physique of a deeply dissociated psyche. In many ways he typified the brain-in-a-vat image from sci-fi movies, someone yearning to live without physical sensation as he taught about joining the higher realms.

Alfred Adler held that one of our greatest needs is to contribute to society in a useful and constructive way, and that's something avoiders have difficulty with. A case in point is portrayed in the film, *Master and Commander*, in which a young midshipman is so bumbling and unsure of himself that a younger boy outshines him at every turn, and he finally drowns himself because his future promises nothing but more of the same.

The contemporary avoider struggles like that because his mind is so often somewhere else, seeking a more rewarding experience. I recall waiting to use the restroom at a local coffee shop, watched a man come out wearing a beatific smile and an array of New Age style clothing, and when I went in to take my turn, I found he had urinated on the toilet seat. That speaks volumes about the avoidant style's inability to "orient to the physical plane," and it brings to mind one of the more reasonable statements ever made about marijuana use (by Patti Reagan, the president's daughter) to the effect that there's already too much unconsciousness in the world for us to afford more.

On the other hand is the button I saw on a young man's jacket reading, "Work free drug zone." It's a great stoner joke, but the price that kind of attitude can exact especially on a teen can be painful. For now, though he's too young to get how he's undermining himself, and he just might go through life blaming a faceless system that's burdening him instead of just letting him drift like a balloon on a string.

There are a number of ways those of us who are avoiders are drawn to exaggerate our fantasy worlds, four that come to mind being drugs, religion, computer games and conspiracy theories. We can be drawn to drugs because we think being dissociated from physical life will lead us to a higher reality. In much the same way, religion provides us with an alternate explanations that are more compelling than the boring and often scary life we're in, while computer games replicate the multi-layered fantasies we already have. And conspiracy theories provide explanations for the anxieties and distrust we've felt since childhood, providing "proof" that "they" really are out to get us all. We hear avoiders speaking of the evolution of human consciousness, but for all their notions, an avoider's sense of reality is generally rather shaky, and obsessive belief systems and paranoia tend to go hand-in-hand.

Most avoiders, though, are simply fantasy-prone, assuming that ultimate reality is to be found within their inner worlds, giving rise to the notion that our imagination has power over the physical world. Whatever may be ultimately true about such things, the avoidant person hungers for magical powers as a substitute for his inability to act competently, to live through magical thinking and wish fulfillment rather than direct effort.

Yet, many of us are distressed by our inability to focus on our physical environment, feeling that, like Silvia Plath, we're living inside a glass jar, unable to touch the world around us, unable to be touched by it. Instead, we'll feel like a jigsaw puzzle with too many pieces missing. That discomfort, though, can be our saving grace, for it can be a powerful motivator to reclaim our lives, and one of the greatest keys lies in unraveling how we'd been imprinted at an early age by people who'd been incapable of facing their own lives. Then, with insight in hand we can start finding the keys to re-choosing our own lives.

Since avoiders have trouble knowing how to be here in the present tense, one of our challenges is to catch ourselves when our mind wants to jump out of gear and spin off into fantasy, compulsive ideation, or simply spacing out instead of staying engaged with the world of flesh and blood.

As avoiders, we often feel we're presented with a Hobson's choice, forced to choose between two things we really don't want. Neither being alone nor being in close relationship feels quite right, yet nothing else seems possible. This is because the original choice we'd faced in childhood was between surrendering to an obsessive parent on one hand, protecting ourselves on the other.

In growing out of this dilemma, we need to be attentive to what's real for us right now rather than being driven by what had happened in the past. It's hard to trust that things could ever be different unless we make a deliberate effort to make it different, which we can do only if we make conscious choices at every step.

In the long run, though, we're all challenged to face the messiness that's inherent in human society, no matter our attempts to transcend it all with high-minded philosophies. We see that dilemma in Hesse's *Magister Ludi*, in which the main character, after a lifetime of intellectual monasticism, realizes that he's missed the vibrant, sensual side of life, and when he attempts to regain it, it kills him.

The challenge, as ever, is for us to be at choice in our lives, to find other ways to respond rather than resorting to old habits, and when we find those choices, it can feel like slowly waking up and getting the fog cut of our heads like a prize fighter shaking off a left hook. And that's a fog that has been there for a very long time.

So, while clingers and bullies ask avoiders, *What's the matter with you, anyway?* as a way of inflicting criticism, it's a serious question every avoider is challenged to answer. Essentially, we have to ask these things of ourselves at a deep level, and answering is never easy.

One of the first things an avoider has to confront is his fear that the glorious notions he's developed may have no relevance whatsoever to his actual life, and that's a difficult confrontation. Beyond that, anyone who has spent a good part of his life floating about like a balloon will discover that on dropping back into his body he'll have to confront every nuance of feeling he's been avoiding, perhaps since he was two years old, if not earlier. Even if the original event happened decades ago, the feelings are always now, and just because we haven't felt them for years doesn't mean they've faded—deep memories are stored in our bodies, and don't just go away.

That means we're likely to face a decade or so of wallowing through the volcanic rage we've hidden away for so long. Most of that hidden rage is because we've grown up feeling victimized, and overcoming an habitual victim stance is one of the greatest demands life gives us. That means developing an adequate self of self, for that's what being victimized deprived us of. The process starts with making more conscious choices in a grounded way, for having choice is another thing we'd grown up being deprived of. Otherwise we'll not only go on feeling like victims, but will victimize ourselves.

For any of us, building ego strength means facing the opposite of our habits, and for an avoider that means taking on physical work, getting close to others without losing touch with ourselves, and reining in our tendency to detach and drift off into fantasy. And when it comes to working out our past, we have to face our shame and self-resentment over having let ourselves be walked over, for not having known how to stand up for ourselves. Eventually that can mean truly seeing how paralyzed clingers and bullies can be, themselves, how helpless they can be in clinging to childish dynamics.

When it comes down to the most basic things, every avoider is consistently challenged to ask himself if his impulse to be in his head is more important than the opportunity to be right here in this moment, experiencing this one amazing instant in life. That's where the avoider's greatest work is, in developing the will and discipline to rein in a defensive strategy they'd developed back when they'd been too little to know any other way to get along. Above all, avoiders have to ask themselves if they really want to go through life interacting with nothing outside themselves, living in a safe reality that really doesn't exist anywhere.

Summing Up – The Wounded Ego

There comes a point when we have to ask what life really means to us. Three blunt ways of answering that question involve expectations so deeply-set they rarely make their way into our awareness: That life is about feelings others are supposed to provide, that it's what we can take for ourselves, or that it's about what we invent in our imaginations. And while those expectations may never become conscious, any way others fail to comply can drive us to fits of indignation and outrage, even despair.

As always, the challenge here is to find new possibilities in our lives rather than repeating the same behaviors, thinking we're being spontaneous and unique. It's a common understanding that we all tend to project our personal dynamics onto the world around us, especially onto other people, and declare it to be Truth, Higher Reality, or even God, so that we wind up basically honoring and worshiping our own nervous systems without realizing it. This is why it can be so important to lay out the ways these human psyches of ours are prone to acting in ways that are really rather mechanical and predictable. It can be a disturbing thing to see, even shocking, but that's one of the greater challenges presented to us all.

Yet, each can be seen as seeking nurturing in their own way: To clingers, manipulating and obstructing others gives them a feeling of being nurtured, avoiders feel self-nurtured by dwelling on their fantasies and intellectual notions, while bullies, perhaps surprisingly, feel nurtured when they dominate, because that's what they'd wanted with Mom.

I recall a film where an older woman is lecturing a younger one: "Family is all you have!" she says. "Without family, you are nothing!" leaving us to wonder if she isn't really saying, "Family is all *I* have. Without it, *I* am nothing." You wouldn't hear an avoider saying that, because his family is where he'd learned to avoid. So, while a move-toward person will agree that other people give us definition, a move-away person is more likely to say that all you have is your beliefs and theories, while a move-against person is likely to say all you have is your country or your team.

Each has its underlying complaints: clingers complain that they're not being doted on enough, bullies complain others won't submit to them, while avoiders complain that they're always being intruded upon. And when it comes to extremes, these can manifest as personality disorders: clingers as borderlines, bullies as anti-socials, avoiders as avoidant personality disorders, perhaps paranoid delusional disorders, and any of them can appear as narcissistic personality disorders.

And we have habitual ways of appearing to others: with seductive eyes full of longing, with a penetrating stare that can look threatening, or with the spaced-out look of having recently been hit on the head with a brick.

Moreover, each style describes ways of trying to identify ourselves to ourselves—by trying to build a sense of self by surrounding ourselves with possessions we can control, by projecting our need for attention onto other people, and by projecting our thoughts and fantasies onto the world at large and calling it reality. And we all do all of it, often all at the same time so that they're really not separate dynamics.

For all our complaints, we're all prone to committing our personal "crimes against other people's humanity," using others as if their lives were food meant for ourselves, using them as servants or slaves, or using them as residents of our imaginary worlds who don't behave themselves properly. Every mother of a two-year-old sees the source of it, for it's the wicked stepmother syndrome all over again: *You're not the boss of me, but I'm the boss of you, and don't you forget it!* Yet for all its naïve beginnings, it's a theme reiterated throughout human history, often with disastrous results.

Adult life requires us to have many psychological resources available, and each of these three styles can be seen as limiting those resources despite our claims to the contrary. Moreover, each style at its extreme constitutes a fundamental betrayal of the human spirit. Extreme clingers betray our most basic notions of love and relationships by making others subservient to our needs, avoiders betray honest intellectual and scientific understanding by being rigidly dogmatic, while bullies betray our trust in honest leadership and governance. Each is also a statement in cowardice: clingers cowardly about their neediness, avoiders cowardly toward hard reality, bullies cowardly regarding their underlying insecurities.

Just as mythology presents a culture's attempts to explain to itself and its place the world, each personality style does essentially the same thing. The intention, then, is to challenge our personal mythology, to expose our internal realities, compelling our psyche to take stock of its habitual assumptions.

The underlying dynamics are hardly limited to humans, for when Russian researchers attempted to replicate the evolution of dogs from captive foxes, they generated three distinct personality types: those who treated humans with hostility, or at least with indifference, those who responded to humans with hand-licking devotion, and those who shied from human contact, preferring isolation.

Returning to Milton Erickson's sense of two people at work in each of us, we see why we're capable of doing certain things while insisting we're not, as if unable to stop ourselves. This also explains why we'll repeat the same things even after it's become clear that they don't work. I once heard a taxi driver talk about how many times he would see a dent in someone's car right where he'd just almost hit them, and it makes me wonder what our Martian anthropologist would think watching us stumble about, convinced we know what we're doing.

One thing that distinguishes humans is our capacity for creating meaning from our experience. Yet we're also proficient at developing blind spots not only to our own behavior, but to that of others like ourselves. So, other-oriented people who consistently manipulate others can't see other clingers doing the same thing, avoiders hiding behind their fantasies can't see how other avoiders ruin their own lives, and bullies justify fellow bullies while refusing to see the repercussions.

Those of us on the receiving end of those behaviors, though, see these things all too clearly, especially when we grow up with parents acting out at our expense, their behaviors becoming the knives in our hearts, the guns held to our heads. Yet we all have ways of trying to enslave one another, enslaving them with bullying rage, with our belief systems, or with our chronic needs, all while blocking out anything that may cause us doubt.

Yet, for all the conflicts, these three basic styles can interact in some interesting ways, for move-toward people have social abilities that avoiders and move-against people lack, avoiders have a wider perspective the other two lack, while move-against people have the motivation to take action that the others lack. The crime against other people's humanity that we all are capable of committing, though, is in assuming that others are wrong for being the way they are, and that we are entitled to impose on them. For their own good, of course.

The challenge is to counter our habitual responses and take on a wider experience of our own lives, or our own selves. That requires us to question our assumptions about ourselves, about others and about life in general, and gain an appreciation for the experience of others and the perspectives they carry. Any style has its strengths and weaknesses, but immaturity can exaggerate things to the point of becoming bizarre and at least slightly grotesque. But life has its ways of catching up with us, and typically we make significant changes in our lives only when the costs of not changing are high enough.

One challenge is to learn what it can be like to do the opposite of those habits, to pay attention and make choices instead of living instinctually. As ever, that requires ego strength, yet it works in a round-robin manner. That is, we ease our way out of immature behaviors and habits by developing enough ego strength to have better range and flexibility, and we develop ego strength by stepping outside our habits. And often the best way to develop ego strength is to be compelled to act as if we already had it—and sooner or later we will.

Yet, we typically would rather do anything but that, and go on running habits that can show up in the most trivial things, such as wanting the salt and pepper at the dinner table: A move-against person will get up and get it for themselves, likely shoving someone out of the way as they do, a move-toward person will want someone else to get it for them, while an avoidant person will keep silent and go without.

Even the world of psychotherapy carries assumptions: Freud taught that we heal our lives by thinking things through properly, Perls taught that all our issues will resolve themselves if we just spew out all our feelings, while athletic coaches and military types insist that we just have to man up and get over it.

We are a mad lot, yet we're challenged to grow enough ego strength to keep our impulses from overriding our better natures, otherwise each style will insist on its own way of defining reality: If I feel it, then it's real; if I think it, then it's real; if I can beat you up, then I'm right. No matter how we try to convince ourselves to the contrary, our feelings are not a true measure of life outside our own ribcage, our ability to accomplish and dominate are not a measure of truth, nor do our fantasies give us a reliable handle on the world outside our skulls.

The patterns that cause us problems were typically developed for good reasons, but will no longer serve us very well as we move through life. But interrupting an unhelpful pattern takes an act of will, and that requires us to distinguish between our inner reality and the hard reality around us, for our patterns don't exist out there, no matter how we may think they do. For instance, if it's our stance to complain that the system is keeping us down, we're challenged to take a hard look at how we're holding ourselves back. We may have in fact been obstructed in childhood, but what's true about that now?

That can be a harsh mirror to face, one that compels us to face what it's like to experience ourselves differently, to experience life differently, so much so that it can seem we might not know ourselves anymore. In our development from childhood to adulthood, our self-experience morphs gradually, but it's a different matter when we have to play catch-up, for interrupting our habits even in small ways can have a far-reaching impact.

For all our pride in our uniqueness, much of our behavior is mechanically predictable, for any of us can act like a wind-up toy much of the time. To quote Rudolph Dreikurs, it's not that we like putting people into boxes, just that we keep finding them there, even if they do slop over from one box to another a good part of the time.

Still, this business of describing three distinct categories is artificial, for while we may lean predominantly in one of those three basic directions, we all have all three tendencies, and they tend to blur into one another. We can even find different parts of ourselves wanting opposing things—one part wanting closeness, another wanting distance, another wanting to just get up and do something. We all have a tendency to try to dominate hard reality with metaphysical fantasies, romantic fantasies, or power-driven ones, and we all have impulses to try to claim everyone else's space, even their interior space, for ourselves, to try to hold the high ground from which we can understand and explain everything, and to try to rule everything as if it were our personal turf.

One of our challenges, then, is to confront some potentially heartbreaking realizations. As other-oriented people we're challenged to see how our notions of love can not only drive other people away, but can traumatize our children; as bullies we're challenged to see how our drive for control can defeat our most precious values; and as avoiders we're challenged to face the notion that our highest ideals may be little more than bizarre fantasies, and can alienate the people we need to be close to. And no matter how hard we try, we can never have enough control, never have enough nurturing, never have enough explanation.

There seems an element of Darwinian selection in much of it, for just as the early proto-humans who could run, hunt and fight the best were the ones who survived, those who could nurture their young in harsh conditions and form workable relationships survived better than those who couldn't, and those who could stand back and figure things out excelled under changing circumstances.

Still, as an old saying goes, virtue starts when our ego feels humiliated. Otherwise we're likely to miss seeing how obsessing on our feelings, living with habitual hostility, or living in fantasy can keep us from growing up. The other-oriented are right in saying that through relationships we learn about aspects of ourselves that we don't get to know when we're alone, avoiders are right in saying that we learn about aspects of ourselves when we're alone that we don't get to know when we're in relationship, and pushers are correct in saying that applying ourselves to challenges teaches us things we'll never get to know if we're always obsessing on our thoughts and feelings.

This takes us to one of the challenges confronting the therapy subculture, for while we can wallow for years in our feelings and in our histories, the challenge for most of us lies in finding the willingness to make different choices no matter what went before. And for all those arguments regarding free will, without being able to confront our habits, those arguments aren't especially significant. After all, we only have free will when we have choice regarding attitudes and behaviors that have been with us since childhood.

And those habits can make us stupid: Stupid with need and childish obliviousness, stupid with aggression, or stupid with fantasy, idealism and (ironically enough) intellectual ideation. We're all living contradictions to some extent, capable of being our own worst enemies when we act out of blind habit, which brings up another misused word: hypocrisy. While it's an accusation we love to hurl at each other, hypocrisy represents the gap we all have between our conscious motivations on one hand, our compulsive, unconscious impulses on the other. It's the reason we betray our own values and ideals at times, and it's the reason we can be abusive without realizing it. This is why it's important for any discussion of personality styles to be applied to ourselves, otherwise it will become a weapon to beat up other people with, and that can make hypocrites of us all.

Again, the overall challenge is to build enough ego strength to be able to have other resources available. And it's about a bodyset rather than a mindset, for our self-sense is held in our physical bearing, not in our thoughts or emotions. So, it's through strengthening our bodily-felt sense of who and what we are that we create healthy relationships, take responsible action, or develop a workable mindset.

Yet when confronted with realities we've been trying to avoid for years, we can feel like a mouse caught out in the middle of a darkened room wondering which way to run when someone turns on the lights. So, if this discussion seems a bit bizarre, well, it is. The problem, though, isn't in what we think or feel, but in what we fail to think and feel; not in what we see, but in what we fail to see; not in what we consciously intend, but in the way our primal impulses take over.

Then there's the challenge to have compassion for people stuck in their own dynamics, especially when they come across as smug and arrogant. It's simply an aspect of human nature to be that way, and we've all done it, but it takes emotional maturity to confront humanity when it looks like it's gone barking mad, especially when it thinks it's acting with the highest of intentions.

Realistically speaking, though, it's unlikely we'll ever stop being driven by habits we've carried since childhood. What we can do, though, is to gain enough personal strength and choice in our lives to restrain those habits, and that alone can make a world of difference.

The Upside-Down and Backwards Theme

We all make mistakes, and we learn the most in life by falling down. We learned to walk that way, after all, and as an old mentor used to say (with tongue in cheek), blessed is he who finds out what doesn't work, because that's the way to find out what does.

There's a dynamic I call the "upside-down and backwards" theme, one that shows up generally in two ways. First, what we say we are doing, and what we're actually doing can be completely opposite to one another much of the time. We may go on about love, acceptance and forgiveness, yet treat others atrociously; criticize others for being stuck in their heads while being obsessively stuck in our own; strive to fight evil in the world only to inflict carnage of our own; try to dominate everyone else in order to prove we're not helpless children anymore, only to come across as helpless children; declare how everyone should be in touch with their inner feelings, yet live in dread of a great many of our own; speak of personal change and spiritual transformation only to become stubbornly rigid when a serious challenge threatens; speak of truth, openness and honesty, only to have to face lies we've been telling ourselves since we were children; philosophize about raising awareness while remaining stubbornly oblivious. Even our theories of psychology show it, for our "rational" mind has an appalling tendency to be resolutely irrational.

This is shadow material, for what our "conscious" self is doing on one hand, and what our shadow side is doing on the other are generally in sharp conflict with one another. "Conscious" minds are, by the way, not very conscious at all much of the time, for there's an upside-down and backward theme built even into our language for describing the way our minds work. And we all have our ways of trying to prove how loving, strong or wise we are while being childishly manipulative, chronically paranoid or nerdy and weird. Everywhere we look, fair is foul and foul is fair.

The other way the upside-down and backwards theme appears is that what we want from life and what life compels us to learn seem so often to be opposites. For instance, we may want more money while life consistently challenges us to learn moderation; we demand others' attention only to find life challenging us with loss; we crave independence only to be assailed with others depending on us; we want power and control only to confront helplessness and vulnerability. Moreover, we all want to hold onto at least some measure of our childhood expectations while life compels us to mature, and it often does so by beating us black and blue.

The Endless Challenge: Developmental Issues in Adulthood

Harsh as all this may be, the point again is that it's in the extremes that we see subtle nuances that affect us all. The challenge is to examine the ground under our feet, for without that we're likely to undermine ourselves, do harm to our fellows, then find ways to blame them for it. Kant said a system cannot question itself because it has no other perspective than its own, yet this is exactly what we're challenged to do. And as Rilke says, if we don't tame our demons, we'll never know our angels.

Delineating human behavior into categories is artificial, of course, but it's a way of trying to get a handle on intangible things. Otherwise, we fail to understand anyone whose personality dynamics differ from our own, and we all have a tendency to become vindictive over those differences—one personality style blaming another, men and women blaming each other, one generation blaming another, each of us committing our personal crime against other people's humanity which we then justify with anything that comes to hand.

The deeper issues, though, stem from the simple fact that compared to other species we're born premature, unable even to stand on our own legs and walk for a year or so. And as children we feed on our parents' lives, complain about them thirty years later in therapy, then feed our own strengths, weakness, and neuroses to our children in turn, only to have them in therapy thirty years later complaining about us. For most of us, though, it's only when we become parents ourselves that we can understand how much of a burden children put on their parents, and only then do we have a chance to take a hard look at our expectations. Failing that, we'll insist on our personal version of reality while trying to flog everyone else, even life itself, into submission.

As an old therapy cliché says, the way out is through, that trying to "rise above" our issues only keeps us from dealing them. On the other hand, decades of psychotherapy have shown poor results, creating a growing sense that trying to work through our past experiences can keep us stuck in them for a lifetime.

More to the point, we learn to handle our pain and distress by developing better ego strength and a self-sense that's larger than all that pain and distress. When we're children, every upsetting experience is overwhelming because it seems so much bigger than we are, but as our ability to handle the slings and arrows of outrageous fortune grows, things that were once overwhelming become less so, perhaps even trivial. This is why a person with low ego strength will be overwhelmed by stressors the rest of us take in stride, and it's why some of us flare with outrage at every slight, for they simply aren't strong enough to carry the experience. It's also why chronic complaining keeps us stuck in old patterns, for it becomes little more than a way of declaring how wrong life is for being the way it is rather than developing enough invisible muscle to pull our way out of our stuck places and learn to carry our lives with competence.

Human Incarnation 101 Revisited

In taking as clear-eyed a look as we can at this human circus, we need to question any assumption that the way we experience ourselves defines the world at large. In this we find three accusatory terms that don't work very well, not only because we're all guilty of them to some degree, but because they are so commonly misunderstood. They are: arrogance, hypocrisy, and ego.

The word "ego" doesn't work very well because what is termed "ego" in the common sense is more accurately described as lack of ego strength in developmental terms, while what is deemed "arrogance" is more accurately described as an inability to act with anything more than childish expectations, expectations that generally fade along with our baby fat, although they don't always. Hypocrisy, on the other hand, is that all too human tendency for our primitive impulses to push aside our conscious intentions, leading us to act in ways that can shock even ourselves.

Human psyches are adept at excluding anything that might upset our personal apple carts, and we're inclined to flare with indignation, cower with fear or lash out when confronted with motivations we like to think we don't have. Yet the bitter medicine we all face is the challenge to stretch our experience of life as far beyond our habitual comfort zones as we can manage.

The overall challenge is to develop a "bodily-felt sense of well-being" that's capable of acting competently in the adult arena. What makes the discussion difficult is that it's an unconscious process, one that's difficult to define. And as much as emotional obsession is a problem, intellectual understanding in itself isn't all that helpful either, for there are plenty of immature sophisticates and intellectuals.

To recap, ego wounds—narcissistic wounds—generally manifest in one of three directions: by continuing our original infantile sense of yearning for other people's personal space, attention and energy; by trying to dominate others just as a two-year-old tries to do with tantrums; and by retreating and creating our own interior worlds as a refuge. Each carries its own sense of entitlement, its own narcissistic stubbornness, and each has its way of justifying itself. Logic, after all, can be used to prove anything if we work at it: It's true because I've made it true, therefore it *is* true.

Developmental psyche refers this as narcissistic wounding because anything that warps our early development can inhibit our ability to develop a healthy way of carrying ourselves. The seductive charmer, the hyper-intellectual and the compulsive aggressor are all hiding behind exaggerated masks developed in childhood. And because our masks blind us to some extent, the more obsessive we are, the less we'll be able to see others as people in their own right.

But even the most competent and accomplished of us has places where our ego hasn't fully matured, and even well into adulthood we may be perfectly competent in one area while floundering in another. So, if we want to better our lives in anything other than financial or technical terms, the challenge is not to rise above our ego, but to further its development so that it doesn't need to act so poorly. Nor is it about education or intelligence, as a person may gain any amount of education, but without sufficient ego strength they'll have a hard time making anything of it.

Then, when we undertake something new—a new career, hobby, diet, or anything of the sort—we'll tend to repeat the developmental process all over again, and any point at which we'd felt stuck in our original emotional development is a place we're likely to become stuck again. For instance, if we adopt a new diet, we're likely become rigidly dogmatic about it for a time, often to the point of seeming obsessive, wanting to impose our latest revelations on everyone around us. Yet, that's a natural phase to go through. Children often go through a phase where they want rules to follow, and they're likely to act as if those rules have been handed down from on high. Diet especially affects us this way because a narrow range of food and tastes is one way we structure our self-sense when we're young, as if eating something alien will make us experience ourselves too differently. After all, only weirdoes eat tofu.

Cutting a bit deeper, we're challenged to look at our notions of love. Kurt Vonnegut, for instance, wrote that Americans tend to look for love "in forms it never takes, in places it can never be," and I once heard a Tibetan lama say that his sense of Westerners could be described as "wounded love," as a chronic yearning for something they'll never find. And it seems a philosophical oxymoron that many Westerners lean toward Buddhism in an effort to find the feelings of love they long for. Yet the Four Noble Truths, which start by saying that suffering is caused by desire, can be interpreted to say that the root of human suffering is in infantile needs having become relentless adult longing. The path, says the Buddhist tradition, is to embrace emptiness, the very things clingers dread.

Beyond the dogma, the Buddhist message can be reduced to the notion that we are challenged to mature enough to face life in its most frank terms, to grow up in the fullest sense, for the more mature we are, the more stable our self-sense, the less dependent we are on things outside ourselves to provide us with a sense of well-being. So, while Western culture has been described as a cult of materialism, it would be more to the point to call it a cult of neediness in which adherents truly believe that their bottomless pits can somehow be filled. And many attitudes around psychotherapy and self-improvement, to say nothing of movies and romance novels, support that notion.

Does this mean that Westerners are inherently less emotionally mature than the rest of the world? In the eyes of some, the answer would be a resounding *Yes!* One place it shows up is in the general condemnation in New Age circles and the self-improvement arena of anything intellectual, reflecting how as small children we simply didn't have much of an intellect to speak of, and anyone bent on regressing to childhood feelings will have little tolerance for anything adult in nature. Using our intellect requires that we take our attention off our feelings, and that can provoke anxiety in some of us. Remember the flower children of the Sixties? Many of them are still around, still drifting along in infantile simplicity, complaining about being oppressed by the system.

For all its excesses, US culture is a fascinating challenge. Over the last century and more it has been described (mostly by European émigrés shocked by the kitsch they found here) as an orgy of destruction besotted with materialism, as a culture of conformity deluding itself with notions of freedom, as a giant prison of freedom, as a cultural pigpen, as a cesspool of selfishness obsessed with financial gain, as a nation of rubes where dullness has been made God, as a nation of gray flannel suits and flowered aprons pursuing mindless routine while fretfully wondering if this is all there is to life.

Critics say many of our cultural values originated not in notions of freedom so much as in having been turned loose in a continent without rules, and once those pesky redskins were done away with, much of the Wild West was run by Hells Angels on horseback. On the other hand, some academics claim the American Civil War was so shattering to the national morale that older values were replaced with cynicism and crass materialism that exceeded anything seen before.

Whatever the reasons, writers like Durant, Hemingway, Fitzgerald, and Hesse have commented on the American tendency toward chronic adolescence, as did de Tocqueville nearly 200 years ago. More recently, Julie Delpy's character in *Before Midnight* realizes that she's married to a forty-year-old American teenager, while Philip Roth writes that the American psyche is possessed of a pretense of sincerity that is worse than falseness, and an innocence that's worse than corruption. Then, Mick Jagger declares, "American girls want everything in the world... and still none of it is ever enough." The same, though, can be said about American men.

As long as we hold to adolescent notions of freedom in which Mom and Dad are authority figures we both need and resent, we'll never truly feel free. This is why those who grew up under tyrannical governments are scornful of Americans' complaints about their lack of freedom, for the key to freedom in a psychological sense is mature ego strength, without which we'll always feel we oppressed without any clear notion as to how or why.

The more mature a person is, the less need for power or control or attention or possessions they'll have. The same is true regarding addictive behavior, for one item missing from the twelve-step programs is that a significant driver behind many addictions is the desperate feeling of emptiness that accompanies an insufficient self-sense. In other words, the challenge isn't so much to stop wanting things as it is to develop our psyches so that we don't have to want so much, where we're not so recklessly driven by impulses.

That lack also results in a failure of both moral and physical courage, for the more mature a person is, the more capable they are of facing difficulties and of supporting the welfare of others. On the other hand, any situation we don't feel able to face head-on is a place where we'll be inclined to distort, manipulate, dominate, lie and evade.

Eastern philosophies add a twist by insisting on the avoider's sense that this world, like the old song about the rowboat, is just a dream. But that brings to mind the story of a Zen monk reciting that life is just an illusion, to which the Zen master whacks him upside the head with a stick and says, "Hurts, doesn't it?"

It's an argument that goes back at least as far as Plato and Aristotle, one that butts heads between our imaginative lives and the demands of hard reality, between our soaring idealism and our fleshly lusts. And again, the underlying issue is that low ego strength distorts our ability to see the world around us, so the world-as-illusion notion appeals to those of us who lack the ability to feel connected to life, and any talk of it all being an illusion will seem familiar, even reassuring.

But all the things we've tried to avoid in life have ways of catching up with us, and that's where the hard work begins, often with a sharp whack upside the head.

The Infantile Tyrant Revisited

Nature has hard-wired adults to the task of attending to children's needs. With an infant, we'll make soft, crooning sounds, open our eyes wide, raise our eyebrows in an exaggerated smile and, in a high-pitched singsong, say, *Oh, you're just the sweetest little baby in the whole world, oh yes you are!* We do that because a baby is hard-wired to respond to high-pitched voice tones, wide eyes, a big smile and a high emotional charge. With a toddler, we'll say, in a less a highly-pitched tone, *Hey little buddy! How ya doing? Is that your toy truck? Cool!* Then, with an older kid, we'll say, in a more level tone, *Come on, let's play ball. Go long!* At every age a child needs to be responded to in an age-appropriate way, and adults are generally hard-wired to act accordingly.

Just as it feels awful to be treated as younger than our age, when someone wants to be treated as if they were younger than their age it goes against our grain in a serious way. That's why a friend once dubbed New Age spirituality as "Montessori for adults." But then we don't have to look very far into history to find tyrants who have demanded to be treated with attention appropriate for an infant.

While it's popular to criticize patriarchal values as inherently destructive and demeaning to women, most of what feminists call "patriarchy" consists of attitudes normal in little boys in that critical stage between the ages of two and five years. So, while women complain quite rightly that men treat them as sex objects, as perpetual cleaning staff, pay them less in the job market, impose a glass ceiling and discount them as equals, a world in which women are at his beck and call is a needy little boy's dream come true.

An NPR article describes male bosses stealing their female employees' lunches from the lunchroom refrigerator or taking an employee's fork to sample her meal right in front of her. Employee as Mommy? It's hardly a new notion. But as children generally we treat our mothers as objects, and it shows in the notions, still a living tradition in some places, that a woman should have no independent life of her own, should leave her home only twice—at her marriage and at her death—and that a wife's body is her husband's property. How else is an insecure little boy to stay in control of Mommy?

So, when we hear writers like Azar Nafisi describing repressed women who are their husbands' intellectual superiors, it's hard not to see most "patriarchal" values as attempts of little boys in grown-up bodies to hold to their original experience of being catered to by women. That puts women in a position where they have no rights, not even the right to be real people, creating a world in which the beloved mother figure is always defeated in her attempts to be herself.

So, is the "patriarchal male" any less insecure than a little boy, afraid that if Mom won't submit to his command, he'll fall apart at the seams? There's an underlying issue that affects boys in relation to their mothers, for just as women have quite rightly objected to men's dismissal of female instincts, many women view a boy's natural inclination to separate from his mother as meaning there's something wrong about him. This is especially true when a boy's natural development compels him to gain more autonomy than a girl typically wants. A little girl knows at an early age she's the same gender as Mommy, while a boy is very aware that he's not, and that can become one of his strongest motivators. It's arguable that this can give girls an easier transition into adulthood than one boys, although individuation and autonomy are complex for both genders.

A little boy senses he has to move away from Mom in order to gain a sense of his maleness, yet he has to stay attached to her because she's still the center of his security, and because he lacks the ability to resolve the issue any other way, he creates a fantasy world in which she's an idealized being dedicated to his existence—part goddess, part slave, part food supply. And for all that a woman may want to be treated as goddesses, a goddess is not a real person. At best, she's a two-dimensional image, and when confronted with the fact that Mom is a person in her own right, a little boy may feel betrayed, leading to the notion carried by many men that for a woman to have a self of her own is an unbearable betrayal.

In other words, feminists have generally mislabeled what they object to, for what they call "patriarchy" is basically male immaturity. It's also true that most of men's complaints against women are about women acting like little girls in grown-up bodies bent on controlling and defeating males. And while feminists have done an excellent job of confronting the male population with its shadow, they've generally done a poor job of facing their own.

When it comes to political power, the mind of a tyrant, like that of a child, reduces things to the simplest terms. For instance, Saddam Hussein once said that Baath party doctrine was whatever he decided it was at the spur of the moment, and Genghis Khan was said to have had entire populations slaughtered because, with childish simplicity, he couldn't think what else to do with them. The mind of a three-year-old generally works that way, aware only of its own wants and needs, raging when it doesn't get its way, reducing others to subservient objects and smashing its toys in the occasional fit of pique.

But that beast lives on in each one of us, and history shows the scars of its tantrums. We all carry infantile expectations and idealized notions of how the world should be, and it's only our mature self-sense that keeps us from becoming tyrants ourselves. Listen to politicians and commentators on CNN and Fox, and you'll see a piece of every one of us trying to pump our balloons up with self-righteous indignation, giving the impression that the louder and longer they shout, the more right they are, a logic tantrum-throwing children have operated on since the dawn of humanity.

CHAPTER FIVE

~THE MALE CHALLENGE
GROWING UP MALE: BOYS AND SEPARATION~

When I was a boy I slept at heaven's gate.
~Robert Plant, *When I Was A Child*

Why, say! You can't grow up yet! You're my baby!
~Thomas Wolfe, *Look Homeward Angel*

One thing many women fail to understand about men is that throwing ourselves into the difficulties of life is something we feel driven to do, for we sense it's one of the few things that can rescue us from any childhood dynamics that are still paralyzing us. It's an atavistic impulse that understands how challenges toughen and matures us, compelling us to seek them out even when they seem a bit suicidal.

The urge to throw ourselves headlong into whatever presents itself is something most men feel, but a highly-avoidant man has a special need to break out of the haze he has lived under. This is so he can re-engage his psychological development, fight through the lingering daze that has kept him indolent and ineffectual, and turn his latent anger into constructive action. Otherwise, the man who believes life should be without challenges, as many in the New Age arena believe, will do little more than read metaphysics and fantasy novels, or watch action movies while a terrible void grows inside him. The price of that failure is to feel vaguely ashamed of his life without having a clue what to do about it until something finally drives him to find a way out of his ineffectiveness.

Some feminist theorists have insisted that boys doted on by their mothers and raised to their mothers' ways are better men than the rest of us, and cite "Momma's boys" who have gone on to become famous, Winston Churchill for example. But the issue isn't all that simple, as feminists tend to seek conclusions that match a woman's viewpoint just as they have accused men of doing. Besides, while Churchill wasn't especially emasculated, even if he was somewhat baby-faced in his younger years, he was noted for some childishly narcissistic attitudes in part because he was bipolar as well as spoiled rotten, and it's little wonder he was once described as half genius, half bloody fool.

Aside from the few who may have excelled, lack of separation from his mother is more likely to send a boy into adulthood unable to adequately engage in the adult world. That will leave him able only to live in a chronically dependent way, immersed in fantasy, hostile toward the world that imposes on him, and perhaps drawn to crime as a way of gaining money with a minimum of effort.

One of the stronger feminist arguments has been that men fear a woman's ability to bear and nurse children, citing the practice in archaic cultures for men to give a boy a new birth in their initiation rites, as if to say that while a woman can give birth to a baby, only men can give birth to a man. The feminist contention is that men want to wrestle the power of birth away from women and claim it for themselves, a tendency they say shows in the medical establishment's approach to childbirth.

Classically, men have shown a compulsion to claim the power of birth (we see it in Greek mythology), and it shows in their tendency to speak of the conception, gestation, and birth of their creations, of their "babies." But that misses the point when it comes to the development of boys into men, for while women rightly complain that men can't understand the experience of a girl, it's equally true that a woman can't truly understand that of a boy.

Most boys grow up feeling shaped and defined by women, sometimes driving them as adults to dominate women as a way of trying to feel in control of their own lives. While that's taking things too far, it's a developmental challenge for boys to go through their first years with only female dynamics to internalize, leaving them hungering for male role models and male feelings. And as he grows, that hunger can become one of the strongest impulses a young boy knows.

Still, many psychologists and therapists argue that forcing young boys to separate from their mothers damages a boy's psyche. It's more accurate, though, to say that the point at which maternal attachment is too much or too little varies from child to child. The question is as to what supports a boy's developing ego strength, for just as a clinging mother can undermine her son's maturation process by refusing to let him separate from her when it's appropriate, too-early separation can have much the same effect. And just as the son who doesn't know how to free himself of Mom will feel a deeply rooted shame over his sense of paralysis, the boy who feels abandoned and neglected will feel shame over his emptiness and loneliness. Moreover, when we grow up having our maturation undermined, we'll likely go on to undermine it ourselves because we won't know how not to.

It's a common notion that initiation into adulthood is one of the things that has been lost from modern culture, rites that would traditionally have come into play at around ten to twelve years of age, taking a boy out of the childhood he knew with women and into the adulthood he would know among men. In some archaic cultures there would even be a change in vocabulary from the language of boys and women to that of adult males.

But initiation was not for the sake of the individual alone, but for the sake of the culture at large, to make teens viable members of the group. Today, though, the culture kids see looks to many of them like a bland, amorphous blur they want no part of. At least that's the way it looks to a kid who hasn't found a way to engage in the world they're growing into.

It's around the traditional initiation age that a father who consistently defeats or simply ignores his son's growing sense of identity is slamming a door in the boy's face, and if that boy doesn't have other men to draw on, he'll not only feel driven away from Dad, but away from masculinity and adulthood in general. Then he'll likely respond either by blindly fighting against any form of authority, or by bowing to authority on the outside while hiding his resentment. The tragedy is that the first response develops into a man who sees masculinity only in terms of rebellion, while the second has a hard time feeling his masculinity at all other than through conformity.

Come mid-adolescence, then, the role of initiation is replaced by a job market that seems to a teenager only to take advantage of people. So it's little wonder that many teens feel contemptuous of the work environment and are attracted to gangs, drugs, and alcohol, for it's the only way they know to feel free and empowered. But they are creating for themselves a reality defined by angry adolescent minds, vindictive and vengeful toward the world around them, not quite capable of comprehending a bigger picture.

The basic blueprint is for us to initially construct our self-sense from things outside ourselves; first from our mothers, eventually from the culture at large, and any way we falter can manifest as a struggle to define ourselves through anything we can find: religion, politics, pop culture and so on, the more radical the better. Or we may try to define ourselves through rebellion, but we'll probably have to learn the hard way that rebellion doesn't give us any true personal authority any more than conformity does, any more than excitement and manic frenzy give us a true sense of personal power.

Lacking significant male presence, a boy has only the world of women to relate to, although it's hardly a mother's fault that she's stuck with a job she ultimately can't fulfill. And if she's emotionally dependent on his remaining a boy, or if she consistently manipulates him into surrendering any sense of himself in order to meet her own needs, he'll likely go through life thinking that giving up his integrity and yielding to others' demands makes him a kind, loving person.

Every child needs to gain a healthy sense of separation—not isolation or alienation, but simply separation—initially from his mother in order to gain his own self-sense. It was with her that we had invested our very existence since birth, yet one of the greater challenges is to learn about the world beyond her domain, otherwise we'll be like a ship forever at dry dock, never quite making it to sea.

Men are sometimes sexually aggressive in the way of infants demanding the breast, and that's an instinct almost always laced with a liberal dose of anxiety-driven rage. This surfaced when Geraldine Ferraro ran for vice president, male hecklers shouting at her, *Iron my shirt!* How dare a woman try to be anything other than a dutiful Mommy? The irony, of course, is that it's an example of men displaying infantile attitudes as if they were something to be proud of.

So, while a woman may think she can raise a boy to manhood, she likely won't understand what her son grows up missing. In particular, many mothers miss understanding their son's need to develop a sense of autonomy and identity away from her, as it's something that lies outside her experience as a woman. As Friday and Tannen have shown us, women have their own problems with enmeshment with their mothers, but because of the gender difference, a boy's need for separation is so much greater that without it he'll be likely to go through life not only chronically dependent, but with the sense of entitlement that women so rightly despise in men.

The Idyllic Mother Fantasy

One of the ironies we face is that much of the rage we see in the world has its roots in the tenderness of infancy. Part of the reason is that, immersed in a universe of two, a little boy holds an idealized notion of his mother based on his memory of having once been a helpless infant at her breast: Mommy is a delicate, angelic being, and he feels for her all the sentiments poets have expressed for centuries, although he isn't yet capable of recognizing the self-centeredness in it.

At the same time, he longs to see himself as a powerful hero who protects his delicate mother/bride against the dangerous world out there. Of course, he's also developing an intellect that will tell him he's just a little kid, and Mommy's a grown-up, but for a few years he can ignore that. In the meantime he's living on holy ground, seated upon the High Throne of his mother's lap like the Madonna and Child.

This is where the foundations of his self-sense are built, feeling nurtured and protected. He also feels something he'll likely carry into his sexual life—at least until harsh reality catches up with him— namely, that she must want him as much as he wants her, that it's just the way the world is meant to be. But when he carries that expectation into his adolescent infatuations, reality can catch up quickly in the form of a teenaged girl's disdain.

Little boys love super-hero fantasies, and movies like the *Rambo* and *Rocky* series, the *Matrix* films and run-of-the-mill martial arts films all play on the theme. A common scenario is where the hero is defeated and humiliated by the bad guys, goes into seclusion to train under the tutelage of a mysterious mentor, then returns to claim victory. No matter the trappings, it's the storyline of a little boy overpowered by older, bigger kids, and hoping to claim his own one day with the help of an ideal father figure to replace the one who has failed him.

It's a powerful image, and there's a body stance that goes with it. Watch a little boy struggling to keep from crying or pumping himself up with rage when he doesn't get his way. Typically he'll hold his arms rigid with his fists clenched, hunch his shoulders and pump up his chest and face. But soften the pose, and it matches the feeling we get when our heart is bursting with infatuation and pride. I recall how at six years old I was fascinated by a Mighty Mouse comic (remember Mighty Mouse?), his inflated chest the epitome of a pumped-up little boy as the bad guys' bullets bounce off. For some of us, though, that becomes our chronic posture. Consider those old photos of Mussolini.

In a little boy's fantasy relationship with his mother, he's the mighty hero, she the delicate maiden, and it's one of the things Freud was looking at when he developed his notion of the Oedipus complex where he saw a boy as competing sexually with his father. But a little boy is actually competing with the man who disrupts his idyllic universe, for Daddy is an intruder who also wants something from Mommy. And while there's a sensual element in a little boy snuggling against his mother, the struggle with Daddy is over security and control rather than sexuality.

I'm sure Freud was right, though, in saying that a little boy's realization that Mommy is a sexual person and is *doing something* with Daddy is a threat to his fragile security. After all, sexuality is a world he can't participate in, one in which her impulses take her away from him. With childish simplicity he'll feel he has to be in control of Mommy or he'll be lost, then might conclude that all female sexuality must be controlled for males to feel secure. So we see men to whom any woman moving her body too freely is advertising herself as a prostitute. She is, after all, stepping beyond her role as nurturer and caregiver, and that's unforgivable to a childish male mind.

But when his own sexuality blossoms, it's in contrast those fantasies. While we all hold at least some sense of love based on our infant experience, to some men sexuality is a betrayal of that original mother bond, a disgraceful thing that destroys the purity of that infantile fantasy. Then, to prove how loving he is, he has to show that he's not sexual like those other guys, for his own sexuality is gentle and loving while every other man's is brutal, crass and filthy. Of course he has instincts that are brutal, crass and filthy, too, but he'll keep all that stashed away in some corner of his psyche and treat sex as something naughty. And every time he has sex he'll feel he's getting away with something. For some, this conflict compels them to celibacy, sensing that sexuality is a vile thing they need to deny in order to be deserving of God's love.

There are several outgrowths of this as a boy grows into adolescence. One is that he hopes for a girl to take Mommy's place as the tender flower in his life while he's simultaneously driven by raging hormones to screw some girl's brains out—quite a lot of girls' brains, actually. This is the classic "Madonna and whore" conflict in which a man can see women only as one extreme or the other. At its heart, though, it's a split between a little boy's fantasy of a delicate female under his protection on one hand, his primal impulse to see women as existing for his gratification on the other.

But it's mainly insecurity in disguise, and an insecure man feels he has to fight to possess and dominate women's sexuality much like a kid in Mom's lap sticking his tongue out at the rest of the male world. After all, if a woman is sexual, who knows where she'll be off to? He wants her to be sexual, but then again he doesn't; he wants her to be pure and untouched, and he wants to molest every inch of her; wants her to be passionate in his bed, a humble drone out of it.

Even the toughest man knows that female sexuality can render him as helpless as the child he once was, perhaps driving him to throw aside reason, fortune and pride to follow that lure—that's Odysseus lashed to the mast while the Sirens sing. Unfortunately, the only way some men know to control their vulnerability is to dominate the thing that threatens to conquer them, often with rage: *Women have bodies we lust after, therefore they are evil.*

Again, it takes ego strength for a man to see women as people in their own right, the irony being that a mother who undermines her son's ego development by infantilizing him is likely to turn him into the sort of man women resent—the chauvinist pig, the seductive gigolo, the pervert, the sex addict.

The Emasculated Man

This leads to the issue of emotional emasculation, the result of a little boy receiving the message throughout childhood that his male body, his genitalia, his natural male energy and inclinations are all somehow wrong, if not shameful. While there are cases of fathers demeaning their sons and treating them as competitors to be scorned, ridiculed and defeated, the most common source of emotional emasculation is the mother, because that's where our deepest imprints originate.

If a mother resents or fears masculinity, her tiny son, needing her for the security she offers, may shy away from his own budding maleness in order to preserve his connection with her. Or perhaps a mother finds her sense of identity through being the mother of an infant, so that her son feels compelled to remain a little boy out of a mixed sense of loyalty and need. Or it may be that the mother had really wanted a girl, or had wanted to make her son into someone compatible with her own feelings. Or if the father leaves or emotionally withdraws, the mother may use her son as an emotional substitute, so that he grows up enmeshed with her, oriented toward her female feelings and needs without any clear sense of his own.

One historical example is that of Robert McCormick, once owner of the Chicago Tribune, whose mother, disappointed at having given birth to a son, insisted on dressing him as a girl and calling him Roberta. Similarly, Ernest Hemingway's mother had dressed him like a girl in his early years, which led to him being a closet cross-dresser despite his manly ways. And Anaya's *Bless Me, Ultima* has a woman declaring what a sin it is for a boy to grow up to be a man. Thus, the traditional male dread of the tyrannies of the petticoat.

Emasculation by men carries a different dynamic. The ideal would be for a man to support a boy in growing into his own masculinity, if only by providing him a role model to breathe in. Without that, he's left with only women as models for his developing self-sense, and if he finds men consistently defeating his growing masculinity, it will leave him feeling adrift. It will also leave him with anger he'll feel powerless to express, since letting it show will get him beaten up and humiliated.

Whatever the cause, an emasculated male is one whose ego development has been consistently undermined: a needy mother defeats him in order to nurture herself while a bullying father defeats him in order to stay on top. And if every time he tries to stand on his own he feels the rug going out from under him, he'll eventually stop trying. Then his isolation will be exacerbated by the bullying he gets from tougher boys looking for a convenient target, and from grown men who simply dismiss him out of hand.

So, he grows up feeling that men can't be trusted, that they'll hurt him any chance they get, and that it's just not worth the risk. Instead, he may lean toward girls or younger boys as friends, or he may simply withdraw altogether. Athletics are too hard, physical challenges are too much to deal with, so he gives up when things get difficult until he has a hard time gaining any sense of reward for physical effort—intellectual effort, perhaps, but not physical effort.

Emasculated men typically feel genderless rather than feminine, and a genderless man usually doesn't realize the price exacted on him until he's put on enough age to look back and take stock of things. Even then, though, he likely won't know what to do about it. What he primarily needs is to force himself to be physically active and gain a degree of competence at it, to cobble together the self-sense he's been denied through physical activity.

Beyond that, he'll have to reclaim the pain and anger he's repressed since childhood at having his developing psyche so deeply undermined. Yet, most likely the people who had undermined him had simply been lost in their own needs. Nonetheless, he's left carrying a bundle of chronic pain and rage at having been raised to be a non-entity, a rage that constitutes a defeated ego's last-ditch attempt at protecting the remaining shreds of its integrity.

That's a long process, and an emasculated man will likely be in his forties before he even starts to make serious headway, and when that can of worms opens, he may have to spend a decade or so thrashing his way through the feelings that erupt as all those repressed feelings take life again. Nonetheless, this is the most important step he can take, otherwise he's likely to remain stuck seeking comfort in fantasies rather than facing hard realities.

All this, of course, runs contrary to popular notions telling us to be peaceful and gentle, for we have to ask if we're being authentically peaceful and gentle, or if we aren't simply faking it because that's what we've been trained to do?

When I speak of emasculation, though, I'm not talking about effeminacy. There's an argument, mostly from the gay community, that some men are naturally effeminate, that it's in their genetic makeup. Emasculation, on the other hand, is a direct result of the way a boy is raised, and while an effeminate man may not have much of a sense of masculinity, emasculated men are not necessarily effeminate. Nor is emasculation equivalent to homosexuality, for most emasculated men are not gay.

In their complaints against men, women often give the impression that what they really want is a woman in a man's body, and an emasculated man almost fits the bill. But then women often find that a relationship with an emasculated man is a disappointment, for while they may feel emotionally met by an emasculated man, it's unlikely they'll feel energetically met. They may start off saying he's gentle and kind, spiritual, and not into power and control like all those other jerks out there, only to discover that he is in many ways more driven to power and control than most other men, just in more subtle ways—through seduction, manipulation, criticism and complaining.

And women will typically find that if they push against an emasculated man in emotional terms, he'll fall down, then fly into a flurry of childish blame. Generally, emasculated men fear forceful interactions because they're not strong enough to stand up to strong feelings or strong language. The lesson they so tragically miss, though, is that it's through pushing against the world and having it push back that our self-sense is shaped. That's something pushers understand innately.

This says a good deal about the New Age propensity for "subtle energies" because subtle states feel safe to an emasculated man. And while many women may be attracted to men like that for their appearance of gentleness and sensitivity, they are unwittingly encouraging a wound, for just as men have traditionally loved weak, wounded women for their submissiveness, many women love the opposite gender equivalent for the same reason. So, just as men have traditionally considered a loving woman to be one who is disempowered, disconnected from herself, out of touch with her sexuality, and with a self-sense largely defined by men, many women feel that a loving man is one who is disempowered, disconnected from himself, out of touch with his true sexuality, and with a self-sense largely defined by women.

But while an emasculated man may revel in the praise he gets from women, he'll eventually feel sick at heart, sensing the lie he's living. Still, he's also likely to seek control by going behind the backs of other men and gain power from women in positions of authority. This is something we often see in spiritual communities, in the alternative healing subculture, and in therapy and religious groups run by strong mother figures. And an emasculated man will seek any position that gives him authority over others, which is why so many are drawn to becoming psychotherapists, professors, spiritual teachers and the like where they get to direct others without undue effort.

One thing that elevates emasculated men in these situations is that they make good followers, good true believers because their yearning for positions of authority drives them to pick up others' creative ideas and imitate them. So, they become devoted parrots, and power-oriented leaders love parrot-like followers.

And an emasculated men often use the authority they gain to lash out at other men as if in revenge on all those playground bullies from years ago. But they'll never go up against another man when he's on his feet, waiting instead until he's off-balance and hurting, then go at him with criticism and finger-wagging, a trait that inspires the same contempt aimed at him as a kid on the playground.

One thing a young athlete has the potential to learn on the football field or in any head-to-head competition is respect for the other guy by directly going up against him. It's a theme that shows up as far back as the ancient tale where Gilgamesh and Enkidu wrestle, after which they become the best of friends.

But the man who's never had that experience will approach other men indirectly, and because he doesn't know how to go head-to-head, he'll seek a one-up position, which is why he'll become a therapist or teacher, as anyone coming to him will be down a peg or two in terms of personal power. But that sense of power may come without a true sense of competence, resulting in the ineffective therapist, the teacher so lost in idealism that he can't see how inept he is.

Sadly, emasculated men can be contemptible, and it seems it's an evolutionary instinct that drives the bully, for if there'd been too many weaklings around in our remote past, the human race may not have survived. We may not have even gotten down out of the trees all those millions of years ago. The irony is that most cultures throughout history have been motivated by emasculated men, for they're often the bureaucrats and administrators, the artisans, religious leaders and intellectuals that give a culture its character. In general, culture is created by those with more imagination than the average bully is capable of, for while macho guys may conquer and defend territory, they're not very good and managing it or giving it depth.

The Bitter Legacy of the Narcissistic Parent

Everything... tries simultaneously to expand
and hold back. It's a mystery.
~Peter Høeg, *The Quiet Child*

They fuck you up, your mum and dad...
~Philip Larkin, *This Be the Verse*

As children we need to feel ourselves at the center of our parents' world, for it's through that original self-centeredness that we build the foundations of our self-sense. It's from there we gain the strength to create and carry our own lives, yet it's just part of being human to have places where we stumble as if stepping into a hole in what had looked like solid ground.

Our psychological blueprint demands that certain experiences be learned in a particular sequence at particular ages, so that when we fail to learn something at the proper time and are then faced with that lesson at a later time, we tend to reject the challenge. There's a time to bond, and a time to move toward independence; a time to cling for comfort, and a time to take care of ourselves and give others the space they need; a time to be given whatever we need, a time to learn to share, and a time to go and get what we need for ourselves; a time to be the center of attention, and a time to step aside.

We all know what it's like to deal with people who behave with childish expectations, then react with defiance when questioned. One of the first calls to greater maturity in childhood is in realizing there are consequences to our behaviors, for it shatters any lingering notion that the world orbits around us. Yet some of us seem determined to defeat that notion with outrage and indignation, as if once the proper time for a particular developmental stage has passed, our nervous system digs in its heels and resists.

As Annie Dillard writes in *Pilgrim at Tinker Creek*, an infant takes in the world with wide-eyed wonder only to acquire within a few years the "cocksure air of a squatter claiming to own the place." That's what we see in the toddler's tantrum: *I've been in this world for two whole years, and I know how things are supposed to be!*

This is one of the things we see in the stereotypical tyrant in a highchair, for as in the Peter Høeg quote above, we want both to engage in the world, yet limit the world to what we understand. That means trying to limit other people to the world as we see it, a dynamic every parent gets to deal with from their child's toddlerhood through his teenage years. That's especially true for teens as the manic quality induced by our hormones convinces us our worldview is vast when it's actually quite limited, and the call to experience anything further can make us flare with outrage.

A teenager is still gaining their self-sense from the world as they see it, and anything beyond that is an intrusion trying to dictate who they're supposed to be. But an adult with that attitude can do serious damage, for his grandiose notions will be the only thing important to him, and he'll become enraged by any challenge to explore the world beyond his expectations.

The theme that follows is that of narcissistic parenting, a dynamic that stands the parent-child relationship on its head, for a narcissistic parent is arrested at such an early level of their own development that they expect their child to meet their needs for them, seemingly oblivious of the notion that a child could ever have needs of their own. After all, why should they have to suffer the indignity of not being at the center of the universe when they have someone else to take up the slack for them, even if that someone else is only three years old?

Like an insecure child, the stance of a narcissist is: *You're not supposed to have a life your own! You're supposed be an extension of me!* That and: *How dare you react to what I'm not doing to you!* So, when their child comes to them for attention, a narcissist will respond with dismissal, sarcasm and ridicule, or with exaggerated praise that only serves to nurture the parent's own need. And a child who tries to stand up for himself will be seen as insolent, for in the eyes of a narcissist a defeated child is a good child. It's reminiscent of some of Charles Dickens' stories. And because of their innate jealousy, narcissistic parents will dismiss their child's abilities and accomplishments, sometimes taking away gifts the kid has been given by others in order to discount him as a valid person.

Narcissistic parents are driven to absorb their child's life as if it belonged to themselves, yet behind their jealousy is their dread of seeing how inadequate they are at facing the adult world—fundamentally they are at war with a big, scary world. It's little wonder, then, that the children of narcissistic parents learn early on to distrust their parents' intentions, and will feel they have to fend for themselves, especially when it comes to emotional needs.

This is Holden Caulfield in *A Catcher in the Rye*, for although his parents are only briefly mentioned, it seems they barely recognize him as a person. In fact, *A Catcher in the Rye* is something of an exposé on the theme. This gets especially serious when children reach nine to twelve years old and start setting boundaries of their own, for a narcissistic parent will attempt to defeat their child's developing psyche out of fear of not having enough control, perhaps out of fear of having to deal with a kid more mature than themselves. So, the driving element for a narcissistic parent is neither arrogance nor power. Rather, it's that frightening hole in the center of their chest driving them to approach other people the same way they had their mother's breast, habitually out to feed their chronic emptiness.

We all have authentic needs, but the level of need expressed by the adult narcissist is a bodily-felt memory of a past need, which is why nothing will ever fulfill it, giving it that bottomless pit quality. It's a bit like watching the movie *Titanic* over and over, hoping that sooner or later they'll miss the iceberg. But old feelings always play back the same way, and demanding that someone else change it for us is to saddle them with an impossible task.

One thing that drives a narcissist is a sense of being deprived, but as long as we're carrying the entitlement appropriate for a child, we'll always feel that others owe us; that we have rights, but others don't; that others demanding rights of their own are somehow depriving us. And just like a toddler, a narcissist feels that being special is something that can't be shared: I win and you lose, or you win and I lose.

Because narcissists assign others an impossible task, they saddle their child with a sense of inadequacy, and because kids have no way of understanding it, narcissist's children assume they are somehow defective. Moreover, a child who lives as an extension of a parent's self will feel limited by the degree of maturity the parent has reached, and will grow up believing life is a minefield that can take you out in a heartbeat, adding to the feeling that they are always somehow at risk, even that life itself is risky.

Lack of ego strength in a parent becomes a wound to their child's psyche just as that lack in anyone from a teacher to an employer to a national leader results in trouble for anyone under their influence. But it's not that a narcissist is deliberately inconsiderate, rather that it never occurs to them to consider because they simply can't. As former New York Times editor Howell Raines says in a different context, people with truncated personalities have the unfortunate ability to inject pathology into the lives of others, and without a lick of guilt.

Learning to pay attention to things beyond our own wants and needs doesn't happen all by itself, for it's an awareness that's gained over the years. And the person who enters adulthood without having gained that ability will likely react as if the need to respect others is an affront, as if it would constitute a defeat to give way over something as trivial as a parking space or who got in line first. What we see in the narcissist, then, is a rejection of a challenge we all face, trying instead to force others to treat them as highchair tyrants whose rages must be obeyed.

This is why a narcissist's child grows up with feeling they're being stalked by an invisible enemy. What's actually after them, though, is a parent's desperation trying to defeat the child's psychological integrity. It's as if a narcissist has traveled only a mile or two on a thousand-mile journey, convinced he's gone as far as he needs to, and that requires him to get others to cater to him, defeating them with tears, indignation and outrage should they fail to play the role he has assigned them.

Oddly, while the child of a narcissistic parent grows up fearing that if he were to ever express anything authentic, something bad would happen, it often proves true, for there are stories of those who finally grew strong enough to confront their parent only to have the parent taken down by a heart attack or stroke. Sometimes it seems the parent's final act of revenge: *Now look what you've done to me!*

For all this, narcissists can be compelling people, as if they give off a bright glow, but it's as if that glow is the energy they've drawn out of other people in their constant quest to fill themselves at others' expense, just as a child does. It's little surprise, then, that those who feel drawn to that narcissistic glow find the price can be terribly high. It's natural that we start out as children with that glow about us, but like those fairy tale princes and princesses, we lose the golden throne we'd taken as our birthright, and are thrown out into the wilderness where we have to struggle to claim our proper place in life. What those tales fail to tell us, though, is that it can take forty years. The narcissist, though, has rejected that task, for losing that golden throne is bewildering and frightening, which is why tyrants dread having their populace turn into real people.

So, narcissistic parenting attempts to break the fundamental blueprint upon which a child's psyche develops, for as the child tries to establish a foundation of his own, his parent tries to claim that foundation for himself. The dynamic even shows up in a seemingly innocent scenario like an adult hugging a child, saying: *Oh you're so cute I could just eat you up!*, for it sometimes carries far more reality than we care to think. And a child's psyche senses it, which is why kids are fascinated by *Hansel and Gretel* and other fairy tales about children being devoured by giants and witches. And he quickly learns that a chocolate sundae never gets to be a real person, never gets to walk away or have a voice with which to say *No!* It's a theme that shows up in ancient Greek mythology, and we see it in Goya's painting of Saturn devouring his children, eyes wide with horror at his own act.

A child of a narcissist is forced to focus so much of his attention on an adult that he won't have enough left over for himself, and when an adult demands, *Look at me when I'm talking to you*, the kid can't look at them and feel the ground under his feet at the same time. Some adults will grab a child by the chin and force eye contact, which compels the kid to dissociate until he's tripping over his own feet and stumbling into the furniture. And thirty years later he'll still feel guilty if he pays attention to his own needs, even if the parent is long dead and gone. It's no surprise that adult children of narcissistic parents are often compulsive multi-taskers, because it's something they've always had to do.

A child of a narcissist will learn to sense others' expectations and adjust himself at a moment's notice, the notion that he could ever be a person in his own right barely having a chance to take root. Instead, he will grow up with a sense that his awareness starts about a foot out from his body and goes outwards, constantly scanning for others' expectations, but with little awareness of himself. And they can be profoundly gullible, easily taken in by con artists because they've been trained to cave in to manipulation. It was originally a survival strategy, but can become so deeply ingrained that it becomes an assumption that others will always use them while pretending they're not.

Still, narcissists see themselves as loving parents, just as tyrants see themselves as loving leaders. And since truthfulness is a threat to a narcissist, their children and spouses learn to lie, afraid that some slip-up on their part may set something off. But to accomplish that they have to switch off part of their psyches, and in time it becomes a habit. Then, when they hear others talk about their needs and aspirations, the child of a narcissist feels only an odd vagueness because the notion that having needs and ambitions of his own doesn't seem real.

He will also believe that love means sacrificing himself for the sake of someone who can't or won't take responsibility for their own life, because notions of self-sacrifice fill him with soaring feelings, at least until the pain catches up with him. It's not surprising, then, that a narcissist's child will go through life feeling that he's not good enough unless he's sacrificing himself for the sake of something—a cause, an ideal, a relationship—yet he'll likely find himself sitting on a powder keg of rage that frightens even himself.

Yet not all narcissistic parents are the angry sort, for narcissism can also show up as obsessive anxiety. A child needs to find his own learning experiences even if it means a scraped knee here and there, but an anxious parent can paralyze him with fears he can't hope to comprehend. So, if he's going to have adventures, he'll have to have them on the sly. Otherwise, he'll imagine great things while doing nothing at all, feeling that life is for others, that others get to accomplish things, have adventures and achieve goals while he watches from a distance. Initiative, after all, is one of those things his hungry parent has taken away from him and eaten.

One response is for him to resort to grandiose fantasies that are at times delusional, telling extraordinary lies about his supposed feats and accomplishments. After all, he's had to lie all along just to get by, so life feels like a lie much of the time, anyway. What's terribly confusing is that the wound he carries is an invisible one. So, the child assumes that his misery must not be real, that there must be something fundamentally wrong with him. Besides, others tell him that: *Your parents are such wonderful people! Whatever went wrong with you?* And because everyone tells him so, he believes them. Yet when he does things well, he'll have a hard time accepting recognition because his history leads him to equate praise with manipulation.

There's a Buddhist aphorism that even were we to carry our

parents on our backs for the rest of their lives, we wouldn't be able to repay them for all they'd done in raising us. But a narcissist abuses every relationship until their child feels torn between a reasonable sense of love and duty on one hand, and a reasonable degree of resentment on the other, especially when they have children of their own to care for.

This is a theme that doesn't just go away with time. Elan Golomb, whose *Trapped in the Mirror* is a seminal work on the topic, tells of taking a long weekend to visit a sick aunt, but getting to spend only a few minutes with her because her mother, who lived in the same city, had demanded all her daughter's time for herself. That's a mild example, but it indicates why even with both parents dead and gone for decades, the adult child of a narcissistic parent can live with a sense that something is always about to undermine everything they attempt to achieve because as children that had been their constant experience.

Many children of narcissistic parents are attracted to spiritual teachings that tell us that an enlightened person rises above all personal needs, but whatever may be ultimately true about such things, the child of a narcissist leans that way for all the wrong reasons. And because they're attuned to meeting everyone else's needs, it's little wonder so many are driven to become psychotherapists and aid workers.

An interesting portrayal of the child of a narcissist shows up in (of all places!) Julie Harris' role in the classic horror film, *The Haunting*, which is actually more of a psychological drama. Harris' character has lived under the domination of a needy mother who, upon her death, has left her daughter yearning to find some place where her own life can finally happen. The thing that haunts her, though, is her guilt that the one time she'd refused to respond to her mother's relentless banging for attention on the wall between their bedrooms was the night the old lady died, as if out of spite. So, when the ghostly presence comes prowling at night, banging away on the walls, she awakens thinking it's her mother.

But for all the examples of parents demanding a child's attention and energy, the avoidant narcissist will insist on defeating a child's needs by emotionally starving them, then blaming them for being so needy. The traditional British school system is criticized for defeating children's needs, for a child can keep a stiff upper lip only by emotionally paralyzing himself, which seems to have gone a long way toward generating that infamously English sense of cold superiority. Similarly, Bergman's film, *Autumn Sonata*, portrays a young woman facing off with her mother who'd insisted throughout the daughter's childhood on remaining distant and aloof. As the mother says, her daughter simply hadn't interested her until she'd grown up, which she has barely been able to do.

Again, it's not that the parent is trying to be cruel, rather that avoiders simply don't know what to do with themselves when pressed with emotional needs, their own or those of others. Generally, they're so preoccupied with themselves that a child's needs are such a violation of their worldview that it threatens their own emotional defenses.

The most blatant example of the narcissistic parent, though, is the tyrant—think of the Queen of Hearts in *Alice in Wonderland*—living in constant outrage, and when that rage is directed at their adult children, their basic message is: *Well, it's your fault that you're all twisted up inside yourself, isn't it?*

Children of narcissistic parents often show symptoms disturbingly similar to those of both incest survivors and children of alcoholic parents, for, metaphorically speaking, a narcissistic parent is both a rapist and an addict, their drug of choice being grandiose inflation which they get by using others. The obvious parallel with incest is that the child is being overwhelmed by an adult's obsessive urges, which is rape in a very real sense, even when there's nothing physical about it.

The child's response is similar to what many incest survivors grow up with: *This isn't happening, I can't stop it or say anything about it, and it's my fault.* But the child also senses, although it will be years before he'll have the means for putting it into words, is that narcissistic adults chronically fear falling apart—they fear falling apart if they don't get their way just as they fear falling apart if they are confronted with their behavior. As a result, their children feel a strange mental block, the result of having to numb themselves since early childhood so as to not say the truthful thing, to not be authentically themselves. They also grow up carrying elements of post-traumatic stress disorder.

The upshot of it all is that children of narcissistic parents have a difficult time maturing. Even if they develop competence as adults, they often do so by becoming followers, whether in business, religion, or what have you. Either that or they become lone wolves yearning to be free of the parasite that continues to eat away inside them.

To truly become free, the child of a narcissist has to reclaim the emotional history he has carried for so long—this is the reason for the descriptions above—and that means wading through the murky swamp of feelings he's been secreting away for decades. And that's rarely achieved before the age of forty. A more immediate challenge, though, is to not pass on the tradition, for the person raised by a narcissistic parent is likely to grow up to become one themselves unless they can unravel their own knots.

That in turn leads to a serious truth for all of us, that we can be adequate parents only to the degree that we can mature our way out of our own childhood expectations of life in general and of other people.

Dealing With the Legacy

Dealing with a childhood dominated by a narcissistic parent means working with patterns taken on so early in life that it's hard not to confuse them with reality. While just getting in touch with old feelings is in itself inadequate when it comes to developing ego strength—in fact, obsessing on them can have quite the opposite effect—there's a particular challenge for the adult child of a narcissist to reinvigorate parts of themselves that hold those feelings, to give those feelings a home.

Chief among the things we have to face are a sense of guilt over having failed at protecting a parent from having to face their own life, and our fear of being attacked by someone ten to twenty times our size whenever they are confronted with a personal truth they can't handle. Basically, we have to reclaim the aliveness and self-sense that were denied us, and at times that means reliving some deep hurts and reengage parts of ourselves that had been deadened when we were too young to do anything about it. As with PTSD, we'll likely find ourselves immersed in visceral memory flashes of incidents that had occurred decades ago, only to find ourselves faced with all the shame, fear, pain, and anger we hadn't been able to face back then.

That presents us with a double-edged dilemma. On one hand, we find the opportunity to develop the ego strength we could have developed years ago, while on the other hand, reliving deeply-troubling experiences without having gained enough ego strength to handle them can be traumatizing all over again.

It can be the challenge of a lifetime to revitalize deadened parts of ourselves, yet we're all faced with the challenge to "grow up" those parts of ourselves and experience ourselves differently. When it comes to a history with a narcissistic parent, we'll assume that others are out to hurt us no matter what masks they wear, and sometimes they really are. So, gaining the ability to interrupt our assumptions and respond to each situation as it is constitutes one of our greatest challenges. Overall, our challenge is the same as ever—to develop enough ego strength to mindfully carry our history.

Shyness

Shyness deserves special attention, for it may be an inherited trait that some of us shrink away from too much attention, drawing back from the spotlight as if from a threat. Alternatively, though, it can result from a chronically overwhelmed prefrontal cortex, and a child will guard against a repeat of that wound by pulling back from social contact unless it feels safe. Either way, shyness is a trait often judged as cold, insensitive and arrogant, although it's typically a reaction against cold insensitivity and arrogance on the part of others. Hence, Holden Caulfield's comment about self-centered girls seeing a shy guy as arrogant.

Shyness is often a result of emotional abuse so early in life that it leaves a person with an expectation that others will always impose on them, that it's just a question of how they're going to go about it, and how long it's going to take them to get around to it. So, on entering a roomful of people, the shy person will cringe, anticipating an attack, and when they're accused of being cold and arrogant, their inner response is: *See? I was right! All they ever do is hurt me.*

I've seen highly respected psychotherapists make this mistake. For instance, in a training seminar a student mentioned something from his childhood only to have the trainer say that his raised voice tone indicated he was arrogant and felt superior to others. The student later confided that what he'd been thinking about was one of the few things he'd felt good about during his deeply-depressed childhood, and that a major feature of that childhood had been that every time he'd felt good about anything, his mother had shot him down for it, just as that trainer had. And that particular trainer had a quality, as do many clingers, that suggests that if you have a good feeling for yourself, you must be arrogant.

That's why shy people feel awkward and bumbling in social situations, sensing something wrong with the way they are, something they can't see while everyone else can. More importantly, most grow up feeling broken-hearted, which makes the criticism aimed at them seem all the more vindictive.

One thing that drives an other-oriented person to instinctively judge shy people as arrogant is that they're unable to fathom any other reason for that behavior. And if the shy do at times come across as overbearing, it's because they're overcompensating by being garrulous, even boisterous, trying to lift themselves up out of the mud.

The challenge for a shy person is generally twofold: to challenge their instinct to withdraw, and to learn to genuinely speak up for themselves, which often means having the strength to tell other people a few personal truths, even if it means coming across as cold and arrogant. As children, the shy often understand that if they were to stand their ground, their abusers would fall to pieces, then attack, so shyness often originates partly as a way of protecting a fragile, self-centered parent. And, yes, even an experienced psychotherapist can go to pieces should they hear a few uncomfortable truths about themselves.

Victims and Victimizers

Accompanying shyness is an assumption that others are out to get us, which was probably for good reasons in childhood, but we're likely to assume it's the way life will always be. Ironically, it's the seductive parent who is most likely to create that attitude in their child, because while a child parented by a bully knows where their abuse is coming from, the child of a manipulative parent likely does not. And because he won't know how to identify the source of that feeling, he'll assume it's coming from everywhere.

Since any feeling internalized at a young age tends to become a chronic way of viewing life, the kid who is the target of every bully on the block will go into adulthood feeling that there's always something preying on him. As adults, then, he'll likely bristle the moment he hears of an ordinance, the rules of a workplace or legal requirements of the slightest sort, and if he sees someone in a position of authority, his automatic assumption is that they are out to victimize others in general, himself in particular.

Then he'll put extraordinary effort into fighting even the most common social agreements, turning trivial issues into a fight for a sense of identity. We might resent large corporations as faceless entities out to control us, and while we may be sometimes right, our challenge is in our inability to distinguish between our assumptions on one hand, the facts of the matter on the other. Because we're likely to assume that any social structure is meant to oppress us, we'll drive through stop signs just to prove we can and violate common codes of behavior just to prove the bastards can't keep us down. Then we'll mock all those "sheeple" for being pawns of the system, failing to see how we, too, are acting like sheeple, while others wonder why we keep shooting ourselves in the foot.

A theme presented in films like the *Matrix* series is that modern culture is a faceless machine that creates a false reality and turns people into drones. But while challenging mindless conformity is a valid issue, fans of the *Matrix* notion tend to act like clones of one another. There is a theme in classical mythology where a hero faces a multi-headed monster that produces another head every time one is cut off. But that monster lives only in our own minds. Are we really being controlled, or are we simply inadequate for the task of facing adult life? But isn't it more thrilling to feel we're victims of some great and profound evil?

Many of us know only to rage at a world that expects us to move beyond adolescent fantasies, able only to see that world as an enemy out to make us part of the machine. So, despite that old Bob Seeger song, if I feel like a number, it's my job to build a better sense of myself instead of expecting the world around me to simply give me one.

As teens we're prone to interpreting even the most reasonable adult expectations as oppression, but what we can't see is that adults are often trying to protect us from ourselves, yet we'll hate them for it. So, while the rebel without a clue sees anyone in a position of authority as an enemy, it's a part of the process of learning to acquire our own sense of authority and cooperate in an authentic way. Unfortunately, though, some of us go on blundering through life in a rage.

There's a facial set we see in some in their late teens and early twenties, the look of someone whose attention is stubbornly set on himself: *Don't expect me to care. I don't have to.* We may see it as being cool or powerful, even as sophisticated, but while self-absorption was natural when we were little, it's a tendency that can have us playing Russian roulette with life, as in the billboard warning reckless drivers with a photo of a revolver with one bullet in the cylinder—*Is your luck about to run out?* Again, it's not so much a thing in itself as a lack of something, not so much the attitudes we have as attitudes we haven't yet gained.

Many of us felt as children that being directed was to be victimized, which led us to either fight back or give up. But a child's greatest learning comes from being engaged in what's happening. The ideal, then, would be for us to learn in early childhood to work our way into the world around us instead of losing ourselves to conformity or rebelling out of habit, learning healthy cooperation rather than obedience for the sake of obedience or anarchy for the sake of anarchy.

Researchers tell us the human nervous system doesn't fully mature until our late twenties, that it isn't physiologically-developed enough to perceive the intricacies of a situation until then, which is why we can be so reckless as teenagers and twenty-somethings—we've got the fire to take on the world, but not enough awareness to handle it very well, although we'll resent anyone telling us so. It's little wonder, then, that so many of our important lessons come the hard way.

While we teach kids to look both ways before crossing a street, they'll likely have trouble doing that on their own until they're older. It's the same with sex in that you can tell younger people about pregnancy and sexually-transmitted diseases, but they're often too disconnected to take it seriously as something that could happen to them: *Remember what you've learned about how you get those diseases that can kill you? Well, you're doing it right now! Get it?*

Then we see kids who've grown up with the expectation right from the start that they are to take part in the family work, and we find relatively little of the obnoxiousness so common elsewhere, while the kid who grows up with a minimum of easy chores that he gets out of half the time anyway will resent the indignity of washing a dish or taking out the trash. Then we see the teenager who, with a look of swaggering insolence, walks out into a busy street, forcing drivers to come to a screeching halt: *See how powerful I am? You have to avoid killing me, now don't you? I can do whatever I want because I'm fifteen and brainless, and by the way, fuck you!* That's why a specialist in adolescent development tells us a sixteen-year-old driving a car can be like a two-year-old with hormones and wheels.

That may be a bit extreme, yet many of us learn early on there's a thrill in going against the grain and getting away with it. But if we go on claiming personal power that way as adults, we'll feel like victims while creating trouble for everyone else. As kids we resent hearing that the age of twenty-one is referred to as "attaining the age of reason," although most of us have done things that in hindsight look like the equivalent of running out into traffic, delirious at having gotten away with it. Personally, I'm not sure how I survived my first two years of driving a car. It can seem nature has set us up to live senselessly between childhood and adulthood, wanting both the power of adults and the lack of responsibility of children, complaining that the system wants to keep us down while victimizing others with ours heedlessness.

Overall, a victim stance is driven by a feeling that's like a hole in our psyche, one that's hard to define, harder still to locate because it's basically a vague awareness that there's something missing from us, that our psyches haven't yet come together adequately. The overall challenge, then, is to fill out that hole by involving ourselves in the world around us, neither rebelling against nor mindlessly complying with the world we find ourselves in.

Without this, we'll go on seeing enemies everywhere, plots against us, corruption that's depriving us of what we're supposed to have. Now that conspiracy theories have become so vocal, especially around the COVID-19 virus, we see a sizeable population who disdain hard science in favor of irrational, fear-based belief systems, and many are willing to resort to violence to prove themselves right. Galileo faced that demented beast, and many others were sent to the stake by it. But why? There seems good reason to hold social media and computer games accountable because they provide a dissociated version of reality that many, especially younger people, get lost in— gaining their sense of reality from an onslaught of questionable information with no physical grounding.

Computers, Rock and Roll and Other Hallucinogens

He just spends his life living on the edge of reality
~Ray Davies, *Rock and Roll Fantasy*

The notion of cool has been destroying the heart for years
~Leonard Cohen

Most of us grow up with the rock and roll fantasy, and it can seriously undermine our ability to mature, for it all too easily addicts us to artificial excitement and the virtually autistic withdrawal that goes with it. A hyperactive trance is still a trance, and if the music is shut off, kids under its sway will either slump in despair or fly into a rage, both of which are significant indicators of addiction.

Even at its best, music has an addictive quality, but just a century ago most people heard it only occasionally, while now it's a constant background drone in our lives. And we've seen the manic quality in popular music increase until it doesn't seem possible to go much further, for what was exciting in the Fifties was boring to kids in the Sixties and Seventies, while geezer rock is grindingly tedious to kids today. And two hundred years ago the waltz was considered far too sexual.

To an adolescent nervous system, manic energy can be a carrot on a stick, promising power and glory if we pushed it just a little more where there's none to be had. It can compel kids to dive further and further into frenzy, not understanding that in spite of their rage they'll always be rats stuck in cages they've created for themselves. So, while rock musicians may be seen by their fans as living gods, they have become like drug dealers, the irony being that their lifestyle tends to eat them up just like it does any junkie. An old Neil Young lyric says it's better to burn out than to fade away, but the truth is that they burn out, then fade away. And while Socrates said that bad music conditions the young to chaos and makes them unfit for culture, it's more to the point that it conditions us to disengage from the life by filling us with a compelling substitute. Even New Age music ("air pudding," as a musician friend calls it) is just as much a drug for those of us who yearn for the misty realms, for it too provides a compelling substitute for real life. So can electronic music and hip-hop, repetitive rhythm and sounds appealing to those of us who are trance-hungry, associating trance with feelings of power and transcendence. On the other hand, those of us who are trance-resistant are wondering what the matter is with all those spaced-out, frenzied kids.

We see a variation in the film industry where audiences demand ear-splitting exaggeration even during the popcorn ads, and anything that requires patience, insight and an appreciation for nuance is intolerable. But patience, insight and an appreciation for nuance are characteristics of emotional maturity, and while they're still to be found in European and Canadian film, they're not often seen in the US fare.

The first target of blame is television if only because it provides an imitation life without our having to get off the couch. Worse, it flattens our experience in a way that can become a sort of artificial maturity. So, while kids may seem savvy, there's such a gap in their psyches that when confronted with hard reality they'll complain that the world out there doesn't match the TV fantasy land. TV also feeds our addiction to constant excitement, images flashing so quickly we can only absorb them subliminally, which is one reason it's thought to induce hyperactive attention deficit disorder in kids. And resurfacing from any significant time under the sway of the blue screen requires a period of adjustment for many of us. Worse, it can leave us annoyed that the world around us can't be changed with the push of a button.

Seventy years ago it was conjectured that captured American soldiers had been relatively easily brainwashed by the North Koreans because they'd already been programmed to gullibility by mass media and advertising, even though television hadn't been a big part of the puzzle back then. It's hardly surprising, then, that research indicates that TV can stunt a child's ability to learn, can build unrealistic expectations, and can lead to hyperactive behavior. It recalls an old cartoon where a man is changing a flat tire in the rain while his kids peer out the car windows. *Don't you get it?*, says the dad. *This is life! We can't change the channel.* And now the Chinese, Southeast Asians and Africans have, with the introduction of television, grown their own batches of lazy, whining and relentlessly demanding children.

Computer games are worse in many ways because they feed a boy's superhuman fantasies while giving him a sense of power that's detached from any physical experience. One result is a sizeable population of young men who are in poor physical condition, live on fantasies bordering on serious delusions, and are impatient with the tangible world because it can't be controlled with a joystick.

Now we have electronic device addiction, the effects of which are only starting to be understood. We see people obsessed with their phones, going through life with their eyes on those tiny screens, even texting while driving, their addiction a threat to everyone around them. And as with any addiction, they'll react with outrage should anyone interfere. Worse, perhaps, the term "social media" hardly applies anymore for there is little true social interaction at work.

Those of us who grow up in this culture have developed a good part of our self-sense based on the advertising, music, TV shows and whatnot, and the price we pay is that our world view is based essentially on hallucinations and fantasies. So, it's little wonder that so many of us have naïve notions of the world we live in. "Techno-narcissism" has become a significant contributor to the childish entitlement we see in so many young adults beyond even what Baby Boomers experienced, for it undermines their psychological development in ways that are not clearly understood. The upshot is that if we're addicted to electronic media, we'll be chronically angry at the world outside our door for failing to be sufficiently enthralling.

So, we see books such as Nicholas G. Carr's *The Shallows: How the Internet is Changing the Way We Think, Read and Remember*, Richard Winter's *Still Bored in a Culture of Entertainment: Rediscovering Passion and Wonder*, and Meghan Daum's *Selfish, Shallow and Self-Absorbed: Sixteen Writers on the Decision Not To Have Kids*. Then we have Norman Doidge reporting in *The Brain That Changes Itself* how pornography creates a dynamic in which the brain reacts more strongly to fantasy than reality. To state it simply, fantasy breeds contempt and rage toward physical reality.

At the heart of this is the challenge, prominent during our teen years, to transition away from expecting our environment to provide us with stimulation toward adulthood where we provide stimulus for ourselves. This leads to the notion that giving a kid a phone takes away their boredom, meaning it deprives them of the opportunity to overcome their boredom by becoming creative.

Strength and Power

One thing that's difficult for a person lacking sufficient ego strength to understand is that while they see adult competence in terms of power and control, those regarded as powerful generally don't see themselves that way at all. Rather, they'll see themselves simply as being competent.

Kids naturally fantasize their future place in the world, playing at adult roles they hope sooner or later to step into, and as they move through adolescence the challenge is to move from childhood fantasies into adult competence. Any failure will leave them still relying on power fantasies, for competent people don't need a sense of power, while those with little competence are likely to remain trapped in magical thinking. Many of the behaviors adults berate teenagers for are the results of a kid's faltering attempts to accomplish this task, such as deliberately walking down the middle of a street, defying drivers to do anything about it. It can feel glorious when we're doing that, yet can embarrass us no end when we recall it years later.

A significant criticism of modern culture is that so many boys grow up with little clear sense of the adulthood ahead of them. They are unable to understand what their fathers do at their jobs, see the culture around them as a bewildering mish-mash they can't sort out, and while they can relate to a NASCAR driver or a rock star, an accountant or an engineer is incomprehensible. And without a sense of where they're heading, many kids are left feeling adrift, unable to get a handle on the world they're facing.

As young men, we're still prone to naïve notions, but an adult still trying to live on power fantasies is likely to look silly. Yet there's support for immature attitudes in the entertainment industry where films by guys like Adam Sandler have promoted the notion that we can grow into adulthood as adolescents, and life will reward us for it. The reality is that life will kick us black and blue, for the eventual price of not growing up can be high no matter how long we may seem to get away with it. But now a father tells his teenaged son how his own dad had once disciplined him, only to have the kid complain: *But he didn't have the right to do that!* Well, yes he did have the right, and the kid's dad is left wondering where his son ever got a notion like that. He didn't get it from him. Instead, he got it from movies, from TV, from song lyrics, and he got it from other kids.

As I'm using the term here, the notion of personal power is a misnomer because it represents a limited understanding of ego strength. It takes ego strength to step beyond fantasy just as it takes ego strength to develop honest relationships and conduct honest business. We begin with a child's inability to comprehend the adult world, too often growing into adults still trying to get by with fantasy-based notions or power, which puts Nietzsche's "will to power" notion in quite a different light. Just look at how many adults are seen as powerful when they're simply good at bullying and manipulating.

This compels us to look at the appeal of the vampire image (the outcast with superhuman powers), the Goth movement, New Age thinking and Neo-Paganism, each with its images of power. Even some in the gay community have pushed the notion of being more highly-evolved version of the human race as in the old David Bowie line: *Homo Sapiens have outgrown their use....gotta make way for the Homo Superior.*

Part of any power fantasy is a child's expectation that we should get to do whatever we want without repercussions. And if we listen to someone like that long enough, we'll learn that the common vulgarism "asshole" means anyone who dares to object to his behavior. To someone with low ego strength, the world is full of assholes.

Countering this is the need to develop enough strength to carry life as an adult rather than relying on notions of power, trying to dominate others instead of working with them. Inner strength is needed to make things work, not power, and without it, we'll leave a debris trail behind us no matter what accomplishments we may gain. And lacking that strength, we'll go on trying to have power, not noticing how much we offend the people we need to work with. Napoleon may be famous, but he had his Waterloo, and was apparently murdered to keep him from making more of a mess of things than he already had.

As children and teens we develop idealistic notions, yet lack enough life experience to realize how unrealistic they are. And our idealism at that age tends to be flavored with numinous feelings of grandeur that can make us resist our need to engage with life in a practical way. And so, as we move from power fantasies toward personal strength gained through raising blisters and bruises, our idealistic notions can become more grounded and realistic, less head-in-the-clouds, hopefully less distrustful of hard realities. Otherwise we'll be driven by an unsettling feeling of incompleteness, then try to imitate completeness by obsessing on religion, metaphysics, politics and whatnot, perhaps bombastically, perhaps living a fantasy-based life that others see as a rather silly.

The Role of Men

There's a shift that happens to most boys when they're ten or eleven years old, before which they may be mother's little helper, only to begin to resist her at every turn, to resent her rules and expectations and resist household chores as gross injustices. Part of what a boy is reacting to at that age is the hormonal surge that floods him with notions of grandiosity and self-righteousness. Beyond that, though, he's solidifying his sense of identity around whatever he's gained from his parents up to this point, especially from his mother, beyond which he'll be internalizing things mainly from his peers and culture heroes. So, the observant nine-year-old can develop into a willfully oblivious fourteen-year-old spewing rage at a world that fails to dote on him. How much of this loss of awareness is due to hormones versus how much is due to narcissistic obliviousness is something we're challenged to answer for ourselves.

Yet, there's a window of opportunity where a boy wants no more from his mother or grandmothers or aunts, but is open to the influence of men, and this is where initiation would traditionally play a role. So, when a ten-year-old is resisting his mother's dictates, no matter how reasonable, he's open at least for a time to the guidance of men to lead him toward adult competence. He especially needs men with adequate ego strength upon which he can model himself, for lacking that he'll fall back on the only things he knows, on the attitudes he's grown accustomed to and the lures of his peer culture.

What he's longing for as he slumps away in a sullen fit with his mother yelling at him, is the world of men. The world of women is one he's trying to grow away from in order to discover his maleness, for while his mother may know how to nurture, that doesn't work for him anymore, while a man, so helpless with an infant, is now in his element. And a boy senses this, that only men can take him from the world of his mother, which he naturally resists even though some part of him wants to hold onto it, and into one where it's natural for him to pick up the work that needs to be done without having to be told. Taking out the trash is, to him, part of the women's world he's trying to leave while building something is part of the world of men being men.

But too much of the time the men are nowhere to be found, so the kid has only his frustrated mother to deal with, driving him to retreat, hanging around malls and convenience stores with other lost kids, feeling that undue effort at much of anything other than getting stoned or laid is an outrageous imposition. But that leaves him in a world full of resentment and raging rock and roll stars, many of them little more than damaged boys, themselves.

It has been noted that girls experience a sizeable drop in self-esteem between late childhood and early adolescence, and boys experience something similar, feeling suddenly inadequate with the onset of puberty. Even the tough kids have that tendency hidden away under their bravado. Part of it is that girls generally mature earlier, leaving boys feeling awkward in the face of these beauties suddenly a head taller and with breasts out to here, but it's also due to our bodies and nervous systems undergoing such a radical change that we don't quite know ourselves anymore.

So, while adults complain about a kid's self-centeredness, he feels helpless to do anything differently, for he feelis like a jigsaw puzzle with far too many missing pieces, and doesn't know how to find them. What he does have is a sense that the people who could help him simply won't. Even the sex education books telling him about his own body are written by women, and that can't be very comforting.

As boys we hunger to be by dad's side when he's fishing, working with his tools, hunting, washing the car, driving, playing cards with the guys, yelling at the football game, and generally grunting his way through life. We hunger for it like we used to hunger for Mommy's breast, and getting into a struggle between the World of Mom and other women and the World of Dad and other men can mark us deeply. Not to disparage motherhood, but a mother simply can't help her son find his maleness. And it's is hardly a new issue, as one of the themes in Homer's *Odyssey* is that the young men of Ithaca act selfishly because they've had no guidance as to how to be men. In fact there's a theme throughout Homer as to whether people are to act in a civilized manner or like barbaric children.

A young man subjected to narcissistic parenting has an especially strong need for male support in developing the things that have been denied him, needs to learn above all that other men can be direct with him, even be a bit rough at times. Women may cringe at it, but here's an Internet joke that has gone around:

> Friend, when you are down, I'll get you drunk and help you plot revenge against the sorry bastard who made you sad. When you are blue, I'll try to dislodge whatever is choking you. When you smile, I'll know you finally got laid. When you are scared, I'll rag you about it every chance I can. When you are worried, I'll tell you horrible stories about how much worse it could be and tell you to stop whining. When you are confused, I'll use little words to explain it to your dumb ass. When you're sick, stay away from me until you're well again—I don't want whatever you have. When you fall, I'll point and laugh at your clumsy ass. This is my oath: I pledge 'til the end. Why, you may ask? Because you are my friend!

Yes, it's a bit adolescent, but there's a tendency as old as humanity itself for men to playfully provoke each other, that while women bond through gossip and chatter, men bond not just through working together, but through roughhousing like boys. Despite the jokes belittling "male bonding" (typically coming from men who lack it and women who feel threatened by it), the trend is for men to provoke each other away from any tendency to fall back into childish helplessness, to help each other move past feeling sorry for ourselves and gain strength and resilience instead, and that kind of reinforcement is something a youngster can only get from older males.

So, men yearn for the crass world of other guys just as women yearn for the one they share with other women. Women may despair at it, but there it is. More than that, boys need men who've been with their own pain, who've faced grief and loss and hardship, and know how to live with male impulses, and that's something no woman can provide.

One scenario between men and women is where a man is thrashing his way through his male challenges while she's essentially asking: *Why aren't I enough for you?* The answer is simply that she isn't, because relationship alone leaves him needing something more. The same was true for the mother who had wanted to hold him back from the world out there, leaving him with a grief he can never tell a woman about—he'll have a hard enough time telling himself. So while his relationships with women may be critical, it's through other men that he gains the maturity to solidify a necessary part of his emotional foundation. As the adage goes, if you let a boy go, he'll come back a man.

But when the adult child of a narcissistic parent starts to awaken from the trance induced in him during childhood, he'll have to wade through a morass of repressed resentment to claim an adult sense of himself, even if it means gaining independence like a grizzly bear, prowling his territory with sullen hostility. Again, what boys and young men need to pull themselves "out of the clutches of women" as the old cliché goes, is the company of men who can provide him with a model for facing life with strength, composure and responsibility, even if it's a bit crude at times.

We see that need in young men everywhere. Some time ago while driving down a back street in a small town, I came up on a dozen teenagers straggling across the middle of the road. Seeing me coming, they slowly drifted off to the side, except for one guy who stood there with that defiant look typical in alienated young men. Then, at the last moment, he stepped aside with a big, open-palmed gesture— *Yo, man!*—the gesture of a bored kid reaching out for some kind of meaningful contact. And there we all are, just driving right on by.

Raging Monsters

Every man, no matter how effeminate, gentle, wimpy or wise, is challenged to face the part of him that will rape for the sake of raping, kill for the sake of killing, plunder and destroy simply for the sake of plundering and destroying. It showed up in the Wild West where lack of cultural constraints gave license to violence, just as it has shown up in the Balkans, the Middle East, and Africa. Destructive behaviors are hardwired into us as a part of the history of our species, and trying to rise above them, numb ourselves to them, or simply intellectualize them away doesn't work. After all, they show up on every playground, in fraternity hazing, in the boardroom, and in inner city gangs, even in spiritual communities.

Feeling sexual aggression doesn't mean we have the right to rape, just as anger doesn't give us the right to be violent, and it takes personal strength to face it without acting on it. In childhood, rage can result from the inevitable loss of our original position as the center of our parents' universe, or from our fragile ego's attempt to defend itself against a parent's behavior. That is, we can either get swept up with indignation at no longer being treated as royalty, or in defending ourselves against someone threatening to undermine our development. We rage both against the wicked stepmothers of the world who oppress us with ordinary expectations, and against an inept adult interfering with our natural development, and the difference is not always clear.

In any case, rage goes hand in hand with low ego strength, and it comes out in any number of ways, especially when it has been repressed for years. Repressed rage can be dangerous, and disempowered men can be extremely angry people. Yet, rage is often a human psyche's last-ditch attempt at preserving what's left of its integrity, and when a person's development is overwhelmed at an early age, he can become an emotional time bomb. So, many of us come out of childhood assuming that being a good little boy means sweeping under the rug all the resentment we've felt at having been humiliated and defeated, and it leaves some of us feeling that the only way to be true to ourselves is to be bad, even to be criminal in revenge for all the wrongs done us. Others of us, on the other hand, are still raging at the world for depriving us of that golden throne we'd once sat upon, and that's a bomb with a short fuse no matter a person's age. Either way, we see it showing up in anything from everyday road rage to genocide, in the thundering tirades of religious fundamentalists, in the insolent teenager and in every petty bully everywhere.

Just as there are three basic ways we act out lack of ego strength, anger takes three basic forms. The most obvious is what we tend to think of as animalistic rage (although animals rarely act that way), that all-too-familiar instinct to attack before being attacked, to dominate before being dominated. History shows us that inhuman behavior is unfortunately all too human, and as George MacDonald writes, "A beast does not know that he is a beast, and the nearer a man gets to being a beast, the less he knows it."

Then there's the angry desperation of the clinger unable to face the feelings that arise when he doesn't get the attention he wants and isn't being nurtured as he wants to be, at which he'll act with the vindictiveness of a tantrum-throwing child. Thirdly is the rage we feel when the integrity of our psyche is being overloaded to the breaking point, perhaps after years of having been victimized by a bullying, manipulative or incestuous parent. This is a fury with a somewhat different flavor, one that says: *You may be able to overpower my body, and you may be able to defeat my will, but the one thing you'll never defeat is my rage.* This is why tyrants from the everyday domestic sort to sadistic dictators are always on the lookout for anger in the faces of those they oppress. That can result in a look we often see in the eyes of subjected people—veiled resentment behind a blank expression. Yet avoider rage can show up in the fire and brimstone fundamentalist, the wild-eyed philosopher and the pompous professor, although what drives it is a hurt little boy.

On a more basic level, anger generally hits us when we feel ourselves starting to come apart, when our balloon is threatening to burst. There's an approximately half-second lag time—a physiological phenomenon based in part on the response time of our adrenal glands during which we start to fall into anxiety if not outright panic, then pull ourselves back together with a burst of outrage. That's why those of us who are particularly unstable become rage-aholics, constantly on a hair trigger.

As Freud implies, focusing on personal gratification can make us blind to each other to the point of outright brutality. So, moral behavior is mainly a matter of truly growing up? And isn't forgiveness, in its mature sense, simply the ability to accept humanity, warts and all? For all that philosophers have pondered moral law, we can reduce it to a simple equation: Moral behavior is what we do when we're not obsessing over our leaky balloons, when we're not driven by a lack of ego strength, when we're not out to gratify ourselves at someone else's expense, when we're able to stand up as adults.

Truly accepting the humanity in others is more easily said than done, for it challenges us to stare straight into the face of the beast. This is why Robert Louis Stevenson's Jekyll and Hyde story serves as an operant myth. Based as it was on a dream, it expresses the fear that if we were ever to touch any of the nasty urges we keep hidden away in the dungeons of our psyches, they would take us over, that there wouldn't be enough good parts of us to keep them in check, that if that cork ever gets out of the bottle, there's just no getting it back in. Do horror movies horrify us because they mirror something deep within ourselves? Probably.

At the Heart of Tragedy

All of this takes a different tone in the aftermath of the mass shootings we've seen in the US, such as at the Aurora, Colorado movie theater and the Newtown, Connecticut elementary school. The inevitable storm over gun control followed, but I find it more important to face the question as to what drives someone to do such a thing.

It takes something wildly pathological to kill anonymous movie-goers, much less small children, but then we saw James Holmes, the Colorado shooter, sitting in a courtroom with orange-dyed hair and a bewildered look—the face of evil some said, but he looked like a lost little boy. But a deeper look implicates us all in some ways, requiring us to take a hard look at the popularity of movies of the *Batman* ilk (which was playing during the Aurora shooting), for I doubt Holmes picked that theater at random. Why are we thrilled by buildings crashing down, cars smashing into each other like toys, heroes bashing about without getting a scratch? Are we all, like little boys, enthralled by notions of invulnerability as we smash our toys—*BAM! CRASH! BANG!*—no death, no blood, no pain, no grief, no loss?

Was Holmes acting out a comic book reality where even the bad guys are role models? Al Pacino as Scarface? Jack Nicholson or Heath Ledger as the Joker? Are movie fans yearning to fly high with the power of the immortals in defense against too much reality? Canadian and European filmmakers have complained that American audiences have little appreciation for thoughtful, nuanced work, wanting sensationalized, childishly unrealistic thrills instead. And we see it in remakes of older films, where an artfully done original is turned into a sensationalistic farce.

Then we see young men in their teens and twenties so obsessed with computer games, so swept up with naïve concepts of good and evil that they have only a vague sense of the world around them. That can develop into a young man so deeply rageful at the three-dimensional world that he can only think of going out and killing people—*BAM! CRASH! BANG!* Only this time there's a great deal of death, blood, pain, grief, and loss, and then reality catches up with him in a serious way. Now he has become a monster. That, I would guess, is what James Holmes was realizing as he sat there in the courtroom.

A harsh question we are left with is whether male violence is simply a matter of testosterone running out of control as many feminists say, or if it's a deeper madness that drives such mindless brutality. Is it simply infantile rage, or is it something more primitive, more primal? Women, too, are capable of rage, except they are more likely to act it out with emotional rather than physical violence, mothers who traumatize their children as if demanding a blood sacrifice to the hungry beast they harbor within.

But it's not testosterone alone that chops arms off children, drags people out of their beds to machete them to death, drives people into mass starvation while commandeering food sent by aid organizations, uses financial aid to feed its elite, or uses business tactics to pillage impoverished countries. There's a monumentally childish selfishness in all this, but while it may truly have been a form of competitive penis envy (as one commentator accuses) that drove men for decades to try to out-produce each other with nuclear weapons long after they had more than enough to eradicate us all, that alone doesn't explain the madness of it. There's a primitive impulse the ancient Greeks called "wolf rage" that loves destruction for its own sake, an instinct that seems older than the human race, which is perhaps why it can be so compelling. After all, if there's anything humans love, it's letting loose to a primal urge, be it sex, excitement, rage or even terror, which is why we love roller coasters. Whatever it is, we all have it, and we need to face up to it.

There's a story of how one woman in the Aurora theater that night told James Holmes something to the effect of, "If you're going to kill me, you're going to have to look at me." That's the challenge we're all faced with, even in everyday road rage, for anonymity and aggression are traditional bedmates. And it's humanity itself that demands, *Look and see me!*

Genders

In many ways, women have an advantage in relationships, and not just because they have a brain better suited for communication. A boy's original connection with his mother, and therefore his blueprint for connecting with women in general, is at such a helpless age that men feel more vulnerable around women than they care to admit. It makes us such saps at times, and it can make us, despite our pretenses, more desperate than women when it comes to our attachments, quite the reverse of how we try to make it look.

While we all gestated inside a woman's body and were cuddled at a woman's breast, the fact that she's the same gender as her mother can give a girl a sense of reassurance in early childhood, while a boy's gender difference from his mother leaves him uncertain, leaning away from her as much as he yearns to be close to her. That's why he'll go through a period where girls are icky, for he has trouble distinguishing between a girl's femininity and that of the mother from whom he's trying to separate. But then her gender-sameness with Mom also means that later in life a woman can have a harder time dealing with her enmeshment with her mother, while a boy naturally understands his distance from her.

As many women learn, men tend to use sex as a way of replacing their mother's breast as a source of nurturing, which is why women have said for centuries that most men are little boys when you get beneath their skin. We may act tough, but we generally feel women are both more powerful than men are, and more real. It shows up in men's magazines where adolescent fantasies cast women as creatures of terrible power, possessed of that greatest power of all—the power to say *No!* Even the toughest man can feel reduced to a needy child by a sexually attractive woman, and that vulnerability can make some prone to violence as their only way of maintaining dominance.

On the other side of the gender coin, it's easy for a woman's instinct for preserving group harmony to get in the way of productive work, insisting on political correctness to the extent that it degenerates into fumbling attempts to avoid anything that might upset someone. The result has been called "totalitarian niceness," something that can paralyze the most casual conversation.

Men, on the other hand, often fear that if they accommodate others too much, they'll only get taken advantage of, and a complaint men often have about women's instincts is that a person focused on conciliation and harmony will get trampled when the going gets tough. And while women complain that men lack nurturing qualities, men complain that women go too far to caretake people who really need to stand on their own two feet.

It brings to mind Freud's comment that after years of psychoanalyzing patients, he still didn't understand what women wanted. He was, women say, a typical man. The politically-correct answer is that women want autonomy, respect and personal power, and they deserve their fair shot at it, not that so many men have those things, really. On an archetypal level, though, women are driven to fulfill their version of archaic blueprints we all run on to some degree: Men want to be like charging spermatozoa out to win the prize, while women want to be the egg that is worshipped and wanted, without which it will wither like a raisin on the vine.

Yes, these are stereotypes, but as much as we are unique, stereotypes have a good deal of influence on us. So, while a man tends to judge a woman on her sexual attractiveness, a woman will judge a man based on the way he makes her feel. We all carry primitive instincts that promise to lead us to glory, but that's just the way archaic impulses are: imbued with a compelling sense of mystery, yet never providing any true sense of fulfillment. As Ovid says, "Majesty and love do not go well together, nor tarry long in the same dwelling place."

So, women complain that men are incompetent around the house and dismal at communicating, while men complain that women try to imprison them while talking a blue streak about nothing at all. And in retaliation for women's internet jokes about adult ed courses for men: *Putting the toilet seat down—You really can do it* and *Having a meaningful conversation—Taking the first steps!*, we see the male response: *Learning to work the toilet seat for yourself—you're a big girl;* and *Silence—A frontier where no woman has gone before;* or *PMS—Your problem, not his.*

Someone once noted that if people could work out whose job is whose, most psychotherapists would go out of business, yet we all have ways of putting unfair demands on each other. While men accuse women of abusing chivalry, expecting preferential treatment while demanding equality, women accuse men of expecting them to play mother to a careless little boy in a grown-up body. Part of the problem is that, given the chance, the human mind falls back on its default settings, regressing to childhood expectations unless it finds enough motivation not to. Yet, unresolved needs can drive us to achieve, to create personal relationships and build communities. Still, one of our challenges is to understand what others can reasonably do for us, and what no one can ever do; what we are realistically entitled to, and what we have no right to expect at all. This sort of thing is generally negotiated unconsciously in a relationship, how much each person is to give and get without feeling slighted or put-upon, and the line between too much and too little tends to be drawn and redrawn.

However, when immaturity is taken for granted, relationships deteriorates. Girlish women complain that all the guys they've dated have all been slugs, but when they get together with someone more responsible, they'll wonder why he won't just hang out with them all the time like those other guys had. And when he challenges her to find a way for him to do that without losing his job, she has no answer because she can't see the world as an adult. She may tell him that love will see them through, but did you ever see *Elvira Madigan?*—young lovers lost in a world they can't deal with.

A boyish man will have similar feelings when he tries to have a relationship with an emotionally mature woman, except that her competence and work ethic are more likely to humiliate than enrage him, and he's likely to run when he realizes what she expects of him.

It's a challenge for any of us to connect intimately with another person while dealing with the stressors life hands us, but an immature person will expect someone else to deal with the difficult stuff. That's why they will try to pull their partner away from responsibilities, often with emotional blackmail, demanding that a partner prove their love by abandoning everything else, no matter the consequences.

Ironically, for all the complaints about men viewing women as sexual objects, the last few decades have shown women's tendency to sexually objectify men as well, for that's what happens when we can't see other people as people. But there's an especially disturbing aspect to male sexuality when it's directed by older men toward young girls, for a mature man will treat a girl or young woman with a protective instinct (a patriarchal instinct, using the term appropriately), while an immature man is still a boy looking for girls. This is Humbert Humbert, the pedophile in Nabokov's *Lolita*.

While women complain that men are always vying for dominance, men accuse them of the equivalent, just with a different style, for many men feel that in the minds of women, men aren't expected to have needs while women get to want everything. Then, if he expresses his own longings and disappointments, she'll tell him he's just a complainer, while she feels entitled to complain about everything.

There's an old tee shirt slogan that asks, "If a man speaks in the forest and there's no woman to hear, is he still wrong?" The cliché is that a woman will make a man wrong because it's the only way she knows to address the chronic disappointment she has carried since childhood, sifting through everything he says for things she can turn into arguments. Yes, men do that too, for most relationship problems stem from a person of either gender struggling to defeat their partner as a way of avoiding the challenges of their own lives, demanding maturity and responsibility from everyone except ourselves.

There's a scene in the old film adaptation of *The Snows of Kilimanjaro* in which Ava Gardner and Gregory Peck are in a restaurant arguing about his job assignment; she always wants him around, while he says that to succeed in his business, there are things he simply has to do. So, she gets him twice over, for while he goes over to the telephone to reject the assignment, she runs off with the foppish flamenco dancer. Then he spends the rest of his life pining for her as she does for him, realizing too late the mistake she's made. A bit of the same dynamic shows up in *The English Patient* where a woman tries to stop her lover from going off to his assigned job. "But this is what I *do*," he says, sounding bewildered. "I do this *every day*." And there's Kevin Costner's *The Love of the Game* in which she feels fulfilled through being with him, while he feels fulfilled through pursuing his career, and neither can quite understand the other.

Yet, when drunk with love we'll declare that we'll give up everything, although when it sinks in we may want to back out of the deal. Then, men complain that she's only happy when he's losing a large piece of his life for her sake, while women complain that he's only happy when he's dashing off in search of some glorious goal, leaving her with the kitchen and the nursery.

We're challenged to accept that we're hardwired to different drives, and trying to make others give up their instincts for the sake of our own leads to emotional warfare. In an immature relationship, though, each person tends to use the other as part intoxicant and part punching bag, each projecting the other as someone who's supposed to fix us and as someone who is out to get us.

There's a flourishing market in relationship advice, much of it quite good, yet life itself is the greatest teacher. The lessons, though, come through the stress and challenges of everyday life, and as a novelist says, even the best marriage ends with making love at night, and has to be rebuilt every morning over breakfast.

Overall, developing ego strength takes eyeball-to-eyeball relationships, often challenging us to face situations where we don't get our way and where others don't see life the way we do. That's what builds our invisible muscle and teaches us to negotiate, compromise, share, and ease off from our habitual stances.

So, what does a mature relationship look like? It's one in which each person is doing a reasonable job of meeting their partner's legitimate relationship needs while doing a reasonable job of taking responsibility for things no one else can resolve for them. Past childhood it's no one's job to fulfill us, and even if they choose to play that role for a while, they'll get tired of it in time. Rather, it's our job to meet the flawed world and the flawed people in it, and to deal with it as best we can in our own flawed way. It's difficult to have relationships with any degree of honesty and integrity unless we're strong enough to face the worst aspects of our own personality, because the other person is bound to throw it in our face whether they want to or not, as will the rest of the world, given the chance.

CHAPTER SIX

~SHADOW DANCING~

I have a secret that I let nobody see,
An evil shadow that's been hanging over me.
~Leslie Bricusse, from *Jekyll and Hyde*

Because we grow through life from Point A to A plus B and so on, no matter how mature and competent we may come to be, those early places are still alive in us—tucked well away, but still there. That's why even the best of us are capable of appalling behaviors at times. The somewhat belabored term that describes this is "shadow," superficially described as parts of ourselves that didn't get our parents' approval when we were little, and so were swept under the rug. But that's a shallow description at best, for much of what is labeled "shadow" comes from infancy and early childhood, and as we grow up, our intellect and personality structures are layered over those early levels, leaving us prone acting on primal impulses we don't even know are there. Beyond that, our shadow also involves impulses that date back over 65 million years to the age of the dinosaurs, and act through our limbic system, as part of our "reptilian brain." In any case, to our intellect, those impulses are simply out of our field of vision, so from the point of view of our "conscious" mind, life works as long as we can don't pay attention to the man behind the curtain.

Our shadow is essentially a collection of blind impulses and primitive instincts that can run us without the benefit of conscious thought. The earlier discussion about three basic personality dynamics—to impose on others, to cling, and to distance ourselves— is essentially about our shadow, about dynamics so deeply rooted that we act on them without making deliberate choices. This creates an added layer of shadow, namely our dread of seeing these things about ourselves, which is why anyone from the adult spoiled brat to the hardened criminal will hide behind a wall of justifications.

Because these instincts are so deeply set, facing our shadow forces us to go against the structure of our self-sense. This is partly because our psyche has a hard time seeing the ground it stands on, and partly because we build our sense of who we are by keeping all those primitive beasts at bay. That is, we build our self-sense to some extent by excluding things. It's no surprise, then, that a confrontation with our shadow can throw us into a panic attack, into depression and despair, or into fits of outrage or hysterics. It can feel like a break in the cosmic order of things, and from the point of view of a shaky ego, that's exactly what it is, bringing to light parts of us that had existed before our self-sense was formed, parts of us about which our conscious self knows nothing at all. As the intro to the old radio show says, "Who knows what evil lurks on the hearts of men? The Shadow knows!"—followed by nasty laughter.

These things can take us by surprise. A personal example was when I once had to pull over on the narrow shoulder of a steep mountain highway, and as I was getting back in the car I noticed a tractor-trailer cresting the hill behind me and gathering speed. I then held the door open with my left hand while starting the car and shifting into gear with my right, thinking, *You know, it would be a good idea if I closed that door.* Yet my left hand refused to budge long enough for me to wonder if I wouldn't have to reach over with my right to get that door shut. Finally I slammed the door just as the semi blew past, leaving me wondering what in the world all that had been about. The answer was that some primitive piece of my brain, probably dating back to the dinosaurs, had sensed energy coming my way and had decided, *Oh, I want some!* Of course, a sixty-five million-year-old lizard brain isn't equipped to understand that sticking your Toyota door out in front of a semi isn't such a clever thing to do, but that's beside the point.

The point is that we can be easily driven by such things, and whether they come from some evolutionarily primitive bit of our psyche or from a suppressed infantile need hardly matters. Most of us, though, come face-to-face with our shadow only by having someone challenge us, often in a rage over something we've done without consciously meaning to. It can also come in those moments when we wake in the middle of the night and find some deeper level of our psyche looking us squarely in the face.

To borrow from popular culture, there's a scene in the film adaptation of Tolkien's *Lord of the Rings* in which Cate Blanchett's character is confronted with her lust for power, and to the author's credit, she doesn't rise above it, come from the heart or control her way out of it. Instead, she lets herself be taken over by it until she knows she's bigger than it is. This may be why many ancient mythologies tell how later gods conquered the original primordial ones, for our developing ego must learn to deal with the primitive impulses that threaten to leak through.

Whenever there is a power imbalance between two people, such as between parent and child, teacher and student, boss and employee, therapist and client, there is a tendency toward what I call "shadow dumping." This is when the dominant person tries, unconsciously for the most part, to drive their shadow into the body and mind of the other as if it were a tangible substance. That's how we wind up carrying our parents' and teachers' neuroses, and I've seen even highly-respected psychotherapists doing that to their clients, spiritual teachers doing it to their followers, academics doing it to their students, all of them pushing their insecurities at anyone they can. They'll do it with anger, with ridicule and shame, and with a threat of rejection, demanding that the other think, feel, act, dress, talk, look, even eat a certain way to appease the dominant person's needs. And the good student, the good client, the dutiful child is one who and goes out into the world acting out someone else's neuroses without realizing it.

The general dynamic is that the person dumping their shadow on others isn't strong enough to face his own shadow, and is looking for a way to get rid of it . One way of describing the process of confronting this is that if we were to dive headlong into our deepest wounds, there at the bottom, under all the pain and fear and anger, we would likely find our parents' shadow staring straight back at us— our parents' or someone else's. The keys to the puzzle are always with us, for parts of the psyches of the people who have shaped us are branded into us for better or worse. Part of the challenge is that when we're young we sense those imprinted feelings and tell ourselves, *This is me! This is what I feel! This is what I think! This is the way I am!,* only to discover that it's not true, that many of those things had been someone else's all along.

So, the admonishment to know ourselves is better stated to say that we need to know our shadow. That in turn compels us to understand our parents' and grandparents' shadows as best we can, for we need to see these handed-down dynamics clearly. After all, parents usually wound their children because they simply don't know how not to. In other words, they do it with their shadows.

Because feelings we've absorbed early in life can seem a bit mysterious, we sometimes regard them as cosmic in nature, as if they'd been handed down from on high. Then it can be a surprise to discover that they were simply someone else's unresolved issue that had slipped into us when we weren't looking. This is why breaking family patterns can seem like a betrayal on our part, and it's why breaking patterns we've been running on for decades can feel like staring at one of those three-dimensional posters, watching it go from a splash of speckles and spots to a three-dimensional image revealing what was right there without our seeing it.

Another area involves what we think of as arrogance. The wealthy and the physically attractive are often subject to that criticism because they often grow up evading the conflicts, struggles and confrontations that compel the rest of us to mature. That is, they can buy or charm their way out of challenges, so they don't learn because they don't have to. But there are certain battles in childhood that we have to lose: We have to let adults stop us from running out into the street or sticking a fork in the baby's eye, and we have to lose our fight to remain wallowing in childhood expectations, for as in the case of Goodall's elderly chimp mother, the child who refuses to let anyone tell him *No!* will likely grow into an adult who believes no one has the right.

There's a notion that kids obsessed with trends like the Goth vampire style and the heavy metal death mentality are acting out shadow aspects of the culture at large. That is, just as orgasm has been equated with death (as in *le petite mort*), people with insufficient ego strength tend to equate intense feelings with self-obliteration, as in the suicidally-inclined romantic poet or the death rocker with his ear buds turned up full blast. It's cool to annihilate yourself and lose yourself to all that infinite something or other. Maybe that's why disaster movies are so popular: *Let's obliterate everything, and that'll be really cool!*

The sad thing is that the zombie/vampire/goth mystique appeals to people who feel dead, and it leaves us wondering why. Is it because they've grown up feeling they haven't been given enough, or because they haven't developed enough ego strength to truly feel alive? At any rate, the shadow side of the culture demands expression, compelling the most vulnerable to act on it, thinking they're being unique. Yet there's just as little freedom in it as there is in the cultural blandness they're resisting, which is why so many of them look like clones of each other. Despite our insistence on individualism, we tend to be rabid conformists, for as long as we're driven by shadow material, we'll be without choice. Even the ardent bully, so certain he has control over his life, is frozen in ways he won't be able to see for himself.

An old saying tells us that what the eye doesn't see, the heart doesn't grieve over, but when it comes to shadow material, that's not at all true. It's just that our grieving goes on quietly, surfacing now and then to bewilder us. Yet, opening the door to our personal shadow can compel us to see all humanity at a deeper level, for it eventually comes down to miles and moccasins, as in the old French saying, *Tout comprende, tout pardoner*: "to comprehend is to have compassion."

John Fowles gives us a model in his novel, *The Magus*, in which the main character is subjected to "the God game" in which a group of rogues set him up, then confront him with his worst character traits. The point is for the reader to wonder: *What if that were done to me?* Tellingly, though, Fowles' character fails to get it.

The point is that until we can see enough of both our own shadow and that of others, all our talk of understanding and compassion will be little more than grandiose posturing. It may ultimately be all about love, higher consciousness and all that, but first it's about growing up.

Containing and Grounding

The cliché is that while girls scream and squeal when they get excited, boys shout and shove, while both giggle and yell and cry and wriggle about like excited puppies when their emotional charge gets too high. That's because they're not big enough (literally and energetically) to hold onto themselves. Yet there's something addictive about it, for we all have the tendency when we are little to become fascinated with our own racket, so that kids on the playground will escalate in volume just because they find it compelling. The same thing happens at rock concerts and political rallies, which can make you wonder.

One reason many Westerners are drawn to Eastern martial arts training is that it teaches them to contain and focus, while the advertising around us encourages us to act with manic frenzy—

remember the Big Mac Attack, or the ad that says: *If you want it, you have to have it?* But the failure to rein ourselves in can lead to misery and mindless violence, and the excuse that we just couldn't help ourselves, while a clever ad ploy, doesn't hold up in court in most cases.

We saw how Helen Keller was wildly uncontrollable until forced to focus (remember the scene where her teacher holds her hands under the water pump?), and that example may have some bearing on the apparent increase in hyperactive/attention deficit behavior among kids today. But then the Germans and British are criticized for over-containing to the point of deadening themselves. Yet what any culture considers moral, dignified behavior has a good deal to do with restraining impulses, mostly around anger and sexuality, although it seems each generation has to hash it out all over again, each calling the previous one oppressive and tyrannical.

Acting without restraint can feel absolutely glorious, at least until the police show up, but that goes against the grain of civil society, and it's an issue as old as civilization. The Biblical tale of the Great Flood and the many versions and variations that pre-date it implies that humanity's inherent inability to restrain itself means we have to be controlled, even destroyed, in order to protect Creation.

Throughout history, entire cultures have swung from too much rigidity to too much laxity, then back again; from a sense that the reins are so tight that creativity and natural expression have been repressed, to the opposite extreme where sloppiness and excess make for an embarrassing mess. As novelist Charles Frazier writes, we're all a bit extreme in our early years, but in the long run life challenges us to "take possession of our old madness." Of course, we usually don't get to see it as madness until we're old enough to look back at the debris trail we've left behind. Or as William Blake writes, energy may feel like eternal delight, but if we can't contain it, our delight is likely to become someone else's misery.

To use the balloon analogy, overcharged children tend to burst and splatter at the slightest impulse, recalling the admonition that children should be seen and not heard, not speak until spoken to. As oppressive as that might sound, we develop our ability to contain emotional energy by having to do it, starting with things as simple as waiting until after dinner for dessert or being quiet while the baby's sleeping, until we're strong enough to contain ourselves appropriately. In the modern school environment, even a simple thing like a return to dress codes (remember dress codes?) has been shown to improve both behavior and grades, for being compelled to act as if we had ego strength actually builds ego strength.

In the same way, being forced to share our toys builds our capacity for sharing, just as learning to make our beds in the morning trains us to order our lives. Sometimes we really do have to crayon inside the lines, just as there are times you really can't have your pudding until you've eaten your meat. And it isn't just a childhood issue, for being compelled to act as if we had better ego strength than we actually have molds us, gradually morphing our self-sense into a more mature shape. That's why rebelliousness can be so self-defeating.

Unfortunately, though, humans tend to go to from Nazi-like rigidity to hippie slovenliness, and now that we've had decades of less rigid educational styles, it doesn't seem to have made for a happier or healthier population or better-educated kids. Moreover, if the kid we see screaming in a restaurant is still like that at thirty, he'll likely be associating aliveness with being out of control. The impulse so many of us feel as teens is to push further and further as if seeking a heavy metal version of glory, but it's an elusive, empty paradise, which may say a good deal about why so many kids feel suicidal. They resent limitations and structure, yet desperately need them; they resent anything that tries to contain them, yet their failure to contain themselves can make them desperate; they find it wildly exciting to be without restraints only to discover they're living in a nightmare.

There have been two opposing notions concerning childrearing in this regard. One is that kids learn to contain only by being compelled to. That's what drives the be-seen-and-not-heard tactic, and the military boot camp where young recruits are forced to shut up, toughen up and focus. It's also the idea behind shock collars, for both humans and dogs hold themselves with a sense of self-restraint, even dignity, when compelled to contain themselves.

The other position encourages children to express themselves freely, arguing that someone who never gets to express himself never truly learns to feel, that they simply learn to behave. So, we see educators focusing on kids' feelings and self-esteem, and it sometimes works in producing inventive, creative adults.

But then Jean Twenge speaks about the narcissism that has

resulted, kids who lack incentive because they expect to always feel special. And kids who never learn to contain an impulse can't understand why they don't have the right to punch out the teacher or throw a screaming fit at the bus driver. And Tina Fey (in *Bossypants*) says it's horrible to be telling children how special they are because they already think that way, and people now in their late thirties talk about how damaging it had been because they'd then had to go out and face a world that expected them to buck up and get over themselves.

Lack of grounding shows up in curious ways, and our notions of spirituality often reflect it. For instance, the words "come from the heart" too often imply the disconnectedness we see in New Agers, the problem being the word, *"the."* Curiously, massage therapists, even dancers, often are trained that way, to speak of *the* arm, *the* leg, *the* head as if they were vague Platonic ideals floating about in the ethers. But, what about *my* heart, or *your* heart?

We express life as we experience it, so if we speak as if we were a collection of disjointed pieces, we'll experience ourselves as disjointed pieces. It's not surprising, then, that so many who tout the come-from-the-heart theme have a glazed-over look about them, yet a simple change of vocabulary can compel them to be more present, feeling their own body more clearly. Ironically, though, it can frighten some of us, for suddenly becoming grounded can be overwhelming to someone who has been drifting like a balloon on a string for decades.

Or we may deem ourselves intellectuals or even mystics with our minds running off into fantasy whenever confronted with concrete reality, and it can cost us dearly. That's what we see in a scene in *The Last King of Scotland* where Forrest Whitaker's Idi Amin tells his victim that the only thing real that will ever happen to him is his death. While that's a bit extreme, the best thing that can happen to some of us is to experience something severe enough to break a habit that ultimately robs us of our lives.

Extreme forms of invasion like rape can make a child afraid of being grounded in his own body because he'll assume it's a dangerous place to be. After all, in his experience, it once was a dangerous place, and the body that has felt that fear has a difficult time letting it go. That's why post-traumatic stress is such a deep issue, and many of us carry lesser versions of it that generally escape notice. So, a person who has learned early on in life to withdraw will likely seek what Scott Fitzgerald calls the "dreadful door to fantasy, the escape that is no escape," which he knew all too well from personal experience.

Bullies and clingers can be ungrounded in their own way, although they're good at making it look like they're not. The overall challenge for any of us is that our bodies carry every nuance of feeling we've ever had since early childhood, that while we may have forgotten the details, feelings are a different matter. So, as we become more deeply grounded, we're challenged to deal with feelings we've been avoiding since childhood, for they're all right here, awaiting our attention. That is, while our minds drift off to the past or future, when it comes to body feelings, everything is in present time, even that two-year-old tantrum we'd rather forget about.

So, becoming more grounded involves dealing with our shadow, for any way we fail to carry a feeling becomes a way we disconnect from our bodies and from hard reality. One of the great challenges of maturity, then, is to reverse that trend, to carry the full weight of our own lives no matter the difficulty.

The Spared Whip

While it's easy to criticize teenagers (a time-honored pastime of adults), adolescence is a transitional phase. The concern, though, is that it's becoming a transitional phase that leads nowhere. As P.J. O'Rourke once challenged teens, *Turn your hat around, pull up your pants, shut your mouth and get a job.* More recently, a business consultant, in frustration, proposed writing a book entitled, *Shut the Fuck Up and Get the Job Done.* Crude? Yes, but that's what it's like dealing with adolescent mindsets in the business world, and it says a good deal about why so many older people have learned: *Don't trust anyone under thirty.*

The most common approach has been to try to force teenagers out of their childhoods, the spare-the-whip-and-spoil-the-child approach evolving into the drill sergeant dragging recruits out to the parade ground at 4:00 AM in the pouring rain, and if some punk doesn't like it, well, he can write home to Momma, now can't he? During wartime, this can be a serious matter when a drill sergeant has only a few weeks to take an out-of-shape kid, toughen him up and get him to cooperate in an environment where adolescent obstreperousness could get someone killed. In that light, the overly nurturing mother is seen as a hindrance because she'll encourage him to regress instead of helping him face the severity of the situation.

Contemporary psychology on the other hand has developed the notion that if a child is given enough nurturing at each level of his emotional development, he will naturally move on to the next; that chronic immaturity results from lack of age-appropriate nurturing at some earlier level, leaving a kid still trying to fulfill that earlier need.

There's a sizeable body of research to support the second viewpoint, yet alternative childrearing and educational practices based on it have had mixed success. It has also led to psychotherapeutic approaches in which adults are encouraged to find their "inner-child," a notion that has gained widespread support in the last thirty-odd years.

Yet, business people, athletic coaches, drill sergeants and youth leaders say too many young men in their late teens and early twenties have nowhere near as much inner strength as that age group did forty or fifty years ago. But human nature is far too complex to pin down in any one way, and it seems both sides of the issue are at least partially correct. That is, while some kids will naturally move ahead given the chance, others drag their heels any way they can. And while a radical teaching method may foster genius in one student, another will use it as an excuse to goof off, just as one kid may respond to consequences in a constructive way while another will react with a *So what?* attitude. Perhaps the best we can say is that it's the individuals themselves that matter, not the methods, for a mature adult inspires the young while an immature one wounds them.

But then I have to be a bit of a psychotherapeutic heretic and say I don't believe in emotional healing, at least not the way it's commonly discussed. My reason is that when people talk about healing childhood wounds, they generally want their lives to be as if all those terrible things had never happened, while the fact is that they *did* happen, and amnesia isn't therapy. And while it can be important to reclaim repressed feelings, therapy practices aimed at re-parenting our inner child too often leave people spinning their wheels for decades.

What we need is not to heal our wounds so much as to gain the ego strength to face them, pick them up and carry them, to develop the strength to embrace the simple fact that our lives were as they were, and are as they are. That is, we are challenged to grow big enough to carry our experiences instead of being overwhelmed by them. That's what ego strength is all about.

Again, our most basic challenge in life is the most obvious of all—that we get born as infants, and it doesn't stay that way; that what we got as children is what we got, and what we didn't get is what we didn't get. Otherwise, we might spend an entire lifetime complaining to a world that really doesn't care. After all, the other seven billion folks out there are too busy trying to sort out the hands they've been dealt to care about ours.

The problem is that most of us don't know how to go about developing that invisible muscle. After all, it's supposed to just happen, not something we have to learn like reading or writing or riding a bike. And it's not about being tough any more than it's about coming from the heart or embracing our inner child. It's not that any of those attitudes are wrong in themselves, just that they're inadequate.

Above all, ego strength is about being able to live fully, about being able to deal with life without being triggered by anything that doesn't suit us. The challenge is to become more present, more alive and in-the-moment, but we have to first develop the ability to carry it all, and that takes decades.

CHAPTER SEVEN

~IMMATURE SPIRITUALITY~

There is no cause so hopeless, no creed so mad,
no idea so ludicrous that it will not attract some believers.
~Bernard Cornwell, *Death of Kings*

The greatest enemy of any one of our truths
may be the rest of our truths.
~William James, *Pragmatism*

It seems reasonable that, lacking scientific means, humanity has attempted to define life through metaphysics and mythology. But we're challenged to understand our basic human nature first, otherwise we'll be putting the cart before the horse, developing metaphysical notions before we've matured enough to experience life very clearly. Among other things, that means our mythology will become a way of positioning ourselves back at the center of the universe. That's why explaining Ultimate Reality has become one of the greatest of human addictions, assuming that spirituality is whatever matches our personal style: As other-oriented people we deem spirituality to be whatever gives us the feelings of nurturing we long for, as pushers we it's a matter of defeating the forces of evil, and as avoiders we see it as anything that exalts the ethereal worlds we carry around with us.

Beyond religious dogma, we generally use words like "spiritual," "sacred" or "divine" when attempting to describe strong feelings otherwise difficult to put into perspective, and even though many of those feelings may be fantasy-based, childishly narcissistic or even delusional, they have shaped human culture from its beginnings. Yet, strong feelings are not necessarily anything of a lofty nature, for as other-oriented people we're addicted to anything romantic, as avoiders we're addicted to the fantastic, while as pushers we're addicted to notions of conquest and victory. Any of us can obsess on what others see as silly fantasies disguised as wisdom.

Our sense of reality is rooted not so much in the world around us as it is in how we internalize that world, so that our spiritual notions can be distorted by our neediness, by our yearning for grandiose feelings, by our need to follow an external lead, for an external structure. And the trance-hungry among us look for something to shield us from the hard edges of life, leading many to seek spirituality through drugs: Indian yogis with their hash pipes, Taoist sages with their opium, neo-hippies calling marijuana "the sacred herb."

It takes ego strength to get past our egos; not to escape or rise above, but to be strong enough to be grounded in our lives. So, a question for both other-oriented and avoidant spiritual seekers is: Why do we seek bliss? Is it an escape? Is it a subtle act of cowardice, a copping-out on the challenges of life? And for pushers the question is: Why do we need to be right? Why do we need to dictate to others? And why is it that human beings can be so vindictively cruel to each other when it comes to notions of divinity?

Metaphysical notions are often considered byproducts of immature psyches, and the theme of the seeker grieving his separation from his god leaves us asking if it isn't his separation from his mother that has him in its sway. In some creation myths, because of a fall from grace humanity was forced from an original state of being fed by the gods to one where we've had to learn to fend for ourselves.

It can also be argued that metaphysical notions stem from early childhood when everything seemed mystifying and magical because our brains yet weren't developed enough to take things in very well. And it's easy to feel nostalgic about that naïve simplicity, so that some of us will block out intellectual understanding and seeing the world through the eyes of a toddler, back when not a lot made much sense. This is Ken Wilbur's "pre- and trans-" argument where people confuse infantile (pre-personal) experience with transpersonal experience, spiritual awareness seen as "oceanic," diffuse and unfocussed as it is for an infant.

But profound feelings can become an addiction; part opiate, part stimulant, part psychedelic. And it can be argued that metaphysical notions are an adolescent compensation for our incompetence at dealing with life, applying supernatural causation to anything we can't understand, which may be quite a lot. Then we are drawn to ancient teachings as if anything old must be both sacred and cosmically true.

In the contemporary scene, we see a mish-mash of teachings telling us to seek our true nature within our humanity, others telling us to transcend our mortal nature, for one of the great philosophical questions is as to whether we are to escape this Earthbound mess or excel at living in the midst of it: do we aim at fulfilling human experience or at transcending it? And while one stance claims to transcend mere psychology, another holds that what we call "spirituality" is our emotional wounding in disguise, seeing life in metaphysical terms while justifying being refugees from reality.

One of the more important challenges in life is not to have answers, but to have ongoing learning, yet we all have a tendency right from early childhood to impose our personal realities on others. Then we see religions where sacred knowledge is revealed only to the worthy: *I have access to the Highest Truths, and you're just a benighted fool.* On the other hand, the Buddhist writer Alexandra David-Neel once asked a Tibetan lama if it was proper for her to translate a secret teaching, to which he replied that the secret was in the listening, not in the telling.

Still, some feel that religious notions are little more than human neuroses taken to delusional extremes. Human psyches are capable of imbuing their emotional wounds with cosmic import, which is why we see people barely competent at managing their lives posing as spiritual teachers out to impart profound wisdom to the naïve masses. Hence, the tantrum-throwing metaphysician, the fist-shaking true believer, come-front-the-heart people reducing everything to childish simplicity.

Most of us aren't anywhere near that extreme, yet if we're going to use words like "spirit," "transcendence," "soul," "divinity" and so on, it's important to stop and consider what we're about. While grand notions and powerful feelings may carry a sense of cosmic wonder, when we worship grandiosity, whether in ourselves or in others, we're likely to create mayhem. Historically, some seriously pathological characters have attained power as if only those blessed by the gods could be so eccentric and so extravagantly cruel. That's why the ancient Greeks created deities to personify strength, beauty, rage, courage, sexuality and so on, assigning divine qualities to primal impulses.

We're all subject to imagery of that sort because they come from the place that generates dreams, the problem being when our internal imagery seems more real than physical reality. Going back to the balloon on a tire pump analogy, our tendency is to apply labels like "spirituality" and "truth" to anything that makes our chest swell or fills our heads with numinous light. It's easy to fall into an addiction to beautiful words, for they can trigger numinous feelings although there may be nothing there but our own fascination. Look, for example, at New Age advertising hawking products as if they contain profound secrets—*Quinoa, the ancient mystical grain of the Incas!*—feeding the notion that humanity in the distant past was possessed of understanding unavailable to our sadly benighted age. By the way, it says nothing at all about quinoa.

It's cliché to say that we cling to belief systems in order to give ourselves a sense of certainty, but it takes ego strength to face uncertainty, without which we're likely to override rational sensibility in a quest for anything to give us the feeling that the world has been explained properly. That's what Galileo ran afoul of, defying the infant's notion that the world revolves around ourselves, for just as the mind of a child views life as if to say, *The world begins with me*, religious thinkers throughout history have hardly done better, as if their midnight ponderings define divine nature, and God had damned well better get with the program.

One notion that has been bandied about is regarding the "spiritual ego," reflecting how insistent and demanding we can become when we latch onto spiritual teachings with low ego strength—"egotism" equaling low ego strength—regardless of how valid those teachings may be. That is, we all too easily use spiritual notions to fill in the weak places in our psyches in ways that can make us oppressive to others.

The notion of spiritual purity can be criticized as the glorious feeling that accompanies a simplistic world view unquestioned and unadulterated by outside influences. As Abelard declares, the believer does not dispute, just as Luther insists that curiosity and doubt are the enemies of religion. And for all its pretense of embracing all truths as leading to the same god, even the New Age culture carries a large dose of the tendency to rigidly fixate on belief systems.

To reflect on an earlier discussion, any belief system, be it religious, political, or even scientific can become a self-object, a thing that "gives me me," so that disagreement can feel like a threat. It boils down to a general inability to distinguish the world around us from our thoughts and feelings, for no matter how vast we like to think our perception is, keeping our inner world tidy can imbue us with a compelling sense of pristine truth. Logic, or at least what we call logic, works at any level if we try hard enough, although it may look to others as if we've simply switched off a sizeable portion of our brain.

One function of mythology is to explain and justify a culture's place in the world, defining itself with a sense of superiority. This is why tribal cultures typically call themselves something on the order of "the people," "the original people," or "the human beings:" *The creator made us first, then the tribes we're friendly with, then our enemies. Where those white guys came from, who knows? Must have crawled out from under a rock somewhere.*

Yet modern cultures also see themselves as possessing divine import, and define reality through their cultural mythology. Americans have our own version, and have run on it for a few centuries: consider Manifest Destiny.

Yet none of this is a condemnation of religion per se. Rather, it's a critique of the way we carry our beliefs, and how we behave when our beliefs are questioned. But children need a sense of structure, and kids raised with religious standards are often more focused, emotionally stable and responsible than those who are not, even if they rebel later in life. As Jonathan Safran Foer has one of his characters say, "Home is the place with the most rules."

So, are our metaphysical notions really about defining the nature of the universe, or are we simply trying to structure ourselves. Psychotic people are often fascinated with creation myths, yet there's that curiosity in all of us, a yearning to know where things came from and how they got this way. But have we been badgered for centuries by immature philosophers and clerics as they try to give themselves a sense of security, perhaps at our expense? Are religions simply ways of avoiding having to face up to life in the truest sense?

While one of the classic questions is why, if there is a loving god, is there evil in the world, a more pertinent question is why people who espouse divine truth, brotherhood and kindness can be so horrifically cruel to one another. The problem, it would seem, is not in the order of the cosmos, but between our ears. One great irony is that much of what we call "evil" results from infantile impulses, and when Augustine declared that children are born sinful, he failed to understand that narcissism is normal at that age, that the problem is when we're still like that as adults. It isn't that humanity risks descending into evil without religion, but that we fail to ascend out of childhood.

To paraphrase something Harold Bloom said with regard to literature, the mind should be "kept at home until its primal ignorance has been purged." This is the cart-before-the horse issue that showed up during the 1960s and 70s when Baby Boomers threw themselves into Eastern religions with such fervor, bringing to mind Alan Watts' comment that devotion to a guru is like having someone pick your pockets, then sell you back your own watch.

Now we hear words like "wisdom" and "enlightenment" bandied about so trivially as to have lost any significant meaning, and we see the spiritual equivalent of spoiled children posing as teachers, followers so desperate for exalted feelings that they mistake infantile grandiosity for elevated consciousness. Then there's Kipling saying that a healthy man doesn't know he has a soul because he doesn't need to obsess on things like that, or Paul Theroux's comment that if you're a good person, you don't need religion.

A natural sense of spirituality comes to us only after decades of hard experience, for without it we're likely to go about with a head full of metaphysical notions and an invisible soapbox tucked under one arm upon which we long to stand and lecture to rest of the world about ultimate reality. Jiddu Krishnamurti said there's an essential problem in human consciousness, a common glitch of sorts, and that until we work that glitch out for ourselves, everything we do will go wrong.

Eventually, it becomes important for those who have grown up feeling brow-beaten by religion to pick apart it all, which is why Joseph Campbell became popular by dissecting the origins of many of our traditions. And no matter the headlines, the debate is not between God and science, but between science and an obsessive adherence to mythology dating back to the Bronze and Late Neolithic Ages.

As infants, our view of the world is one of seeing our parents as gods and goddesses descending from on high to change our diapers, the family house as a mysterious castle, the family dog as a being possessed of great and dreadful powers. The problem is when we remain in that archetypal simplicity, for if I see you as an archetype, I can't afford to let you be a flesh and blood person, or my illusions will suffer. Yet archetypal simplicity is one of the things that attracted people to Nazism, and it shows up in American jingoism.

A curious challenge is when an early memory surfaces from the cluttered basement of our psyche, and our rational mind simply doesn't have any context for it. This is because such memories come from a time before our rational mind had taken shape, making them seem mysterious, perhaps divine in nature, especially when they carry a high emotional charge. As infants everything had seemed of cosmic proportions, and our first altar was Mommy's body. This seems why some of us deify oceanic experiences, for that's the way we had experienced everything during our first few months.

On the other hand, none of this is to say that we don't have transformative experiences, just that we too often give cosmic labels to some fairly meager things. There are experiences worthy of being called transcendental, although they are both more straightforward than the complex metaphysical talk we hear, and far more difficult to embrace than all those starry-eyed folks would have us think.

It's a common complaint that religious hierarchies throughout history have been obsessed with power and control, but it's more to the point that they have tried to control their own anxieties by controlling everyone else, just as we all do as children. There's a general attitude that implies: *If you don't believe what I believe, then you're bad, wrong, stupid, evil, or just plain crazy.* That's what I call "the Big Five:" bad (or unloving in the New Age version), wrong, foolish, corrupt or insane. And it's hardly limited to religion, for we all carry ideals as to how the world is supposed to be. Underneath it all, though, is a child's fear that if the world is different from me (which it is), isn't obeying my will (which it won't), or isn't pleasing to me (which it will only in our dreams), then I'll fall apart at the seams, throw a tantrum, burn someone at the stake or put a bullet through their brain. Even at our best, our drive to create personal meaning can have us fail to appreciate others' experience, and can have us seeing others' lives as violating the very fabric of the universe. And if we obsess on our need for glorious feelings, the rest of the world will become either a confusion or a frustration: bad, wrong, stupid, crazy and evil.

We're good at worshiping anything that gives us a dramatic inner experience: our excitement, our intellect, our emotional highs and sexuality, even our outrage, and the challenge to grow beyond that notion compels us to grow up. Despite the popular notion of the "spiritual warrior," the greatest learning in life comes through the common drudgery that humbles us all. So, you're a manifestation of unconditionally loving eternal spirit, but now you've incarnated as a human being and it's stupid and it sucks, doesn't it? And the warrior in us is the part that knows to do what has to be done just because it has to get done, especially when we don't want to. As Rilke says, difficulty is a friend to the soul.

Just as luxury can cause us to resent an uncomfortable experience, youthful mysticism can drive us to resent this life that burdens us with gravity and appetite. Are we, as Emily Dickenson says, covering the abyss with trance? Some of us can become lost in our need for isolation, becoming trance-hungry, desperate for a mystical dream to shield us from all those slings and arrows. But while spiritual literature is full of wise sages living in caves and mountain huts, the modern day equivalents generally prove to be sadly damaged people.

Novelist Bernard Cornwell offers the notion that a person can't truly gain wisdom until they've experienced three wounds—one to the body, one to the heart, and one to the mind. And just as Odysseus is recognized in the end by an old wound, we're all individualized by our own. All things considered, it seems all the philosophies and spiritual teachings revolve around a center point without ever touching it, and that we only reach that center point by being jarred out of our spinning minds, perhaps in shocking ways. And the more naturally spiritual a person becomes, the more we discover an experience that is independent of teachers, magical formulae and scripture.

One of the best statements I've heard regarding natural spirituality comes from Jack Munighan's description of Hemingway's work as revealing the "deep, grave, majestic essence to reality," to which I would add that it's right here for us once we stop to take notice.

Another is attributed to Lao Tzu:

> *If you don't realize the Source, you stumble in confusion and sorrow. When you realize where you come from, you naturally become tolerant, disinterested, amused, kind-hearted as a grandmother, dignified as a king. Immersed in the wonder of the Tao, you can deal with whatever life brings you, and when death comes, you are ready.*

CHAPTER EIGHT

~PERSONALITY STYLES~

The heart is a rage of afflictions
~Leonard Cohen, *The Book of Mercy*

Personality styles are like opinions:
Everyone has one, and they all stink.
~anonymous

The overall intention here is to recognize ways our habitual ways of being can undermine us. The challenge, then, is to simply stop doing those things, which, habits being what they are, is easier said than done.

And while much of this can come across as criticism and accusation, it's just that we need to look into the mirrors life confronts us with, to be as present to the moment as we can, at choice in our lives and interacting with the world at hand rather than with our past history and the habits we've been carrying for years.

The intention of this next piece is to take this theme deeper by delving into specific personality dynamics. Just as each generation and culture has its self-explanations and justifications, so does each personality style, and those personality styles can be alarmingly predictable despite our notions of being unique. In truth, many of our behaviors are almost mechanically predictable.

Humanity is simultaneously a glorious, noble, infuriating and heartbreaking affair in which we are all afflicted with what has been called "inattentional blindness," making us selectively blind to anything that violates our personal sense of how things are supposed to be. But then we are all challenged, as an old saying goes, to solve the question mark of our own personality. One difficulty is that because our personality style was largely developed before we had a sophisticated thinking process, it rarely occurs to us to question it. Instead, we see our underlying traits as having always been there, so that bringing any of it into question can seriously rattle our self-concept.

To some extent our personality style is based on repeating the patterns of our family and culture, yet it's also a collection of habitual ways of responding to childhood hurts, like scar tissue. We also tend to act out ways that had given us feelings of well-being as children. Whatever its source, because our personality style is habitual, we have a hard time seeing it for ourselves, although others can. And in taking that hard look, we need to, as in the fairy tale of Rumpelstiltskin, "name the thing," to put words to things otherwise difficult to pin down.

With this in mind, we're going to look at a personality typing system called the Enneagram, a system with roots reputedly more than a thousand years old, and has in recent years been used by the psychotherapeutic community and the business world alike. While its early history is uncertain, there are vague references to a possible use of the system in thirteenth century Europe, although details are lacking. While Georges Gurdjieff made his own use of the system in the early 1900s, the Enneagram was put forward in the 1950s by Oscar Ichazo and his Arica School, and Helen Palmer and other writers have since brought it into popular culture.

The system breaks personality styles down into nine types, numbered one through nine, depicted in a nine-pointed diagram—"enneagram" simply means a nine-sided shape. And styles tend to bleed into one another, creating "wings", so that a Five has a Six wing and a Four wing.

Unfortunately, as with many popular themes, there's a tendency for some of us to become Enneagram junkies, treating the system almost as a religion. Like any system, though, it's simply an attempt to make sense of ourselves. It's also a "negative" approach in that it focuses on our "primary blindness" (as Enneagram teacher Father Richard Rohr calls it), ways we habitually behave without thinking about it. This is why Rohr comments that when a person figures out what style they best fit, they'll typically get depressed for a week or two.

Yet it's not about self-flagellation. As a therapist acquaintance says, what brings many people into therapy is that they feel they have to pay someone to have an authentic relationship, while with the Enneagram we have the potential to develop a more authentic relationship with ourselves and, hopefully, with others. However, it requires us to be brutally honest with ourselves, for this is a system that points out our most problematic traits. Is that harsh? Perhaps, but not as harsh as what life does to us otherwise.

With this in mind, I'll be limiting this discussion to the characteristics of each style that pertain to adult immaturity, generally focusing on the worst aspects, for describing the extremes brings out nuances that affect us all at least in subtle ways. As ever, though, this isn't to point blame, but to expose aspects of human nature that are right in front of us, but which we don't see very clearly.

Roger Bacon once noted that every place is the center of its own horizon, and that's true about personality styles as it is about geography. The challenge, then, to take a hard look at the thing that calls itself "me," and that's never an easy thing to do, for parts of us remain invisible until they are seen under a strong light. And it involves all of us equally, otherwise the system will become a weapon in our hands, everyone else becoming a target.

No matter their positive traits, our personality dynamics create stubborn blind spots that will continue to trip us up until we can do better job of looking for them. The potential of the Enneagram, then, lies in the notion that we can't know what changes we need to make until we see what it is that needs changing. Yet even then the process remains mysterious, for it lies outside our awareness for the most part. What's required is that we find choice points and exert the willingness to make use of them, which means changing not only how we experience ourselves but how we experience life at large.

So, we have nine personality styles that at their extremes create most of the interpersonal, if not international, problems we face. Despite the issues inherent in any way of categorizing human beings, this can be an impactful way of seeing things about ourselves that otherwise remain outside our field of vision.

ONE

Moral indignation is jealousy with a halo.
~H. G. Wells

You better watch out, you better not cry,
You better not pout, I'm telling you why…
~old Christmas song

Ones are those of us whose favorite role is dictating to others, decreeing how things are supposed to be, expressing not our own rules, but *the* rules, God's rules, the way things have to be. And sometimes we'll do it with such indignation that we'll be convinced that it's God's outrage that drives us, not our own. And if a One says something is holy, then, by God, it's holy, for blasphemy is anything that violates a One's version of Truth. A One's anger, though, stems not from a violation of scripture or of some higher authority, but from a violation of their own sense of reality, and it can embarrass them for they really want to be kind people, not raging tyrants.

Typically, Ones are reacting to rigidly authoritarian parents. What so often underlies their tyrannical impulse, then, is that when a young One sees other kids doing things he's not allowed to do, rather than face the resentment he holds toward the parents who have immobilized him, he resents those other kids for being adventurous and free. This is a One's way of pumping up the balloon in the center of their chest, not just holding fast to rules for their own sake, but dictating them to others, often with a mask of serenity and superiority.

But Ones aren't necessarily religious, rather it's that religion offers them a way of acting out their personality style. Whatever the case, with their instinct to rigidify human behavior, Ones are the mainstay of cultural traditions, for in their worldview, the way things have always been is the way they're always supposed to be. That's why most older cultures have a One-ish flavor, as we see in the Far East from Kamchatka to Borneo and all across Japan and Mainland China, cultures where it's expected that the head of the clan is to be unquestioningly obeyed. This is why Mao became such a revered figure, for Ones want a divinely-ordained earthbound government to replicate divine rule, a notion we see in the histories of medieval Europe and in ancient Egypt, in the Vatican, and in the Forbidden City. Our word *cosmos*, by the way, comes from the Greek word for order, although the actual cosmos seems a rather chaotic affair.

One-ness shows up in cultures that worship ancestors, for Ones want to keep things the same, to walk the same paths as their forefathers. In these cultures, men traditionally teach boys how to behave properly and become men in turn, just as women have traditionally taught girls how to behave properly and become women by passing down strict rules of conduct. This is why traditional elders complain that their young, influenced by the outside world, no longer know how to act with the dignity and responsibility demanded of them. It may look like oppression to outsiders, but the imposition of structure is an important factor in traditional lives, and this is the One's forte. Moreover, strict moral codes like *sharia* are based on the notion that people are incapable of impulse control, and it's in their best interest to be regulated.

The drawbacks became obvious during China's Cultural Revolution when no one was willing to tell Chairman Mao that his policies were not only failing, but were often delusional. But while people have often had to suffer the lunacy of rulers rendered insane by power, the basic justification in the mind of a One is that most people are too irresponsible, misguided or untrustworthy to be allowed too much freedom.

While modern-day Westerners chafe at the notion, it makes sense that pre-technology cultures would organize themselves that way, for too much dissension could threaten the survival of an entire community, and trying to do things by consensus could lead to disorganization and inaction. So, Ones are good at keeping things going and getting others to get things done, but they may do it in a way that makes them look like demanding children, and if they're in a leadership position, they may inspire someone else to topple them.

The greatest criticism of One cultures, though, is that they can be intellectually and emotionally stultifying, each generation a clone of the one before, that no further thought, learning or understanding is allowed. This is why traditional tribal cultures have a hard time with the technologically-based world. The modern world has shifted people's reliance on cultural values to reliance on individual choices, and individuals often don't make responsible choices. A large part of what drives a One's indignation, then, is their fear that if people don't live as they should, everything will fall apart, which is often quite true.

A criticism of US foreign policy throughout the Cold War was that Americans failed to appreciate that, given their respective histories, the word "freedom" implied chaos to the Russians and Chinese, and the fear that lack of strict control will allow everything to go to pieces is an attitude that opposes social reform in many parts of the world. To anyone with that history, the rule of law and order is more important than individual license, the ideal being for the populace to bow to the social order, just as Confucius, taught. This is why ancient Chinese literature tells us how ritualized behavior harmonizes our lives, and that the emperor rules not so much as himself, but as the most current representative of divine authority.

But One-ness easily degenerates into power cults and military dictatorship. To a One, there are clear-cut rights and wrongs, and those rights and wrongs are more important than individuals, perhaps more important than life itself, driving things like *seppuku*, the samurai's ritual suicide, where a person's life is subject to the dignity of the master.

As one small example, I recall an Asiatic college professor refusing to give partial credit for a test question where a student had made a simple arithmetic mistake although his line of thinking had been correct. Unlike most Westerners, the prof's response was, "But it's *wrong!*", for in the world of a One, there is no such thing as being partially right. This is why Ones will split hairs over rules to the point of driving everyone else to distraction, but they do it because they're trying to define the nature of the universe even in what seem to others to be petty matters. This drives the tyrant's instinct to control information, creating a world where only the official version of truth is allowed. Hence, the bizarre versions of world history Chinese students were taught during those decades of isolation.

Any rigid stance can become One-ish, from religious fundamentalism and propaganda-dependent political systems to the everyday family autocrat. We even see it in the scientific community, for Ones anywhere feel threatened by the slightest hint of doubt. One of the challenges a One faces, then, is that others may see them as being out of touch with reality, and some political figures throughout history have truly been deranged. The witch trials of Europe and New England, and the atrocities of the Cultural Revolution and Khmer Rouge are the results. The Inquisition burned people at the stake, convinced it was to save their immortal souls, and we hear of Chinese Communists so obsessed with forcing "confessions" from people that they were mollified with even the silliest confessional statements just because they needed *something, anything,* to fulfill the need.

Stalinist thinking was much the same, upending cultures all across Eastern Europe and Central Asia, imposing a staid, two-dimensional blandness as if human minds could be bred like cattle. Then, as if in self-fulfilling prophecy, the collapse of the Iron Curtain left many of those regions to deteriorate into genocide and crime just as the fall of the Roman Empire led to the Dark Ages.

But then extreme One-ish groups like the Taliban yearn for a Dark Ages of their own, convinced God's wrath directs them to repress all who defy them. It follows, then, that just as modernity is a threat because it introduces uncontrollable influences, intellectualism is a threat because it dares to raise questions. Questions, to a One, represent moral weakness just as curiosity represents rebellion.

Ironically, intellectuals can be quite One-ish, convinced that anyone who disagrees with them is an imbecile. Even anti-religious systems like Communism are like that, Marxist-Leninist ideology taking the place of God, *The Communist Manifesto, Das Capital,* and Mao's *Red Book* receiving Biblical reverence. And one sardonic joke of the Cold War was the name of the official Russian newspaper, *Pravda*: literally, truth.

Holding to any given teaching, to any set of rules, can fill a One with a numinous sense that's compellingly addictive, so that even Marxism can be an opiate for the masses. On the other hand, the ideal of rebellion holds an aura of glory for some, which is why Fidel Castro was still shouting about his revolution a half century after he'd won it.

The vision of hell many of us were raised with is a One's notion, a place where souls suffer the rage of a vengeful god for having broken the rules, if only in their most secret thoughts. Yet for all their self-justification, Ones imagine hell for others while hiding the atrocities they commit, themselves. We see it in tyrants from the petty domestic kind to international ones, their stance being: *This isn't happening, you don't see it, now go away!*

While that's One at its worst, most Ones don't point anything more deadly than their forefinger at other people, yet they carry a sense that if others don't behave as they're supposed to, they deserve to be punished. But even as stern-browed patriarchs, they are, under the skin, fearful of Mom and Dad's disapproval, even though Mom and Dad may have died decades ago.

A One's notion of love follows in that they feel loving as they inflict rules and punishment just as they'd felt loved by the parents who had punished them all those years ago. Accordingly, the One's version of God is a heavenly tyrant wielding demands and threats of retribution, a god placated with good behavior and sacrifice. This is embodied by the god-king, for to defy him is to defy divine order, as in notions of a country being an extension of its ruler, the state representing the "march of God in the world." It's ironic, then, given Communism's contempt for religion, that there was little difference between the divine emperor in his Forbidden City and Mao with his Red Guards. And that degenerates into a society in which the slightest criticism of the government can lead to a bullet through the head in a back alley.

But most Ones don't aspire to such heights. Rather, they want to dictate the rules of a power higher than themselves, for the law is the law, no matter how irrational. Yet they can be seriously irrational, seemingly unable to understand that people resent being treated like sheep. And they treat themselves that way, fearing and loving their god as they'd once feared and loved their disapproving parents.

Amy Chua's controversial *Battle Hymn of the Tiger Mother* demonstrates many of the positive elements of the One, particularly their ability to teach children to focus their lives as opposed to the general wishy-washiness of modern American culture. Yet Chua admits to having gone too far at times. A One's challenge is to learn the difference between guidance and tyranny, between reasonable social structure and obsessive control, otherwise they'll see even the most reasonable disagreement as an insult, and respond with outrage. Moreover, Ones fail to understand that their moral strictures are often a substitute for mature ego strength.

Still, the people they are hardest on are themselves, for they are driven by a chronic sense of disappointment in others, in life itself, and most of all in themselves because they know they'll never live up to the impossible standards they've set. Overall, a One is challenged to face how faulty we all are, to accept that people aren't just cogs in the social machinery, aren't children to be punished for every infraction or subjects to be dictated to. But to do that, Ones have to face the fear they've carried since early childhood of being attacked with punishment and blame for violating the rules of a world that was too bewildering to comprehend back when they were little.

So, the immature One represents the demanding child in each one of us trying to rule the world from his highchair, anxious about anyone who fails to act the way they're supposed to, expecting that his very existence defines reality, and that he's entitled to dictate what others are allowed to do, think, feel or know. The underlying challenge, then, is to recognize that each of us is just another warm body on the planet, and no one owes it to us to live their lives according to our expectations. And in achieving that understanding, Ones can soften their stance until they can truly become the guiding lights, the pillars of their communities that they long to be.

TWO

I can't live if living is without you…
~Harry Nilsson, *Without You*

To love another person is to see the face of God…
~Boublil & Natel, from *Les Miserables*

As a fundamental representation of the move-toward dynamic, Twos are the ultimate relationship people, at least in their image of themselves, for they yearn for closeness, for eye-to-eye contact, to be immersed in another person's attention and be at the center of that person's life. As stereotypical clingers, they'll feel entitled to others' energy, attention and personal space, longing to fill that dreadful hole in the center of their chests by merging into others. In doing that, they'll play at attending to others' needs while actually they are attempting to find their own center within someone else's life. The problem is that even when someone lets us merge with them, the center we find there isn't our own—it's theirs. That can lead us to become endlessly demanding: *I keep trying and trying, but the person inside your skin keeps insisting on being you! Where am I supposed to find me?*

As a result, Twos are often accused of being emotional parasites, although it's more to the point that we're driven by an impulse that's out of place and out of time. There's a scene in the film, *Lantana*, in which Barbara Hershey's character, on hearing a man complain that making love to his wife is like trying to fill an empty well, teeters on the brink of a panic attack, for she realizes how true that is of herself. Those few seconds reveal a hidden side of the Two dynamic, that much of what drives us is both our fear of facing our own emptiness and our fear of facing the affect we've had on others.

Twos often have a poor sense of humor, for they take their needs so seriously, as if it were a matter of life and death, and have little latitude when it comes to playful teasing. Nor do they have much tolerance for irony, recalling Harold Bloom's comment that you can't teach a person to appreciate irony any more than you can teach them to appreciate solitude. Twos typically have little tolerance for either, and will fill their lives with small rituals, trying to control their feelings by making things predictable.

Mediterranean cultures in general have a Two-ish quality. Leo Buscaglia, for example, the lecturer popular in the 1980s, expressed a Two's notion that love means living like a pile of puppies tumbling over each other, and many in the New Age circus have been Twos: Shakti Gawain, Gangaji and Ram Dass come to mind. It was another Two who admitted (rather bravely) that no matter her intellectual understanding, her emotional expectation was that other people existed to meet her needs.

Gertrude Stein once said it's important to know what is our business, and what is not, but that challenges Twos who have felt since early childhood that they have to attend to everything going on with everyone else in order to feel secure in their own lives. And that their behavior can drive others away is something they refuse to see. The woman who'd thought her friend had gone crazy when he was simply exhausted from a hard day's work, and the therapy trainer who'd labeled a student as arrogant for having a good feeling for himself are classic Twos. After all, in their world anyone who doesn't give them all their energy and attention must be simply crazy or arrogant.

Because they yearn to fill their chronic emptiness, Twos are often overweight, and although they often seem quite grounded in their bodies, they also want to push their way into everyone else's body as if their own space simply isn't enough. The negative trait of the Two is said to be "pride," although a better word is "entitlement," as they assume the world around them is theirs to fill with themselves, just as they assume the way to change their feelings is to badger someone else into changing theirs.

As Twos, we can be like the Greek mythic character, Echo, always reflecting the people we are close to, yet constantly monitoring, adjusting and fiddling with them in order to get ourselves right. On the highway we'll glom onto other cars as if trying to get someone else to drive our car for us, then do the same thing in relationships, trying to get someone else to lead our lives, then complaining they're not doing it right because we're chronically dissatisfied.

Twos often come from a childhood where they'd been allowed little personal space, growing up enmeshed with others so chronically that individuality feels disorienting, and as they were never allowed to develop personal boundaries, other people's boundaries can feel like a threat. Or they may have had their enmeshed childhood cut short by the birth of a sibling, leaving them with a sense of loss they don't know how to face. Either way, while a Two may resent the lack of privacy they grew up with, feeling separate can be so upsetting that it will drive them to intrude on others, searching for something that will be enough to fill their emptiness.

If we were one of the younger kids in a family and the only way we got attention was to be underfoot, we will try to replicate that feeling as an adult; not because we're trying to be obstructive, but because it's our most familiar place to be. So even when we're trying to be helpful, we too often do it prying where we're neither wanted nor needed as if unable to distinguish between being helpful and being a busybody.

As Twos, though, we'll complain that this entire discussion is unfair, because we see ourselves as always giving and loving no matter the cost to ourselves. But we try to attend to others' needs as a way of avoiding our own emptiness, and it's the obliviousness that accompanies that impulse that causes problems: *If I sense that you need something, and if I put myself in charge of it, then I'll feel secure.* But while Twos complain that they ignore their own needs by attending to the needs of others, they are actually ignoring a far deeper need, their need to establish their own core sense of identity. Otherwise, the Two dynamic is a matter of needing to be needed.

In many ways, Twos are in a difficult situation. For instance, we'll often have a problem with "image constancy," meaning that we need to be reassured that our significant others still exist whenever they're out of sight. In the same way, we see our "locus of control" as being in the other person's body, mind and feelings rather than in our own, driving us to try to control our own experience by controlling others. Then, as parents, we'll dread our children's developing autonomy, fearing a piece of ourselves might up and move out of town one day.

The New Age subculture is largely a Two phenomenon where issues commonly arise between people who are meditation oriented and those of a come from the heart stance, for Twos feel isolated, even threatened, when others do anything that holds them in their own quiet space. In the same way, Twos feel threatened by intellectualism, as someone immersed in their own thoughts isn't emotionally available. In a Two's world, spiritual experience is when another person lets them in, the bed becoming their shrine, followed by the coffee table or any other arena where they get to merge with others. In effect, they worship their own Two-ness: They call it love, they call it cosmic awareness, and they call it God.

Yet, as Twos insist, we don't come to fully know ourselves in isolation because relationships, even unhealthy ones, bring out aspects of ourselves we seldom come to terms with when we're alone. To give them credit, Twos get quite a lot of things right about relationships, but they're generally right for the wrong reasons, for the Two's ideal relationship is a bit like one person in two bodies, two people losing themselves in each other. True relationship, though, requires two people with their individual integrity.

Yet, as much as Twos can't tolerate not being able to get into someone else's space, they can have an obstreperous side when it comes to defending their own. After all, if we're always trying to blur ourselves into other people, we're the ones who are in control, while if they try to get into our space, that's a different matter. So, while as Twos we yearn to merge, it only feels right if we are the ones initiating it, otherwise we'll sense we're losing control. And that can have us trying to imitate personal boundaries with anger and defiance.

As small children we naturally have Two tendencies, dependent upon others' attention and care, assuming Mom and Dad's lives belong to us, and assuming they have no need for anything themselves. As kids it's the only way we know to be, and the challenge faced by a Two is one we all face in growing to adulthood. But because their personality style is natural early on in life, it's hard for a Two to understand why they should ever have to change. To them it can seem unnatural, not understanding that they are operating from a blueprint most of the rest of us have added to over the years. So, Twos can come across as the most appealing personality style of all because their behavior reminds us of our own infancy, yet they are handicapped in trying to relate to the adult world the same way a child relates to its mother. That's why they will often speak with a gently seductive tone, imitating the way a mother talks to her baby.

Sometimes the kindest thing to do for a Two is to give them tough love, for while Twos typically say the hardest thing for them is to be in a relationship where their needs aren't being fulfilled, it's far more difficult for them to be in a relationship with someone who prevents them from Two-ing all the time.

The challenge for Twos is to face their assumptions regarding what others realistically owe them, what others really want and need from them, and what others don't want or need at all. That in turn requires a Two to face their self-centeredness and the anxiety that underlies it, and that requires him to face the separateness imposed on us all by adulthood.

In the long run, it's only by developing a more mature self-sense that a Two can truly deal with their chronic longing. And in doing so, they can gain a deep sense of human connection free of desperation, touching the core sense of relationship that we all sense and feel driven to bring into our lives.

THREE

The hustle, the con, these have been elevated
to a very high position in our morality.
~Leonard Cohen

Girls go crazy for a sharp-dressed man.
~ZZ Top

The difference between you and me is
I make this look good.
~Will Smith in *Men In Black*

Threes are those of us driven by success, by the need to look good in the public eye, by the need to shine and excel. They look polished, professional and confident, they are charismatic, they are hard workers, and they can step in front of a microphone and deliver a polished spiel without effort. They'll never have a hair out of place, but they'll assess every scuff on your shoes, every one of your out-of-place hairs, and for God's sake! Where'd you ever get that suit?

Walmart or something?

Suze Orman, Joel Osteen and Deepak Chopra come across as Threes, as do most of the talking heads on TV. As kids they'd often had to step into adult roles at an early age, perhaps because of illness, alcoholism or incompetence at home, in which case they'll likely have a price to pay later in life. More often, though, they're simply driven by a need for praise and recognition, and their way of getting it is to learn at an early age what others want to see, and adjust themselves to it. In effect, they've been in front of the cameras right from an early age. The price they pay, however, is a loss of any sense of authenticity, for to look good they've had to develop a highly-polished mask while sweeping under the rug anything that didn't come up to snuff.

But we all find that the things we sweep under the rug have ways of coming back to haunt us, and a Three's greatest fear is of being unmasked, of having their unseemly side exposed. For this reason the negative trait of the Three is said to be deceit, for they feel they have to keep their polished veneer in place at any cost. Moreover, the seedier side of the Three assumes they should have whatever they want, and are entitled to do or say whatever they have to in order to get it.

The Greek word *persona* originally meant the mask an actor would wear to designate his character, and it was in this spirit that Alan Watts commented that the once-popular book, *How To Be a Real Person*, should have been called, *How To Be a Genuine Fake*. At their worst, Threes will habitually scan another person for a way to take advantage of them, assuming that if they can get away with something, they're entitled to. The traditional stage magician comes across as a Three, epitomizing the slick operator always looking for a way to put something over on you. Then we hear them saying, "Now, I'll be honest with you...", leaving others wondering, "You mean you weren't before?"

Motivational speaker Tony Robbins is a classic Three. He looks great, preaches self-confidence and success, and he tells people they can simply get rid of any feelings that don't fit. That's what comes naturally to a Three, and they can't understand why anyone would have trouble with it. Werner Erhardt, creator of the EST seminars (now Landmark Education), is a Three, and the LGAT (large group awareness training) scene he spawned is criticized for masking manipulation behind a sensationalistic mask. Bill Clinton is also a Three, and we've all seen his unmasking, but so are many politicians, far too many of whom succeed through deception and superficiality, giving birth to the comment that a statesman is a politician who is dead.

Another of the most abused words is "integrity," for Threes will use it to mean whatever they want, failing to understand why others are put off by their slick cockiness and insincere glad-handing. Ask a Three what it takes to succeed, he'll typically respond that it takes hard work, and while Threes are typically hardworking people, we may see their businesses shut down because of dishonest practices.

This is the nasty side of the Three, and it shows in their attitude that manipulation and little white lies are simply the way to get things done. I'm reminded of a salesman trying to convince me to buy something over the phone, saying: "Look, we have a truck coming through your area, and there's still room on it for one more..." while I silently guffawed. He didn't know that I live at the end of a long road ending at the foot of a 14,000-foot mountain. But the robot calls telling us the police are looking for us or that the auto warranty we never had is about to run out have become signs of the times, as is the degree of fraud happening all over the globe.

Martin Kihn's humorously disturbing book, *A$$hole*, tells of his trying to make himself into a Three, describing manipulative tactics as softening people "into the right frame of mind to be victimized," which is how little white lies become very big ones as in the savings and loan scandals, the Enron and Arthur Anderson debacles, and the subprime lending disaster. In the mind of an extreme Three, lying and cheating are just the way to do things, and when it all starts to go south, they can't admit to their failures until there's nowhere left to hide, which is what happened with Enron and AIG.

Despite that history, Threes have a hard time understanding that other people can't do those things because it makes them cringe. After all, Threes have been sweeping things like cringing feelings under the rug since they were too young to remember, so none of it makes sense to them. Much of the contemporary business culture is a Three phenomenon, and it shows in the predatory corporate executive wearing a sophisticated mask while behaving like a pirate out for plunder. The famous line from the film *Wall Street* that "greed is good" is a Three's anthem.

Threes feed the fashion market where their need to be stylish makes for big business, and they'll buy an exotic car because of the image it presents rather than because they actually like it. Yet Three-ness isn't necessarily synonymous with financial success. Rather, it's that Threes are experts at dressing for the occasion whether in a three thousand dollar suit or in purple hair and body piercings. It's no surprise, then, that a Three's notions of love and spiritually usually involve shining in the proper light despite their underlying motivations. Machiavelli expressed the Three theme in declaring that a prince doesn't have to have good qualities, only that he has to appear to have them.

The United States is considered a Three culture because we can be so obsessed with form while lacking in substance, and because we take pride in our material success, technology and lifestyle. We also have a jingoistic mythology that both amuses and frustrates the rest of the world. Yet we can be terribly naïve when it comes to acknowledging the repercussions we inflict on that world, even on each other. And while in some countries it's considered treasonous to question the authority of the leader, in the US it's considered treasonous to question a leader's motivations. That's a Three trait, for Threes hide their true motivations even from themselves.

There's a particular hunger that drives a Three for while Ones want your respect and obedience, and Twos want your attention and love, Threes want your money and recognition, often seeing both in the same light. They're the sleazy salesman, the gigolo, the huckster, the con man and the slick politician. It's little wonder that Threes are so successful in American politics, as our culture is geared to them.

Because they have a Two wing, Threes can act like they're your best friend, like they have only your best interests at heart, while back in the sales office or the smoke-filled room they'll roar with back-slapping laughter at how they'd taken you for a sucker. But the bottomless pit of need we all carry tells a Three he's never successful enough, and nothing matters more—not integrity, not the law, not respectability, not even love. So he'll live by the little boy's credo that nothing's illegal if you don't get caught.

At their worst, Threes are like children with a high sense of entitlement, which how salesmen are often taught to think: *I have your product, you have my money, and if you don't buy from me, you're stupid.* And because they grew up thinking that way, they'll assume that looking good entitles them, as if acting a role sincerely will make it real.

The version of God that attracts Threes is one that rewards material wealth, although how it's attained hardly seems to matter. And the manipulative salesman, the devious lawyer and the corrupt politician truly believe they are honest while believing in a god who punishes sin, yet praises appearances, meaning that if you have anything unseemly going on, just don't let it show.

Predictably, the challenge for us as Threes is to come out from behind our masks and be authentic, no matter how it goes against our grain. But as Threes we can be deeply shadow-phobic, perhaps more than any other personality style. With their emphasis on making amends, Twelve Step programs bear the mark of Threes striving for redemption as does the work of John Bradshaw with his focus on hidden shame, for what gives a Three such pride early in life can cause disgrace later on.

In broader terms, Three-ness represents a challenge for all of us, for human psyches have an inherent tendency to pose inauthentically, the ones we con the most being ourselves. That's especially true when it comes to notions of love, spirituality, morality and integrity, notions we are all adept at warping to suit our purposes.

So, in finding their authentic center, their authentic sense of self, Threes can find the common ground from where they can present themselves to others in a way that can be powerfully compelling, making them strong, focused leaders capable of inspiring others to be at their best.

FOUR

Oh, I hate you some, I hate you some, I love you some
I love you when I forget about me.
~Joni Mitchell, *All I Want*

It is not what France gave to you,
but what it did not take from you that is important.
~Gertrude Stein, *An American in France*

Fours are the eccentric, artistic types among us with their flamboyance, their love for being unusual, especially for attention.

They may dress like fashion models, like overdone floozies, or they may look like they've dressed in whatever they'd fallen into when they rolled out of bed in the morning, but whatever it is, it's a practiced look. Their socks may not match, but they were carefully chosen. Cindi Lauper and Lady Gaga are classic Fours. They love to be unique, they love to feel special, and they love luxury sometimes to the extent that the lack of it will make them indignant. They can be fastidious to a fault as well as demanding: Frederick Chopin and Oscar Wilde are historical examples. And they can be loud: Ethel Merman, famous for her brass band vocal style, Lucy (from the *Peanuts* comic strip), and Carol Channing are Fours, but two of my favorite portrayals are Ava Gardner in *The Night of the Iguana*— flamboyant and in your face—and Leslie Manville's role in *Another Year*—flaky, depressive and disorganized.

Fours can look like Twos at times, for they share a great many traits, although Twos generally have a softly seductive look about them while Fours carry either the look of someone about to receive a birthday present or the look of a cat ready to pounce. And their tendency to be exhibitionists has them impulsively putting themselves on display. Because as Fours we're driven to feel special, we will, like Twos, drag out any situation where we're holding the attention of others, but while a Two will want one person's attention, a Four will want an entire audience. So, while a Two will try to strike up a relationship with the cashier at the checkout line, a Four will get up to the front of the line, then create a small circus with themselves as the center attraction. Like the *Princess and the Pea*, they can make the tiniest issue into one more reason to feel disappointed and betrayed, which we see in Sandra Bullock's character in *Crash* when she realizes she wakes up angry every morning, and doesn't know why. And although there are plenty of male Fours, it was for the female version that Shakespeare wrote that Hell hath no fury like a Four who has been dismissed as less than special. Orhan Pammuk has one of his characters say that if a poet is happy for too long, his poetry will become banal, for while Twos long to lose themselves in someone else, as Fours we love the feeling of longing itself. Having is boring while longing to have is dramatic stuff, so much so that sometimes the perfect lover is the one who has left, or is about to leave, and they're often about to leave because we've been driving them crazy.

Remember the woman dancing in the fountain in *Under the Tuscan*

Sun, or Goldie Hawn in *The Banger Sisters?* But our drama addiction will keep relationships in an ongoing state of chaos, for if things stay on an even keel for too long, "too long" perhaps being only a matter of minutes, things will get so tedious that we'll just have to do something about it. True to her Four-ness, Marie Antoinette once said she was terrified by boredom. The same can be said about cultural trends, for the nineteenth century Romantic Movement has been described as one of infinite longing. That's the drug of choice for those of us who are Fours, for we get high on drama, and dread stability like death itself. This is why Fours are at their artistic best when they're yearning for what they don't have.

Ironically, while Fours say they crave happiness and solace, they rarely do, for despair, rage and anguish are just as good as romantic ecstasy when it comes to getting high, and they'll often do it with a frantic sense of urgency. We see it in their art: Joni Mitchell, Alanis Morissette, Michael Bolton, Elton John (remember the glasses?), Bette Midler, Celine Dion (remember *Titanic?*), Liz Taylor (remember the husbands?), Prince (who couldn't seem to find a name special enough) and Liberace (remember the sequins?) are all Fours. And Flaubert was revealing something of himself in describing people lost in their anticipation of happiness, yet in love with their sense of martyrdom.

While Twos and Threes learn to get their way through seduction, as Fours we learn if we scream loud and long enough, people will cave in and give us our way. So, the Four impulse can make us compulsive tailgaters, for we've been chronically demanding for so long that it just seems natural. Beneath it all, though, not getting our way is so excruciating that we'll do anything to avoid it. This is one of the things that feeds a Four's sense of being special, because even as young children we get the notion that while everyone else has to toe the line, we don't have to. And we'll sense that the more out of control we are, the more alive we are. That's why Fours drive recklessly, seemingly unable to constrain themselves even after a string of accidents and speeding tickets. While there are plenty of male Fours in the world, truckers will tell you that the most dangerous drivers on the highway are women between the ages of seventeen and thirty-five, chronically incensed at having to share the road with all those jerks who are supposed to step aside for them.

So, a Four is likely to walk right into you as if you weren't there, then say it's your fault. Yet, like Twos, Fours generally aren't consciously selfish, rather that they're acting on their version of how the world is supposed to work. Ironically, Fours are likely to get into miserable relationships because their sense of drama draws them to troubling if not dangerous partners. Yet, unlike Twos, Fours often yearn for privacy, and will fight to preserve their private space.

The Enneagram refers to Two, Three, and Four as the "heart points," yet while we may assume that refers to loving behavior, all three are driven by the neediness and self-centered entitlement we'd all felt as children. And all three express an innate resentment at being deprived: Threes with contempt, Twos with seduction, Fours with flamboyant indignation.

Many Fours are artistically brilliant, but they can pay a high price for it, and the entertainment industry is full of stories of Fours storming off stage or out of the studio in a rage over being asked to cooperate with others' creative ideas. And just like in the daytime soaps, arguments often end with a Four storming out and slamming the door after having had the final, glorious say. Or it's like the old *Saturday Night Live* skit where John Belushi is pounding his chest, wailing, "*This is my art, man! This is my art!*" But Fours who slam doors like that will likely have to go back and apologize, for they'll realize they need that job or that relationship, just that in the heat of the moment their need for drama had simply been too much to resist.

Some of the greatest artists in history have managed to get away with some fairly outrageous behavior, Renaissance geniuses like Michelangelo, Brunelleschi, Caravaggio and Botticelli being classic examples. Part of their genius is that Fours tend, like landscape painter Albert Bierstadt, to dress reality up with an exaggerated vertical scale to give it that sublime power the everyday world lacks. The torch song, the drama of the stage and the romance novel are all Four-ish, for to a Four, exaggeration *is* reality. Or as an old adage says, art is proof that life itself is not enough. Remember that scene in *Titanic* when the girl's hand slaps up against the car window and splays out? Fours love that stuff! More than that, they *live* for that stuff. They also love the notion of a glorious death, Roland dying with horn in hand, birds singing, leaves drifting down. Or Cyrano de Bergerac declaring that the one thing death couldn't take from him was his panache, for if there's anything Fours have, it's panache.

To others, though, they can seem deceitful if not delusional because they'll exaggerate in such extreme ways. If something happens twice, they'll rage that it'd happened six or seven times—*and then this happened and that happened and then you do know what he did?!*—because it's so much more satisfying that way. At times their version of an event can seem so distorted that others will assume they're either lying or are simply crazy. It's just that as Fours we have a hard time separating our emotional experience from our physical experience, and it's our emotional experience that we're paying the most attention to. This is why Fours are often deemed borderline psychotic when, really, they're just being Fours.

Yet, their obsession with personal gratification can serve them in some ways, for their chronic search for refinement and perfection make them connoisseurs and experts at anything involving style: the fashion scenes of Paris and New York are their hunting grounds.

While young children tend to be like Twos, most of us as teenagers feel like Fours for a time, lending credence to the comment that being a poet requires a combination of inexperience and arrogance. Rimbaud, Chatterton and Rupert Brooke all wrote their important work as teenagers, while Byron (mad, bad and dangerous to know) seemed a perpetual adolescent. Brooke, for his part, thought we should all commit suicide at the age of 30 because he couldn't imagine life without all that adolescent grandiosity. But he died young, so we'll never know how he would have felt about it when he got there. On the other hand, Chatterton did kill himself, acting out an adolescent impulse we see carried out by far too many kids today.

Because Fours have a hard time containing their feelings, they'll assume the very notion is a mistake. Really, though, containing an emotional charge can build it beyond a Four's tolerance—they'll spew their feelings out because they have little tolerance for holding a high emotional charge, and not being able to scream and shout can make them feel like they're about to burst. Then they'll quote chapter and verse about how emotional excess is the only way to feel alive.

In addition to appearing unstable, Fours can become "emotional flashers," exposing their sexual exploits as a way of shocking complete strangers or inciting jealousy in their lovers. Besides, many of us love being told to repress our passions, for it gives us an excuse to flaunt our sensuality and shock people. I'm thinking of films like *Sirens, Chocolat* and *Dirty Dancing*, which had to be set in the past because they simply wouldn't work in contemporary settings.

Much of the impetus that drove the "Me Decade" of the 1970s came from Fours, and the Gestalt therapy popular back then is a Four's delight. Fritz Perls, who developed Gestalt, had Four-ish traits, and it's little surprise that he developed a form of therapy that matched his personality style. With its flair for dramatic imagery, the New Age movement is largely a Four phenomenon where spirituality is all about dramatic feelings.

Ironically, for all their talk about feelings, Fours can spend an inordinate amount of time in their heads, looking to find the right poetry, the right words, the most artistic way to express themselves. It shows in spiritual teachings full of tediously convoluted detail, in rambling descriptions of the complex interplay of universal energies, just as it does in the college professor discoursing with great passion about some arcane subject no one else cares about in the least.

While Fours excel in artistry, they generally do poorly in task-oriented work, putting in an eight hour day while accomplishing only two or three hours' worth of results because they'd spent so time focusing on their feelings. And they can look ditsy because there simply isn't enough attention span left over to pay attention to anything else. In the same way, they are directionally-challenged when it comes to using a map. The stereotypical "dumb blonde" is a Four, although it really doesn't have anything to do with being dumb, blonde or female, as there are plenty of men who fit the description. It's just that most people who bleach their hair are female Fours.

One of the worst traits of a Four is jealousy, for in their need to feel special they'll assume that if someone else has something desirable, then they must have been deprived. So, a Four throws a tantrum in a restaurant when someone else gets a better table, gets angry at anyone with a better car or clothes, and becomes indignant at having to wait in line like everyone else. In the same way, we'll take up two or three parking spots or take up extra room in crowded airport waiting areas just to prove we deserve it. We're hard on waitresses, handymen, nannies or anyone else in a service position because, failing to feel special enough, we'll be looking for someone to blame. Above all, we yearn to be like a movie star getting out of the limousine while the flashbulbs go off—*Here I am, everyone!*—when all we're doing is going to the grocery store.

Four-ness, like Two-ness and Three-ness, can be described as an emotional process obsessed with itself. So, our redemption comes through our willingness to face our addiction to drama and our need to feel special, to gain the inner composure to face boredom and stability, to embrace our commonness, our ordinariness, and the plainness of life in general. That in turn will confront us with heartbreak and disappointment we've been carrying since childhood as well as the underlying depression we've been carrying just as long. And because we have a Three wing, we're challenged to face the ways we deceive ourselves about our own motivations. In the long run, though, we're faced with the irony that our passionate grasping at life has actually deprived us of a good deal of what we've wanted all along, which is to truly feel alive amidst the ordinariness of life.

In developing a truer self-sense, Fours can bring out an expression of the passions we all feel, passions that are core to the human experience we all share, yet can do so wisely rather than impulsively. And in doing so, they can reveal to the rest of us nuances of life that are so easily overlooked.

FIVE

I must be wise, I must try to analyze
each change in me, everything I see.
~Leslie Bricusse, *from Jekyll and Hyde*

Engineers aren't boring people.
They just get excited about boring things.
~tee shirt slogan

There's a scene from *The Simpsons* in which a woman, in a dry, nasal tone, tells little Lisa something to the effect of: *I can assure you that although there's no change in my patrician façade, my heart is actually breaking.* That's a parody of a classic Five.

Fives love the world of words and ideas, concepts and theories far more than the messy one of flesh and blood, distrusting physical experience as a teacher while valuing rationality and the Socratic dictum to seek reason unfettered by passion. Extreme Five-ness is epitomized in the notion that words are our only true reality, that to order our thought processes is to order our universe, that we can make life right the same way we order our bureau drawers.

Well, we can order our mental universes that way, and the way we use words does create our inner reality to some extent, but Fives extend the notion to the universe at large as if words when properly assembled and understood will lead us to a revelation of great truths. Consider the notion of the world having been given form through the spoken word or the uttering of a sacred syllable. After all, in developmental terms our intellectual experience of the world around us actually is given form through language.

But then we see professional journal articles with wording so convoluted that you can read a sentence a half dozen times and still not be quite sure what they'd been trying to say. As Bill Bryson tells us, a conference of sociologists once defined love as "the cognitive-affective state characterized by intrusive and obsessive fantasizing concerning reciprocity of amorant feelings by the object of the amorance." Hmm... wonder if you could fit that into a love song. And thinking of Dreikurs' comment about not wanting to put people into boxes, actually the Five in us really does want to put people into boxes. It's comforting to have them there.

Fives can be guilty of what Freud called the narcissism of petty differences, for to a Five there's always one more question to ask, one more thing to say, another word to use. We see it in college debate teams where words are reality, and that once said, there's no opportunity to revise them. The complaint, *But that's not what I meant!,* doesn't have a place in the Five world. William F. Buckley, both applauded and feared for his "polysyllabic enthusiasm," was a Five, but Fives can confuse convoluted verbosity with sophistication, leading us to explain and explain, still feeling we've not said enough. Nor does intellectual obsession necessarily make us intelligent, for Five-ness can demonstrate what novelist Elizabeth Peters describes as a combination of erudition and naïveté. Still, Fives often share a notion that if we say something enough times, then it's true.

As Fives, we can become so lost in our own worlds that we'll insist that the world "out there" must simply be wrong, although to others we'll look a bit loopy because our detachment can lend us an oddly eccentric air. E.M. Forster shows this in his scathing parodies of British culture as in *A Room With a View* and *Howard's End,* both containing murder scenes so vaguely described as to seem like philosophical dissertations rather than violent events.

As Fives, we are arch-avoiders, and because we feel so easily intruded upon, we crave jobs where we get to sit in a closed room with someone shoving papers under the door while we shove our finished work back out the same way. Much of the tragedy associated with Hurricane Katrina was a result of what has been called "proactive dereliction" on the part of detached paper shufflers, and it's the Fives among us who believe that a computer could someday demonstrate artificial intelligence indistinguishable from a human mind. If Twos and Fours represent an emotional process obsessed with itself, Fives represent an intellectual process fascinated with itself, seeing intellect as existing for the sake of intellect alone. For some it seems there's little difference between a flesh and blood person and the classic "brain in a vat," lacking any physical experience at all. This is why intellectuals are often ridiculed, as no one likes being lectured to by someone so lost inside his head that he's unable to button up his shirt properly.

Writers like Umberto Eco and Jorge Luis Borges typify the Five's tendency to create mental worlds, reducing life to words and numbers, and we see in films like *A Beautiful Mind*, *Proof*, and *Pi* how it can lead to outright psychosis. That's why it's so disturbing to hear young men addicted to computer games claiming that they have moved beyond the rest of mankind, and are evolving into a superior species.

One notion behind the development of "talk therapy" in the late nineteenth and early twentieth centuries was the belief that mental illness could be cured by convincing a patient to see reason. Now we hear techniques for creating world peace by getting people to think in a certain structured way at the end of which they would conclude that fighting was wrong. And that's the world Fives live in, one where thought reigns supreme, no matter how naïve it may be.

Yet for all that they are criticized, Fives can have an appreciation for nuances the rest of us miss, for they are often the thoughtful contemplative or the quiet scholar: the Dalai Lama and Jane Goodall are Fives, as was Mohandas Gandhi. Generally, though, they are aloof intellectuals, absent-minded professors, ivory tower people and statisticians, the folks with cluttered libraries at home. A.A. Milne's Owl is a Five. They're great at juggling statistics, and they tend to speak in nominalizations (words that turn actions into things) as in: "The fetching of thrown sticks is a behavior in which dogs enjoy engaging."

Yet there's an assumption that disconnected language implies sophistication. Moreover, while Twos and Fours act as if their feelings define reality, Fives assume that if they think something, then it must be universally true. Ironically, it was Nietzsche, himself a Five, who said Socrates had made reason into a tyrant, while Alan Watts (another Five), described the typical philosopher as an "intellectual yokel" gawking obsessively at things that sensible people take for granted.

Science and mathematics appeal to Fives because factoids and the unchanging nature of numbers lie outside the quicksand of feelings and needs. After all, two plus two always equals four. But as much as we may love science, we can be so obsessive that we'll create stumbling blocks for everyone else. For instance, the 212 degree Fahrenheit scale, the 5280-foot mile, the twelve-inch foot and the 746 watt horsepower are horribly awkward to work with, yet Fives can be so insistent on irrelevant precision that they'll create headaches for everyone else.

As Fives we can give the impression that we're more interested in theories, information and concepts than we are in relationships or anything that requires physical activity. And with their impulse to download their entire thought processes, they are prone to delivering tedious lectures as conversation. So, when we read Herodotus' infamously lengthy digressions, well, maybe he was a Five and simply couldn't help himself.

But Fives can get so wrapped up in their heads that they fail to apply what they know to anything practical, making them, as Flannery O'Conner describes one of her characters, too smart to be successful. Moreover, because ego strength is a bodily-felt experience, lack of physical involvement can to hold back a person's maturity. Joseph Campbell, also a Five, spoke of how people who spend years in post-graduate studies have a hard time maturing because the academic atmosphere holds them in a dependent role, and it shows in how many footnotes they rely on, always relating to someone else's authority. They can also be what my father (himself a Five) called "stupid intellectuals," people for whom the world would be just fine if they could only get the wording right.

Fives are often high-strung with a high-pitched, pressured way of speaking as if struggling to keep up with their fast-moving thoughts, although some are quite the opposite with a flat, tedious voice tone. And while they're often accused of arrogance, it's more likely they are simply withdrawn, shy and socially inept, so involved in their inner worlds that they don't realize why the things they say are often unintelligible.

And because we over-contain our feelings, those of us who are Fives have a hard time when pushed into our emotions: the classic film, *The Blue Angel*, portrays a Five being blown away by a flaming Four. English culture has a generally Five-ish flavor with its tradition of relying on nannies to deal with the messy business of raising children, then shipping them off to boarding schools where they're instructed to maintain a stiff upper lip. After all, despite one's feelings, one simply does not conduct one's self in an unseemly manner, now does one? That's why Evelyn Waugh describes the upper class young Englishmen of his day as having been forced into premature dignity, but at a cost. That implies a secondary meaning to Forster's *A Room With a View*, that the culture itself was like a stuffy room with the curtains drawn.

On the other hand, withdrawn people often come across as rude because they've grown up feeling so invisible that it doesn't occur to them they can have an effect on others, and often overcompensate in ways others find offensive. But Fives can truly be offensive as their version of the Captain Bligh syndrome is to hold contempt for anyone they see as their intellectual inferior, which means just about everyone. Consider the bombastic professor, his voice dripping with sarcasm, as in the Thomas Mann character regretting that he's fated to "inflict his malice on such insignificant objects," meaning other people.

Because intellectual scorn pumps up a Five's balloon, endless bickering has marked intellectual discourse for centuries. For example, a men's group leader I once encountered related how he'd grown up with an alcoholic father telling him, *You shit-for-brains! You'll never be a man like me.* Yet his own message amounted to: *You shit-for-brains! You'll never be an intellectual highbrow like me*, even when he had his facts wrong.

To Sartre, hell is other people, which is why Fives retreat into intellect to escape pain and humiliation, then aim contempt at others, and they love Socrates' cave analogy to claim that they alone see the light while the rest of us are benighted fools. This often happens between fathers and sons, which is why we see such hopelessness in the works of Franz Kafka, who had a vindictive father. Many of us carry a sense of persecution for no apparent reason, a sense that no matter what we do, someone else will always find a way to make us wrong, and it can drive us to nightmarish fantasies. How many of us, after all, have ever imagined waking up as a giant bug?

Still, Fives aren't necessarily intelligent. Rather, it's that they use their minds as a remote control on the rest of themselves. And while some are walking libraries of facts all neatly categorized, others are a mismatched hodge-podge of stuff. They are either extremely neat or extremely sloppy, staunchly anal-retentive or anal-expulsive, either struggling to order their homes the same way they order their orderly thoughts (remember the character in *Good Morning, Vietnam* who loves collating?) or letting their homes become disordered jumbles just like the insides of their heads: as we think, so we keep house. Beethoven and Socrates were both farty, smelly slobs, while the ancient Cynics fitted the mold of the Great Unwashed, as did both Dylans—Thomas and Bob. So do many contemporary computer geeks and scientists, going about with "interestingly willful hair" as Bill Bryson describes them. So we have the Five who can conceptualize quarks and gluons, but can't balance his checkbook, while Agatha Christie's Hercule Poirot personifies the anal retentive fop—intensely observant and fastidious to the point of being a bit mincing.

Yet, while Fives may be eggheads, they have an absolute ball in their own way, and they can be outrageously funny. Peter Sellers was a Five, and the humor of Monty Python is Five-ish as is English humor in general—from *Three Men in a Boat* and Saki's short stories to contemporary Brit-Com; from Graham Greene's *Travels With My Aunt* to Elizabeth Peters' Peabody and Emerson novels. What many people don't like about that kind of humor, though, is that you have to take the time to appreciate the subtleties, and you may need a backlog of historical information just to get the punch lines.

Einstein once said, in explaining how he'd come up with the theory of relativity, that while children often think about time and space, it was his own delayed emotional development that had allowed him to go on questioning well on into adulthood. Fives especially have fun playing with intellectual notions, for who but a Five would name a sub-atomic particle a "gluon" (after a stripper's glue-on tassels?) or designate pulsars as LGMs: Little Green Men?

There was once a study in which research physicists and psychotherapists were asked to describe their work, and while the therapists strove to be tediously serious, the physicists described their work as fun. Here they are exploring the nature of reality a hair's breadth after the Big Bang, and they're having a blast doing it. Fives also play with words the same way they play with reality. As a National Public Radio Sunday Puzzle asks, name a six-letter animal, change the second letter to the next letter of the alphabet, read the result backwards and you'll get the name of what US city? That's Five. But then they can get carried away as Salman Rushdie discovered when his flippancy made him the target of a *fatwa*.

With a strong Four wing, Fives can take on an eccentric air—the bohemian intellectual with his beret, goatee and bongos (the 1950s beatnik look); the wild-haired, tweedy professor of the 1970s; the greatcoat and cigarette holder of the pre-war gothic look; and today's neo-Goth computer geek in a hoodie. They can also be the wild-eyed radical incensed by all those idiots out there who won't listen to the solutions to mankind's problems they carry around in their heads.

Fives can be both emotionally and financially stingy because they learn at an early age to hoard things (ideas, energy, time and affection, as well as money) from a world that constantly intrudes on them, fearing that otherwise they'll never get to have anything, not even good feelings, for themselves. So, they love isolation, and under stress will withdraw into themselves, which was how they'd learned to get nurturing as children—from themselves. As children, many Fives used the same strategy as the monks who'd built those windowless towers we still see in the Irish countryside as a defense against Viking invaders, hoping that if they hid up there, surrendering hearth and home, the enemy would eventually go away. But the invaders never did go away, so they learned to stay up there in that one place no one could get at them. That's why Fives feel threatened when someone demands to know what they're thinking or feeling, as if demanding the right to get at them in their final refuge.

If Fives have spiritual inclinations, they'll likely be drawn to meditation and contemplation because teachings like Buddhism justify their withdrawal, giving them license for numbing all those annoying feelings. But just as the ancient Greek notion of *apathea* is not the same thing as apathy, and the Cynics weren't sarcastic, Fives tend to misinterpret teachings that appeal to them. As Christians they're attracted to Augustine and Duns Scotis, stuff that put most people straight to sleep, just as they're attracted to the notion of enlightenment through the revelation of arcane secrets. Their God is the *logos*, the embodiment of rationality, the secret revealed, and they take literally the Biblical line, "In the beginning was the Word..."

Many Fives, though, are atheists, seeing soul as a manifestation of reason. That's a notion both Albert Einstein and Steven Hawking expressed regarding scientific theory, as if having a few good notions here on this little planet of ours makes us masters of the universe. And it shows up in our common language where we refer to things as "universal" when they actually apply only to our small world in this one moment in history. I can't help but wonder if the folks out there at Alpha Centauri know we've defined all these universal truths for them. The Enneagram itself is a Five creation, as is our legal system, as Fives love linear, step-wise logic.

Sex is often a dilemma for a Five. Leonardo DaVinci and Isaac Newton both insisted that sex and intellect were at odds with one another, that celibacy leaves us untouched by the messiness of the sensual world. And Rene Descartes, with his *Cogito, ego sum* (I think, therefore I am), was known to lie in bed until noon, the stuff inside his head being more fascinating than the sunny day waiting outside. But then he drew the response that "I think, therefore I am" is a statement by someone who underrates a toothache.

Among the ancient deities it was wise Athena, born without benefit of passion, who remained unaffected by Aphrodite's lure. Yet, some Fives become the randy bohemian casually sleeping around with a philosophical air, disdaining all those fools yearning for 'til-death-do-us-part. And it brings to mind Lily Tomlin's line that if love is the answer, could you please rephrase the question?

Fives represent the avoidant personality style, and a drama that gets played out in the spiritual and psychotherapeutic arenas is between Twos and Fours on one side, Fives on the other, for when clingers are upset, they'll reach out for comfort just as they always have, while Fives withdraw just as they always have. So, we see this seesaw effect between avoiders and clingers, for Fives typically became Fives because they'd had a demanding, invasive Two or Four for a parent, while many Twos and Fours had Fives for parents, and Fives typically make poor nurturers. Then, when Fives *do* get in touch with their feelings, as Twos and Fours are always telling them to, they'll likely find that they've been carrying a lifetime of repressed rage at all those Twos and Fours who've been flooding them with insatiable demands since before they were old enough to walk. On the other hand, clingers love to rage passionately at Fives for under-nurturing them.

Fives feel their greatest love through sharing their sense of wonder, and they feel frustrated and hurt that others can make no sense of it. Ultimately, though, they redeem themselves through allowing themselves to touch and be touched, which brings them up against the pain that drove them into their heads in the first place. It can make them feel vulnerable and fragile like a chick breaking out of its shell, a challenge they've been putting off since childhood. Then, a Five's challenge is the same as a Two's—to face their underlying neediness and sense of loss—and that's likely to involve facing all the pain, shame, self-loathing and rage that drive the avoidant personality style, feelings they've been avoiding by living in their heads for so long.

And once having gained mastery over those feelings, a Five can attain a quiet understanding of life, of humanity in particular that can truly be called wisdom.

SIX

Suddenly – Look at me! Who is this creature that I see?
~Leslie Bricusse, *from Jekyll and Hyde*

The only thing we have to fear is fear itself.
~Franklin Delano Roosevelt

As children, most of us had a fair list of fears: of dogs (that tongue!), of witches and goblins, the boogie man in the closet and the monster under the bed to name a few. Stephen King, who would jump into bed as a kid so that hand couldn't reach out from down there and grab him, has made a career of that fear.

Developmentally speaking, children fear abandonment because their balloon will go to pieces if they're left alone for more than a few minutes at a time, which is why it's deemed child abuse. Beyond that, they fear being overwhelmed by adult demands and anger, by things that are too big and loud, and by anything that's incomprehensible to them, all of which can burst a kid's fragile balloon. And that's our greatest fear of all—our fear of having our psyches go to pieces.

While all nine Enneagram styles are fear-based in their own way, Sixes are people for whom fear is an habitual way of being, commonly a result of having grown up under anxiety-producing circumstances. So, as Sixes we often have a wide-eyed, deer in the headlights look as if we're about to jump out of our skin—jump out of our skin, fall apart in tears, take a swing or pull a gun.

While a certain amount of anxiety is normal in children because of our low ego strength, those of us who are Sixes live throughout adulthood with constant fears that others have trouble understanding. And while other people tell us to just get over it, chronic anxiety is such a part of a Six's sense of identity that it's as if we put our fear on before our socks in the morning, and without it we wouldn't quite know ourselves.

When it comes to extremes, we're the people with five locks on our doors, who live with the shades drawn, who thrill at conspiracy theories, who are absolutely certain that everything from earthquakes to AIDS and COVID-19 are products of the CIA, multinational corporations or the aliens, maybe corporations *and* the aliens *and* the CIA working together. No matter what may actually be happening, as Sixes we carry an underlying assumption that there's something sinister going on all the time, and even if we're occasionally right, we're stuck in a posture of chronic anxiety under what others see as trivial stressors. But it's not necessarily that we lack overall ego strength, rather that our weak spots are very weak. Obsessive-compulsive disorder is a Six characteristic, a dynamic that tries to control anxiety through repetitive rituals.

Fear is dominant in some animal species that are prey in the natural world. For instance, in response to criticism of the meat-packing industry, animal behavior expert Temple Grandin comments that cows heading to slaughter aren't generally frightened at all, yet if you were to toss a paper cup into the chute, it could shut down a slaughterhouse for the rest of the day. In the same way, to a Six, it's the unexpected, the sudden thing that inspires fear.

Most Sixes, though, are simply timid. With that big-eyed waif look she sometimes let show, Princess Diana was likely a Six, and with his litany of witty neuroses, Woody Allen is probably a Six with a strong Five wing. Then there's the stereotype of the fussy, fluttery neurotic. The *All in the Family* character, Edith Bunker, is a Six, while Captain Queeg in *The Caine Mutiny* shows the more paranoid side.

But it's not just about fear, as some Sixes learned as children that a timid kid may get more nurturing, just as it's the scared kid who stops a school outing or camping trip dead in its tracks, giving him a sense of power that's just too good to let go of. Sometimes Sixes get their way because others cave in just to stop their anxious complaining, so that for some of us, being scared equals being in control.

Like Fives, Sixes are often highly anal-retentive, but while Fives try to impose logic and order on their environment, Sixes try to alleviate their anxiety that way, and if something's a bit out of place, it can deeply upset them. Don't go moving the furniture or knick-knacks in a Six's home unless you want to invite a storm.

It works to some extent in the business world to be that orderly, but no one likes being set in order as if they were part of the furniture. And while others work to get things accomplished, a compulsive Six, can become so fixated on order that they'll make it difficult to accomplish a goal. Along with Fives, Sixes are the people who create those stacks of forms we have to fill out.

Sixes have ways of trying to make others feel the same fears that they do, which is what religious leaders, politicians and conspiracy theorists do. Or they do it by badgering: *My God! You were supposed to be here ten minutes ago! How could I know what happened? I was about to call the police and the hospital and the FBI!* And all because you'd had to stop for gas. Just as all personality styles project themselves onto others, Sixes send a message that implies: *You have to change so that I don't have to feel all these chronic feelings I pretend I don't have!*, no matter that they've had those feelings since before they can remember. Just as it's common for us all to try, unconsciously at least, to slough our feelings off onto others, Sixes want to drive their anxiety into other people's lives as if it could be injected like a drug—I've even seen psychotherapists try to push their anxieties onto their clients as if that were somehow helpful. Children of Six parents get an especially strong dose of it, as if the parents are insisting, *I have to control your life because I'm scared of my own.* So, we see a five-year-old getting on a friend's bike and getting it right the first time, only to have his anxious parent drag him away in a panic. Then, when he's forty, he'll feel anxieties he can't explain, and can't ride a bike.

What we've been looking at so far are "phobic" as opposed to "counter-phobic" Sixes, for rather than being timid and cautious, counter-phobic Sixes try to defeat their anxiety with a belligerent air, often playing the daredevil just to prove themselves to themselves. At the extreme, they're the paranoid gun nut, the radical militiaman holed up in the woods with an arsenal, the guy with a yard full of Rottweilers. Benito Mussolini with his ludicrous posturing and Adolph Hitler with his shrill speeches were counter-phobic Sixes. On the healthier end of the scale, novelist Tom Clancy is probably a counter-phobic Six.

Sixes of either type are known for their loyalty to organizations, causes or any other scenario that can give them a sense of security. They're often good corporation people, but they can also be cult followers giving their leaders fanatical adoration. Like Twos, they can be compulsive caretakers, but while Twos seek to merge with other people, Sixes are seeking safety as part of a group. We see this in Communism's use of the term "comrade," French revolutionaries calling each other "citizen" in order to create a group mentality.

We see a peculiar case of the counter-phobic Six in the current conspiracy theory trend. While Sixes are generally driven by fears they've had since childhood, conspiracy theorists have been so entrenched in that backdrop of fear that they no longer experience is as fear. Instead, they experience it as reality, then feel driven to convince others to believe the same fear-based notions that mainstream culture is lying to us all. Then, in a classic turn-around, conspiracy theorists tell others to release themselves from the "bondage of fear," meaning that you want to wear a mask against a deadly virus because you're just afraid of other people. Well, people also started using condoms when AIDS became a threat because they didn't want to die from what was then a 100% fatal disease, and is still a threat. And while accusing others of lying, the conspiracy theory world has consistently bolstered itself with fabrications, apparently because validating their fear-based reality is more important than anything else.

The psychiatric diagnoses those of us who align with conspiracy theories are significant, such as Paranoid Personality Disorder and Paranoid Delusional Disorder (or simply Delusional Disorder), for while difficulty in distinguishing between inner and outer realities plays a part in all personality styles, for Sixes it stands out dramatically.

On a lesser note, Enneagram aficionados within the Catholic community admit that the rest of the world sees Christianity as a Six religion with its hyper-vigilance regarding evil, salvation and heresy. But while it's common to accuse the traditional church hierarchy of being obsessed with control, it's just that Sixes try to protect their narrow sense of reality, anyone not toeing the line making them fearful.

The great challenge for a Six, predictably enough, is to gain the courage, the ego strength, to trust life, for while there are pitfalls and dangers for all of us, the chronic anxiety of a Six is rarely about tangible threats, although it may have been back in childhood. So, an initial step for those of us who are Sixes is to hold our fears for ourselves instead of trying to inflict them on others, and to assess what's real versus what lives only in our nervous systems. The difficulty is that containing our fear can send our anxiety right off the scale at first, but the way to become stronger is by facing that challenge, and that's where the greatest courage is required, although it may be the last thing in the world we'll want. Otherwise, we'll fail to develop better ego strength, and go on feeling wracked by irrational fears and incapacitated by undiagnosable ills.

The great hope for us, as Sixes, is to face our tendencies early on, to consistently ask ourselves if our fear has any basis in the present moment, or if it's no more than a bodily-felt memory that has no present reality. Is the world really full of scary things, or are we simply assuming it is because we're always afraid? The counter-phobic Sixes among us seem a long step ahead in this because we'll throw ourselves into danger just to prove we can take it, yet our underlying anxiety is still there, and coming face-to-face with it in ourselves rather than out there in the world is a step we'll still have to take.

The great gift of the Six personality can, in the long run, develop into an acute awareness—not as fear, but as a finely-tuned alertness to life in all its nuances.

SEVEN

Thought it was to fly.
But I learned it was to land that required the skill.
~Semih Yalman, *"To Land" (from Black Butterfly)*

Eddie Valiant: "You mean to tell me you could have taken
your hand out of those cuffs any time you wanted?"
Roger Rabbit: "No. Only if it was funny."
~from *Who Framed Roger Rabbit?*

While rambling on about his spiritual yearnings, a young man once asked me if he could feel so ecstatic in a fit of laughter, why he couldn't feel that way all the time? One answer is that our nervous systems aren't very good at maintaining extreme states, and besides, someone has to wash the dishes and pay the bills. But what he really wanted was a rush of rising energy lifting his face into a big grin and bubbling out the top of his head like champagne. In short, he was a Seven.

It seems it's about Sevens that Schiller says a man is nowhere more himself than when at play, for Sevens love the relentless pursuit of excitement, laughter and giddiness, anything that gives them that rush of bubbly feelings. They're the class clowns cracking jokes at every turn, often with seriously inappropriate timing, and they'll carry that reckless buoyancy into adulthood, often with manic fervor. They'll memorize comedy routines, punctuate their sentences with sound effects (*Wham! Zing!*), and they'll stand out in a crowd with their chronic smile, or the look of a grin about to happen. And because they feel things so viscerally, they'll play out feelings in a way that can make them buffoonish. Most stand-up comics are Sevens, as was the late Steve Irwin.

As we see in the film, *Amadeus*, Mozart was a raging Seven, as was Davy Crockett, judging from the stories about him, and so was Salvador Dali with his compulsion to warp reality—warping reality, is a Seven's favorite pastime. Mr. Bean is a Seven, although his alter-ego, Rowan Atkinson, comes across as a fairly level-headed chap. But then the likes of Robin Williams and Jim Carey have taken on roles that go to disturbing extremes, while Jim Morrison went to dark excesses while describing himself as having the soul of a clown. On the darker side, Jeffrey Epstein was probably a Seven, a potty-mouthed life of the party guy accused of some seriously depraved behavior. Sevens like Ringo Starr can be loveably goofy, but then Sasha "Borat" Cohen is also a Seven, and that's all we need say about that. Ben Franklin was apparently a Seven, his most renown accomplishments having been achieved in his later years after he'd gotten over the worst of it. Then there's Charley Chaplin who once declared, tapping the side of his head, that it was the greatest toy ever created.

Sevens are at the beck and call of the striatum, a part of the brain associated with creative surprise, which is why Dr. Seuss famously said that nonsense wakes up brain cells. For a Seven, every day is April Fool's Day, as in the bumper sticker: *I don't suffer from insanity. I enjoy every minute of it.* Then there's the notion that comedy is mental illness with timing. And it's hardly limited to humans—border collies are Sevens at their lunatic extreme.

But Sevens aren't necessarily funny or creative, as some can't tell a joke to save their lives. Rather, it's likely they grew up in families with deep conflicts, and they learned to serve as a distraction to the family problems, not realizing the price it would exact on them. As a result, they like putting a pretty face on things, trying to be light-hearted and buoyant, then getting so stuck in it that they can be offensive at times, not knowing when to switch it off, or simply not knowing how.

Because of their underlying anxiety, Sevens epitomize the Peter Pan Syndrome, since they resist aging with a passion because mature behavior seems a form of slow death. Ironically, though, they'll also feel like they have an elephant sitting on their backs, that being the price they've had to pay for providing light-hearted entertainment to the family they'd grown up in. A greater irony is that while Sevens can be like adults playing at being children, Twos, Threes and Fours, so critical of Fives and Sevens, can seem like children playing at being adults, posing the question as to whether one is really any less mature than the other. Sevens *act* childishly and are often unable to unhook themselves from childish impulses while Twos, Threes and Fours are defined by neediness normal in children. Beneath the airhead giddiness that Sevens often exhibit lies a deep uncertainty, for the world they grew up in was a difficult one to trust, and while chronic need drives Twos, Threes and Fours to seduce and manipulate, it drives a Seven's notion that life is an ongoing joke of bizarre proportions.

With their low boredom threshold, Sevens love the variety of experiences and toys available to them, making it difficult for them to choose any one thing, any one relationship, any one course in life, any one career. And they can't have just one of anything because there are so many out there, and they're all so wonderfully different. Just look at Jay Leno's car collection. And Sue is such a wonderful girl, but what about Diane and Jane and Sally and Joan? The newest thing is always more exciting, the latest self-help book, the latest guru, the newest gadget attracting Sevens with enthusiasm. Enneagram literature refers to Sevens as "epicures," but it's a bit of a misnomer, for it's just that if something's good, more must be better. And different is better, which is why Sevens will throw themselves into something that's completely out of character just to have had the experience at least once.

Because of their reckless sense of adventure, Sevens can't resist pushing a button or flipping a switch just to see what it'll do, the perpetual Adam who has to eat the apple just because someone told him not to. Worse, if they know something is likely to send someone else into a rage, they'll do it just for the sake of doing it, compulsively twisting a knot in the tiger's tail. It's as if the more frivolous they are, the more alive they feel, driving them to violate social strictures simply for the sake of creating a little disruption, just because they can. The joker is always wild, often with a wise-ass smirk.

Because they are so fantasy-oriented, Sevens tend to dream up grandiose, unrealistic future plans, partially to keep from having to put their feet on the ground, partially because they don't know *how* to put their feet on the ground, and as a result they can be terribly gullible. Because they'd rather not have to work a real job (wearing a suit and tie can feel like being assimilated into the Borg), they can be prone to every get-rich-quick scheme or screwball investment gimmick that comes along. And because they'll do almost anything to avoid punching a clock, they're drawn to any kind of work outside the mainstream—athlete, musician, surfer, skier, rock climber. Sevens find things like surfing and skiing and rock climbing more important than trivial things like financial security, and outlandish adventures can become holy quests because they provide the thrill drug Sevens crave, and everything else pales in comparison. That's why they can take to gambling, certain the winds of fortune will sooner or later blow their way, providing them with money without their having to work for it.

Yet, Sevens can view life with the hostility of a street punk, and some are attracted to notions of anarchy, although true anarchy would terrify them. It's just that they want to live like a kid playing hooky, and for all their grandiose notions, they can be terribly foolish. As a Sevenish race driver once commented, the line between heroism and stupidity can be quite thin.

At their worst, Sevens can be drawn to thievery. While Twos, Threes and Fours can become kleptomaniacs because they feel that they deserve whatever they want, Sevens seek to have things without having to exert undue effort. Pirates, highwaymen, and other parasites on civilization since before recorded history have had a Seven nature, acting as "labor exploiters," taking advantage of others' efforts. So, while Threes will fleece you because they see it as a matter of success, Sevens may filch from you because they're basically indolent, sometimes stealing things they don't need just for the sake of the adventure. And they'll do it a smirk, the mark of a smartass out to get something for nothing.

Actually, Sevens will do a lot of things just for the sake of the adventure. Mark Twain's Tom Sawyer and Huck Finn are classic Sevens, as was Twain himself. On the other hand, the image we have of the medieval troubadour singing his way into the hearts of the village girls, then skipping over the horizon when one of them shows up pregnant is a Seven. George MacDonald Frazier's character, the randy and cowardly Harry Flashman in the hilarious Flashman novels, is a Seven, as is the Baron Von Munchhausen.

Children typically act out in response to family stress, so while the cliché is that Sevens act the way they do in order to avoid pain, many learned at an early age to keep others from feeling *their* pain, fearing that if the family was confronted with its own misery, everything would fall apart, which may well have been true—as long as everyone was laughing, they weren't fighting, drinking or sinking into depression.

So, Sevens develop a peculiar way of manipulating a group, and when they tell a joke or pull a prank, they're drawing attention to themselves the same way they'd tried as kids to pull others away from their own pain and rage—while it looks self-centered, the original impulse was a form of self-sacrifice, which is why chronic despair underlies much of the Seven personality style.

Because their childhood role was to deflect adult conflicts, Sevens typically don't have a very good model for constructive argument. Since in their experience disagreement implied total victory on one side, total surrender on the other, many Sevens react to conflict either by caving in without even trying to stand up for themselves, or by running away. Or they'll lash out, and if that fails, *then* they'll have to run because they don't know what else to do.

At the very least, a typical Seven's outlook is that there's a slightly bizarre joke going on all the time, which is why Seven-ish thinking tends to be convoluted and fantastic to a degree that can seem a bit perverse. For example, Joyce's *Ulysses* regales us with puns, deliberate spoonerisms, stream of consciousness passages and constant word play, all of which provide a peek into a Seven's mental processes: *Bless me Holy Farmer; I beg your parsnips; Don't be casting nasturtiums on my character.* The same thing shows up in Malachy McCourt's rendering of the Catholic prayer: *Blessed art thou a monk swimming.* But then Ireland is a Seven culture, for who but an island full of Sevens could have come up with leprechauns and the Blarney Stone, upon which the locals are rumored to urinate when the tourists aren't about. Freud, by the way, was convinced the Irish couldn't be helped by psychoanalysis, which gives the Irish a good chuckle to this day. Then there's John Lennon's gibberish lyrics to *I Am The Walrus*, the works of Vladimir Nabokov where even perverse scenes are made funny, and painters like Dali where fantasy blurs into reality until it's difficult to tell which is which. But then Sevens often don't quite know which is which.

But for all their horsing around, Sevens can have a keen sense of how serious things can be. We hear it in stories from war and concentration camp survivors about how it was the Sevens who had helped them make it through desperate ordeals by cracking jokes while others were literally dying on their feet. For all that Sevens can be airheads and goofballs, their serious side is why Seven actors (Christopher Lloyd and Robin Williams come to mind) can play deeply disturbing characters without having to reach very far under the surface to come up with it. And because their attempts at humor can be a bit vicious, nightclub comedians who poke fun at people in the front row sometimes get punched out for it.

Then we see *Confessions of a Dangerous Mind* in which former game show host Chuck Barris portrays himself as a secret CIA assassin, which he stands accused of having fabricated. But that fits the type, for as much as Sevens love outlandish experiences, they will fantasize outlandish experiences as the next best thing, then try to convince the rest of us that it's real. This would seem to play into the conspiracy theory arena with its paranoid dramas and fabrications.

A Seven is also the guy having sex with his friend's wife while the guy's at work, and she's attracted to that Seven because he's so lighthearted, because he appreciates her so much, and because he's always around. Of course he's always around because he doesn't have a job, and he panders to her the same way he'd done with his Mom, but it works, at least for a while. And while she doesn't know any of this yet, she eventually will.

Sevens are often attracted to New Age thinking with its head-in-the-clouds attitude and its tendency to be a grab bag full of all manner of philosophies. While Ones use religion to be right, Twos to merge with other people, Threes to look right, Fours to feel exultant, Fives to have big answers, and Sixes to feel safe, Sevens use it as the biggest playground of all. It's a Seven's tendency to gather things up like a beachcomber, seeking an overview perspective, and for all that some people have attempted to unite all world religions and philosophies, a Seven may actually do it someday.

If this seems like a lot of examples, it's because Sevens are chameleons, always trying on different aspects of life. In fact, they can look at times like any other personality type, often because they have very little self-sense. One of their greater challenges, then, is to find something that truly works for them rather than chasing one thing after another. Their bigger challenge is to contain their effervescent energy, to interrupt themselves whenever they drift into fantasy, and force their feet down onto solid ground. And the best way to do that is through work. In other words, the best education for a Seven is to wake up early, go to work, work all day, come home, pay the bills and stop complaining. That, and stuffing a sock in his mouth when the next urge to crack a joke comes up.

Failing this, a Seven is likely to hit middle age with a sense of loss over his failure to have truly engaged with the life going on around him. Ultimately, though, a Seven has to confront the heartbreak he's been secreting away since childhood along with a Six-like fear that everything will go to pieces if he doesn't keep it all light. That means he'll have to stop goofing around, get out of his fantasies, and, like Fives, face the repressed rage he's been harboring for so long.

And, like Fives, Sevens can eventually come to a quiet overview of life, which is what they've yearned for all along.

And how do I know? Because I'm a Seven, in case you were wondering.

EIGHT

I had to fight all my life to survive. They were all against me...
but I beat the bastards and left them in the ditch.
~Ty Cobb

Go ahead, make my day.
~Clint Eastwood in *Dirty Harry*

If you've ever seen it, you'll have a hard time forgetting the movie scene where Jack Nicholson's character fumes, *You want the truth? You can't handle the truth!* Nicholson, like the character he plays, is an Eight. So was John Wayne: *Fill your hands, you son of a bitch!*

On first meeting someone, the typical Eight will size them up for a potential fight, challenging them if only with the grip of their handshake or the look in their eye, and if they sense the other person is too strong, they'll hold back and look for an advantage. An Eight's basic assumption is that others are weak and incompetent, and that they have the right, perhaps a duty, to dominate. Overall, they assume life is a constant struggle for domination, driving them to treat others with contempt if not naked aggression.

A simple interaction with an Eight can be challenging, a bit like holding a conversation with a sledgehammer as one businessman said. Extreme Eights can be like John Travolta's character in the movie *Get Shorty*: *I own you. And I really don't care all that much. I can walk away, or I could put a bullet through your head. It's really pretty much the same to me.*

Some, like pathological tyrants seen throughout history, are so hyper-vigilant that if you are less than obsequious toward them, they'll attack. As President Kennedy once said about the Soviet

Union, you can't work with people whose attitude is that what's mine is mine, and what's yours is negotiable. With outright Eights, though, it more like: *What's yours is whatever I feel like letting you keep.*

And they're like that right from early childhood, seeing life through the red mist of rage and treating the world as if it were their personal punching bag. Even as a little boy, the Eight stands out from the rest, already fascinated with his ability to intimidate others. He may be the hulking brute of a kid skulking around the playground like a thug, or the wiry one strutting around with his chest out, his back concave, hips rigidified into an odd stork-like walk as he circles the other kids with clenched fists and jutting jaw, looking for a victim. Then, as an adult, he'll drive a 4x4 truck jacked up with huge tires and six headlights because it gives him the feeling of power he craves. I remember a truck like that tailgating me at seventy-plus miles an hour in heavy traffic, and when he blew past to tailgate the next car in line, I got a look at his license plate. It read: AMMO.

Eights try to reduce the complexities of life to the notion that the way to solve a problem is to force everything and everyone into submission. But as much as they try to command respect, they'll draw hatred, not that they're likely to care. They may be able to create a business, but it's difficult to find employees willing to put up with them, or other businesses willing to work with them. What generally happens in a successful enterprise run by an Eight is that a secretary or office manager eventually falls into place, more through trial and error than by deliberate design, to soften the boss's impact on everyone else.

Eights have a hard time understanding that throwing our rage, or even the threat of it, at others doesn't make us powerful—it only makes us look dangerous. As Steven Pressfield's characterization of Alexander the Great says, "virtue is written in the blood of the enemy." So, while Eights may be successful in financial terms, they'll be unsuccessful at being decent people, and they are generally poor teachers, for they talk *at* people, not *with* them. Moreover, they are likely to see their child's developing self-sense as a threat, for while Fours may compete with their child for the right to feel special, an Eight is likely to feel that a child is just someone else to push around.

At their best, Eights are simply forceful and direct. Actors Gene Hackman and Anthony Hopkins are Eights. But then Josef Stalin, Slobodan Milosevic and Saddam Hussein typify Eights at their worst, people so obsessed with brute force as to justify devastating entire nations. And while Sixes like Hitler scream, tyrants like Stalin and Hussein are serene as they order someone packed off the Siberia or sent back to their family in a plastic bag. True to form, when asked how he felt about being called the "Butcher of Baghdad," Hussein responded with psychopathic logic that to be a leader you sometimes must be tough.

Sparta was an Eight culture, shame-based and driven to gain fame in battle, and we see their modern day equivalent in sports. The coach I remember from high school was a bully barely more mature than the kids he humiliated daily, yet I've seen choir leaders act that way, and anyone who wanted to gain from their expertise simply had to put up with it. Bull Meecham in *The Great Santini* typifies the extreme Eight's attitude that a real man is an infantile brute out to stomp the world into submission—in other words, only Eights are real men.

Rough as they are on others' feelings, Eights can sometimes have effective methods, if a bit severe. We read of a five-year-old who had badgered his father for a guitar until he finally got one, although the family was quite poor, but after a week when the kid hadn't touched the thing, his dad smashed it. It was a rough strategy, but the kid grew up to be an excellent guitarist, the lesson being that either you do it or you don't, but don't waffle. Eights hate waffling.

And they have no tolerance for disagreement, expecting everyone to either yield to them or fight, because to an Eight, life is an all-or-nothing proposition. And it's all too easy to get into trouble with them, for while Twos scan their environment for someone to merge with, Eights scan theirs for anyone looking at them the wrong way. Klingons are Eights—all of them.

Aristotle said a man's character is demonstrated nowhere so much as in warfare, although any extreme situation will bring out our character in ways normal times will not, which is why some of us are driven to seek out extreme challenges. But war also brings out the predatory sadists who, like little boys torturing insects, use it as an opportunity to unleash their demons. Still, Eights are the people you want on your side in a fight, but while others may lose a war, Eights lose the peace by making enemies of the people they need to work with.

It brings to mind an old science fiction story in which humans are in a raging war against an unseen enemy that somehow always manages to fire back at them with the same increased armament every time the humans step up theirs. It turns out, of course, that there's no enemy there at all, only a force field that bounces back everything fired into it, but Eights get so wrapped up in their Eightness that they can't stop.

Bullfights, dogfights, fistfights, anything involving contained warfare is meat and potatoes to Eights. They love bleeding as they push on to victory, heeding no pain, feeling nothing but the joy of battle, even if it's only a backyard project. We see it in Tom Berringer's character in the film, *Platoon*, shouting at a dying soldier to suck up his pain and stop being such a wimp.

But if we can imagine life a hundred thousand years ago, toughness, aggressiveness and the ability to withstand pain have been vital to the survival of the species. These days, though, it starts with things like the game we used to call "Six Inches" where we would take turns punching each other in the shoulder from six inches away, and the first to flinch lost. It's something many boys feel driven by, as if testing each other's ability to face the world, and while well-meaning parents may try to keep violence-oriented toys from their kids, they'll find little boys making guns out of sticks. That primal urge is an Eight's forte, an essential energy that has motivated human evolution for millions of years, for they're the ones who got us down out of the trees a few million years back, the ones who learned how to survive the Ice Ages, which explains the Eight's sense that weakness is a threat to everyone's survival. The Eight's problem, though, is that they tend to live as if survival were always an issue, and defeat is not an option. Neither, unfortunately, is cooperation.

Eights are generally not religious people unless they see it as a way of gaining dominance, yet a deity they can respect is one who throws them into life with the commandment to figure out how to deal with it. Like the rest of us, Eights worship their instinctual impulses, assigning them a supreme place in the order of things, which is why the god of the Eight is a god of war, the god of the red mist. That's why in the Norse tradition the man who died in battle went to Valhalla where he would spend all eternity fighting to his heart's content, while he who died without glory went, literally, to Hel, the goddess of death.

A keyword used to describe Eights is "lust," a word with more than just a sexual meaning. In general, Eights are driven to thrust themselves against the world with passion. Zorba the Greek is an Eight with a strong Seven wing, as was Anthony Quinn who played him so well. Sexually, Eights go for what has been indelicately called "sport fucking," gentle intimacy not being their strong suit, and they love vulgarity. An Eight has the ability to focus on a romantic partner in a way that can emotionally overwhelm a woman by being so intensely *there!* But he's also the guy who hits her when she dares to defy him in some way, only to have him crumble with guilt: *I'm so sorry, baby. I don't know what came over me. I promise I'll never do it again.* But of course he does it again, yet his intimate intensity when he's not being violent keeps her hooked.

Eights can be compelling people, which is why they often become business, religious or political leaders, attracting a following of people longing to absorb the sense of raw power an Eight exudes. But while an Eight may play the role of defending the downtrodden, if he comes to feel he's been protecting a wimp, he'll turn on them with all the contempt he has for the weakling. Then he'll become the tyrant that someone else has to overthrow for riding roughshod on everyone just like the last one had.

Yet people who ride the cusp between Seven and Eight can have a buffoonish side. Teddy Roosevelt and J.P. Morgan are historical examples. The Norse god, Thor, is represented like that, fiery-tempered at times, a bit of a dim bulb at others, for Eights can be so focused on pushing other people around that they don't stop to think things through. Hence the stereotype of the dumb brute. So, while Fours may get labeled as ditsy because they have a hard time taking their attention off their feelings, Eights get labeled as intellectually stunted because they can't take their focus off their aggression.

As any woman who has been in a relationship with an Eight man comes to know, behind his bluster is a little boy posturing to keep the world at bay. Yet that can be a hook for some women as they're maternally geared toward catering to the demands of a little boy, confusing maternal instincts with sexual ones. And like angry little boys, Eights love a partner they can dominate, yet want someone who will take care of them—they love the person they can control, yet despise anyone they can push around. And they love patriotism because it provides a higher authority they feel bound to obey, and will despise anyone who fails to have the same motivations. Overall, an Eight demands respect while giving none, postures as a tough guy while acting like an insecure child.

But most Eights aren't warriors or outright bullies. They're simply overly strong-headed and insensitive, and most of the battles they fight are fairly trivial. Yet the peace they lose can be significant, although they'll pretend none of it matters.

To mature, an Eight is challenged to confront not only the sense of entitlement he takes for granted, but the fear if not outright paranoia that hides behind it. No, he doesn't have the right to push people around, and no, he doesn't have the right to treat others like doormats. And just because he wants to attack the world around him doesn't mean he's entitled to do it.

It's not uncommon for men in their sixties and beyond to have to look back at a life of walking over other people only to deal in their elder years with a deep sense of regret if not shame. It's reminiscent of how Socrates, apparently inspired by the fact that he'd been on the losing side of a war, said that an unexamined life isn't worth living. Most Eights, though, don't have a philosopher's motivation, and go into old age still warring against a world that both fears and despises them. Age, though, is one of the few things that can inspire an Eight to confront himself, as he may eventually have to ask himself if it's more important to win or to be a decent person. Even Ernest Hemingway came to realize that winning isn't what it's all about, and said so in his later works. But while a younger Eight may convince himself that dominating others makes him a person deserving of respect, sooner or later he may have to confront a sizeable list of people who have no respect for him at all.

On the other hand, a mature Eight can gain a protective sense that, in a man, could be called "patriarchal" in the most positive sense, and provide leadership in a way that is neither domineering nor contemptuous.

NINE

Take it easy, take it easy...
Don't let the sound of your own wheels drive you crazy.
~Jackson Browne, *Take It Easy*

I'm out of bed and I'm dressed.

What more do you want from me?
~ *Tee shirt slogan*

During the rule of the British Raj in India, the fastidious English were faced with people who'd been slogging along in their own way for millennia, and weren't especially interested in changing much. So, while the always-punctual English Fives complained that they couldn't get their trains to run on time when they had people like that to work with, most of those people didn't seem to care if the trains ran at all. This is a drama that has been played out whenever technology-based cultures have met archaic traditions, for people in isolated or underdeveloped areas, even within the US, tend to be Nines.

Nines are those of us who love to drift along with the breeze and take life as it comes. The cliché is that they are naturally spiritual, natural peacemakers, and as such they represent one of humanity's most natural tendencies. But it's a sedentary impulse with many problems, for like Sevens, Nines can be lotus-eaters, longing to dream their lives away, yearning for a world populated only by folks like themselves where no one is pushing them to do anything too taxing, while someone else puts his back to the wheel. The placid Buddha and the chubby Ho Tai are Nine figures, as is Winnie the Pooh.

The headlong rush of modern culture can reduce everything to a blur, which is what Nines react against, their ideal showing up in the Hawaiian *aloha* spirit or the Navajo sense of *hozho*—a soft, expansive way of embracing life. Yet the extreme Nine represents a degeneration of those values into a nebbish trance state. Melville's scrivener, Bartelby, is a Nine, and his is an extreme Nine's fate. But while Nines complain rightly enough that the rest of the world is dashing madly about, we read of Nines two or three hundred years ago—when things moved quite a bit slower—who couldn't get up in the morning and get much of anything done, farmers so "Nined-out" they couldn't get around to milking the cow in the morning, couldn't get crops planted in the spring and couldn't get the harvest in come autumn, as if the sun, moon and stars simply moved too fast for them. As a Nine once complained to me, this world just isn't made for Nines, and he's right. So, while it's unfortunate that modern culture is so frenzied, it seems if we were all to wake up as Nines one morning, a large percentage of the human race just might starve to death through lack of motivation.

There's a story that went around the New Age culture several years back in which a group of jungle tribesmen were taken on a trip by anthropologists only to have them all sit down at one point and refuse to go any further because they said they had to wait for their souls to catch up. While it's a touching story, it leaves us to question if it isn't simply that Nines lack the ability to move too quickly or for too long without losing all sense of themselves, that they have to stop and re-gather themselves after any significant degree of effort. It's little surprise that an element in some of their creation myths is that it was the introduction of ambition and greed that upset the harmony of the universe, for it's a Nine's assumption that ambition equals evil, greed and cruelty, which, considering their Eight wing, has a certain validity in Nine cultures. On the other hand, ambition also means having the motivation to move beyond habitual behavior, which extreme Nines find bewildering and threatening. So, while we see archaic cultures revering the ways of the forefathers, always looking to repeat the past, it can lead to what one writer calls "bovine torpor."

Overall, the Nine style presents humanity with a basic challenge, for we have to ask both individually and as a culture about the cost of progress versus the cost of not striving for much of anything at all. Archaeologists suggest early proto-humans went through a period of nothing much happening for a million years, just as the few remaining archaic cultures (Eliade's term) we see today have gone largely unchanged for centuries.

It's no wonder Nines are easily overwhelmed by modern culture. They're the people we see driving the interstate white-knuckled at forty miles an hour, or trying to cross a city street against traffic, looking terrified and confused. But it also means that planning things more than a few months out is a daunting challenge for a Nine-ish economy, which can be a major handicap in the business world. This led a journalist from a struggling country to declare that his people, including himself, needed to stop expecting their government to take care of them and start taking responsibility for themselves. So, while business people from Nine-ish countries demand inclusion in the global economy, their inability to manage long-range planning undermines their ability to come up to snuff, and the rest of the business community simply isn't willing to accommodate them.

At times a Nine's greatest desire is for the world to simply grind to a halt, and some seem determined to make it do exactly that by being deliberately obstructive. Extreme Nines don't just want to go slowly, for if the speed limit is 65, they'll go 50; if it's 45, they'll go 30. In other words, their instinct is not to go slowly, but to resist. We see it where a mother is trying to cross a busy street with her kid dragging along behind and fighting all the way, oblivious of the danger. And that kid is likely to find that resisting gives him such a sense of power that as an adult he'll sit for a moment when a traffic light changes to green just to reassure himself that he's driving on his own volition, not because the light is telling him to go, and certainly not because the guy behind is honking his horn. In fact, the guy honking his horn is likely to become a target of a Nine's rage: *I dare you to get impatient with me. I just dare you.*

Fundamentally, the Nine's resistance is due to their fear of losing their self-sense, and it shows up as a dread of stepping too far beyond their comfort level. That's why they will impulsively hit the brakes when the traffic light goes from red to green, even if they're not moving, as if freedom and open space are something to back away from. Limited options and lack of effort are reassuring to a Nine, so when life challenges them to take action, they'll look for something else to do, as if responding would mean a loss of self. A lot of us do that as teenagers, much to our parents' frustration.

So, while Fours may stand about in an emergency, anxiously flapping their hands, Nines are likely to freeze and stare in confusion because they have a hard time coming out of their haze. I was recently in the checkout line at our local library, and when the woman ahead of me was called up to the counter, she dropped her gaze to the floor and her entire body went slack for a moment before she stepped forward. That's Nine. Or you may see several employees behind a store counter, only one of whom is working a register while the checkout line goes down the aisle and around the corner. That's Nine, too.

Nines may learn as kids that when everyone else was getting ready to jump into the car to go somewhere, the one who took ten minutes to tie his shoelaces got to control everyone else with minimal effort. So, they develop passive-aggressive tendencies as a way of coping, priding themselves in how many cars are backed up behind them on a winding road, accelerating to racing speed when others have a chance to pass, then slowing back down when the road curves again. And they'll walk in slow-motion as if on display, then flare with indignation should others push their way past.

When Nines speak of dignity and pride, of serenity and peacefulness, they're describing their way of pumping up their balloons with deliberate slowness. Or more to the point, they're describing their way of protecting themselves from a world that feels overwhelming. On the other hand, with their Eight wing, they're capable of extraordinary rage should anyone violate the haze they've surrounded themselves with—some are capable of appalling violence when faced with serious problems because they just can't find any other solution. And stealing is far easier than constructive effort, which is why Nine-ish cultures tend to be graft- and corruption-based. So we hear aid workers, after working in a Third World country following a natural disaster, describing the population's habitual helplessness and sense of entitlement combined with a flair for unpredictable violence.

One question we have to ask about Nines in general, then, is whether they're really laid back and easy-going or if they aren't simply disconnected and secretly spiteful. This is what Paul Theroux describes in his novel, *Lower River*, portraying an extreme found in sub-Saharan cultures. But then J. D. Vance says in his *Hillbilly Elegy* that while one stereotypical image of a Welfare Queen is an angry, indolent and entitled black woman, the many Welfare Queens he'd known were all white—angry, indolent and entitled.

For all their resentment toward the mad rush of the world around them, the Nine style has been described as "self-forgetting," resulting in a slothful lifestyle while blaming others and demanding that someone else fix things for them. There's a fundamental human challenge in this, as archaic cultures typically see themselves as having existed since the beginning of time and therefore as sacred in nature. That's why they'll see anything new as a betrayal of the gods, just as western Christianity has in the past seen anything violating the way things have always been as inherently evil. It has been said that even in the countryside of Shakespeare's England anyone who could read and write could have been considered an enemy of the common people, a notion found in some parts of the world to this day.

While many Westerners today may see archaic cultures as

mystically appealing, others see them as intellectually stultifying and paralyzed by superstition. So, while Nines may wish for a return to the simplicity of Stone Age tribalism, they'll also see those who have gained from hard work and education as having betrayed some core aspect of humanity. This led Will Durant to comment that young people today with delayed emotional development are likely to take an "imaginative refuge" in the imagery of primitive societies as a way of escaping modern life.

Nine-ness can work fairly well on a tribal or village level, but not on an urban or national level, at least not in a modern context. Communism often appeals to Nines because they feel disenfranchised, oppressed, even enslaved by people more enterprising than themselves, not understanding how much they've disenfranchised themselves. But their notion of a communal society seems little more than a way of getting taken care of as if in parody of JFK's comment about the Soviets: *What's mine is mine, and what's yours belongs to everyone, especially me!* And anyone not willing to play along is just being selfish, for Nines can be like dry sponges trying to absorb whatever they can from the people around them. When a Nine asks to borrow something, they typically have no intention of ever giving it back.

Like Twos and Fours, Nines have a penchant for putting themselves in other peoples' way, but while Twos do it in a silky, seductive way, and Fours in a bristly, demanding way, Nines do it like a St. Bernard flopping down in a doorway. I recently watched a bulky young man in a restaurant amble for no apparent reason away from the counter where his parents were paying their bill, across the foyer to stretch and yawn in front of the entrance, his arms stretched wide like an elementary school crossing guard, his back to people coming through the doorway. It wouldn't have looked so odd if it hadn't been such an outlandishly deliberate act.

Benjamin Disraeli once said we are not creatures of circumstance, but the creators of circumstance. But a Nine's favored way of responding to many situations is to not respond at all, or as little as possible, hoping that if they do nothing long enough, it'll all just go away, or maybe someone will feel sorry for them or get frustrated enough to do things for them. But then they'll feel bewildered, even threatened by people who do take action, and are likely to try to coax others into sitting down and doing nothing just like a Nine would.

Thomas Friedman has referred to this in his *The World Is Flat*, relating how even when Third World leaders promote progressive programs, their own legislatures will often undermine them, apparently unwilling to risk an innovative solution that may take too much effort.

Nines can make themselves invisible by blending in with the furniture, then blame others for treating them that way, for self-sabotage is a Nine's forte, and where we're all challenged to react and adapt to changing situations, a Nine's impulse is to resist and resent. Their suspicion and resentment toward the world at large, especially toward ambitious and successful people, is a hallmark of Nines, for they love to stay rooted to one spot both physically and psychologically, insisting that a world that demands too much from them is a world that is inherently wrong.

Because so many poor, under-educated racial minority people are Nines, this tends by White culture to be seen as a racial issue, yet it's a personality dynamic that crosses racial and cultural lines. Hemingway's diatribe against Spanish men in *For Whom the Bell Tolls* and Cuban men in *To Have and Have Not* are his reaction to impoverished, uneducated Nines with aggressive Eight wings, which can be found in any culture. And it's no surprise that Nine-ish cultures are prone to domination by tyrannical Eights because anyone with enough incentive will wind up in charge whether they want to be or not. Conrad's *Lord Jim*, *Heart of Darkness* and many of his short stories are about this, and if someone's drive is to dominate, they'll find Nines easy pickings. It's also makes graft and bribery major factors in Nine-ish cultures: *Why work when I have so many other people to take advantage of?*

One thing Nines are challenged to learn is that rage is not power. Rather, it's what helpless, dependent people resort to when they don't know what else to do, and for all their placidity, Nines can carry deep rage, as does anyone feeling chronically disempowered. This is what we hear in Rudyard Kipling infamously describing people in what we now call the Third World as half devil, half child. Imperialist and racist Kipling may have been, but his comment can be made about Nines of any nation, race or gender.

Yet, it isn't that Nines are lazy. In fact they can be extraordinarily hard-working. Rather, the Nine's challenge is their overall sense of inner sluggishness. "Sloth" is a term used to describe them, although it's easily misinterpreted, for while Nines can be hard-working, they'll likely need someone to put the work in front of them without which they're likely to just wait for something to happen. Entire countries can fall to the fate Will Rogers spoke of in saying that even if you're on the right track, you'll get run over if you just sit there.

In Western culture, people often become Nines because of harsh childhood environments from which they'd had to shield themselves, their only defense available being to surround themselves with a mental fog through which nothing could reach them. Alternatively, people raised in isolation or in poverty often become Nines simply through lack of stimulation, for the person never challenged in childhood rarely learns to respond to challenge as an adult. The stereotype of the country bumpkin hostile to outsiders is a Nine.

For all the criticism, ridicule and blame aimed at Nines, most non-Nines are simply bewildered by Nine-ish behavior—bewildered, frustrated and enraged to the extent that they readily judge Nines as being inferior. It's unfortunately common for someone to go out of their way to help a Nine only to wind up angry at his unresponsiveness to his own problems. So, Nines find that others give up on them, communities tiring of being caretakers for the chronically helpless, people in shared group situations watching their belongings, energy and money disappear into the communal void, romantic partners complaining that being with a Nine is like swimming with a cinder block, aid workers getting back on the plane in frustration and despair, sometimes in abject terror.

The conflict Nines have with the rest of the world is fundamental because in many ways they represent the bedrock of humanity. We all know the urge to stop and smell the roses, and we all know the tendency to follow the dictates of tradition in the face of a technological culture that may not be able to sustain itself in the long run, anyway. We also thrill at scientific advancements and technology, yet feel the stress they bring, leaving us torn between losing ourselves to our frenetic lifestyles on one hand versus simply vegetating. It's a fundamental dilemma, for Nines represent a confrontation between modern humanity and its roots. As Graham Greene has one of his characters say about Vietnam, the people there had been living that way for thousands of years, and would be doing so long after the Western powers had disappeared. That, after all, is the Nine's forte.

While we as a culture are confronted with the cost of aspiring too highly, we have to consider the cost of failing to aspire at all. We all were once convinced by the childhood notion that if we needed something, then we had a right to it, and it was someone else's responsibility to provide for us, just as it was someone else's job to deal with the debris trail we'd left behind. Then, many of us were faced with that again when we went through a Nine phase during our teen years when it felt like everything was too much to deal with, and everything was unfair. And when we responded to common household chores by whining, "*Whyyyy?*", the answer is because we're moving into an adult world, and are challenged to be responsible like everyone else. Some of us, though, can spend a lifetime resisting that notion.

One of the great tragedies of world history is how technologically-advanced cultures as far back as the 15th century ruthlessly dominated Nine cultures, resulting in European colonization of the Americas and what we now call the Third World. And now we see issues of immigration where people are fleeing Nine-ish cultures that have failed to manage themselves, leaving their people to escape the poverty, violence, corruption and all manner of social ills that extreme Nine-ness creates. That leaves technologically-advanced cultures questioning how much Nine-ness they can absorb, fearing that immigration brings with it the very issues that had made those home countries such as mess. And all sides of the issue demonstrate an avoidance of responsibility: developed cultures irresponsible toward the consequences they've had on the Third World, Third World governments irresponsible toward their own people, and immigrant populations acting irresponsibly toward their host countries.

All this is accentuated by extreme Nines' expectation that any need on their part implies a right while seeing others' rights as tyranny and oppression—the mostly white hippie movement back in the Sixties held much of that attitude, as does today's neo-hippy culture. Their rage, though, reflects their underlying helplessness, and the only way they know to deal with it is to lash out and tell the world how wrong it is. Again, there is the double-edged question as to whether Nines really can't manage things for themselves, or that they simply dig in their heels and refuse. It's an age-old question, but Nines can often take it to imply that if others can take action and get things done, then they are obligated to provide for Nines. In its worst sense, the implication is: *If you have things that I don't, it's your fault, and you owe me.* And as stable nations feel flooded by immigrants escaping nightmares back home, the social repercussions can become significant. Yet it's hardly a new issue, for the ancient Romans, Greeks and Egyptians had their versions.

Yet, immigrants are looking for ways to salvage their lives, and are often willing to take on work people in their host countries refuse, and that can leave them feeling used and abused even while providing for the needs of the people who reject them. And Nines in Third World countries had felt used when European colonizers showed up with ships and guns a few centuries back, just as country folks feel to this day when the city slickers and developers show up in town. History has a way of coming back at us like that.

Those of us who are not Nines have a challenge to see Nines, even at their extremes, as equal human beings. This has been an issue throughout history, and not just across racial or cultural lines, for there has always been a tendency for non-Nines to see Nines as inferior, and the scars are obvious. But then every personality style has its own self-undermining ways, and its ways of justifying itself. We all have ways of resisting the life we find ourselves in, especially during out teens when we're likely to see even the most common demands life puts on us all as oppressive and wrong.

Yet, Nines offer the rest of humanity a much-needed mirror considering the helter-skelter lives so many of us create for ourselves. As Nines, our challenge is to interact with the world around us, to be responsible for our place in the world, and to apply ourselves beyond our habitual comfort level. That means starting with even the slightest challenges: setting goals for ourselves, making plans and carrying them out, focusing on completing things rather than applying minimal effort and walking away when it seems too much. While it may seem trivial to some, we see programs in Nine-ish communities teaching people those very things in order to help them out of the ruts they're in.

But to do that, most of us as Nines will have to wade through layers of resistance, for it confronts us with the reasons we'd numbed ourselves in the first place. We are challenged to own up to any passive-aggressive tactics, any tendency to feel powerful by resisting and obstructing others, any way in which we avoid effort, then trying to manipulate others into being responsible for us. And to do that we are likely to face a wide range of difficult feelings we've been avoiding for years—mainly despair, rage and the fear that drives it all. Those of us who are people of color still have to deal with serious racial prejudices, yet for all our complaints about being kept down by "the system," even white Nines are challenged to face how the thing that keeps us down the most is lodged inside ourselves. Most importantly, we're challenged to see that what we shield ourselves from is life itself, for it's our own aliveness that we resist more than anything.

And when a Nine can truly embrace life and aliveness in a deep way, they can become the peacemaker, the spiritual light, the solid rock for others that they have yearned to be all along.

PUTTING IT ALL TOGETHER

We are so small between the stars,
so large against the sky
~Leonard Cohen, *Stories of the Street*

It could be that the purpose of your life
is only to serve as a warning to others.
~despair.com

So, what can be the point of dissecting ourselves like this? Is it just about guilt and blame, wearing the hair shirt? Or is it about gaining ammunition to point out everyone else's faults? Well, this is tough, but then it has to be, because most human conflicts come down to a matter of raw impulses running into each other.

No matter our resistance, there are times that simply realizing what needs to change engages a mysterious process that can be profound, percolating away under the surface of our awareness until it surprises everyone, especially ourselves. At the start I said this is all about mirrors, for life consistently presents us with reflections we typically avoid until something forces us to face all the things we've tried to not see about ourselves. This is what this work is about, for in order to make significant change in our lives, we have to know what it is that needs changing. And while it's not easy, what life does to us when we refuse its mirrors is harder yet.

As before, we typically stand within a bubble created by our own personal dynamics so that while we think we're looking out at the world around us, we're actually looking at ourselves projected onto what we think of as reality. Some of us will fight to preserve and defend that reality, even with appalling violence, convinced we're upholding noble causes, even cosmic truths. All of us, not just the fantasy-prone, are prone to assuming that whatever is in our head defines reality, for any of us is susceptible to mistaking fantasy for intellect. And the urgency and rage we're likely to display rise out of the fear that our "reality" may turn out to be deluded, and that is fear, indeed.

Yet, the naivete we experience when we're younger can be compelling because it's so often accompanied by glorious feelings and a sense of magic and mystery that can make a stable, grounded attitude seem dull and lifeless. That in itself can have us resenting adulthood as a betray of the aliveness we feel, not realizing the cost it can exact on us. Yet, with environmental degradation becoming such a significant factor in today's world, we're all challenged to face the combination of need and entitlement we bring with us out of childhood. So, while one of Leonard Cohen's more accusatory songs says, "...*take the only tree that's left and shove it up the hole in your culture,*" it speaks to many of the passionate feelings we all have at some point, especially in adolescence, expecting others, even life itself, to fill the holes we don't want have to feel. Cultures, after all, are simply expressing the dynamics common to their populations.

I have mentioned the work of Alfred Adler and the field of coaching based on his work, yet the approach I've taken here is distinctly non-Adlerian. This is because it's easy for us to avoid the life challenges that can move us forward in our lives without our realizing it. Yet one of Adler's stances that runs throughout this work is the dual need to develop our individual lives while participating in a social group. But staunch individualism can turn to social irresponsibility and arrogance while being part of a group consciousness can lead to individual irresponsibility, even cultism. Current ideologies such as the sovereignty movement and conspiracy theories indicate an inability or outright refusal to embrace social needs while the notion that we're all one is too often distorted by being so disconnected that the world around us becomes a blur, or by obsessing on feelings to the extent that it all becomes a blur in a somewhat different way.

Another notion Adler and Rudolph Dreikurs promoted is that we make our own meaning of what we experience, especially as children when our understanding is so limited. And the meanings we make can undermine our lives as adults, even when we make those meanings as adults.

All things considered, there are a few basic things to face regarding these human psyches we've been born with. For one thing, human psyches, even at their level best, are a bit squirrely. And history has shown us that we humans are often not very nice people, especially when we think we're being noble and righteous.

A crude synopsis of the developmental process we're faced with is that in childhood we develop notions of how life is supposed to be based partly on our early experiences, partly on a blueprint imbedded in our nervous systems at birth. Our challenge, then, is to develop more depth and range to our experience of life, and to grow the invisible musculature to carry that experience. Otherwise, we're likely to try to dictate how others are supposed to live their lives: *You're not supposed to be the way you are, you're supposed to be the way I want you to be!* That's a common dynamic for a small child, and it starts the first time Mommy puts us down and walks away, leaving us with the realization that she's not really an extension of ourselves after all.

The challenge is to expand our blueprint, and that can be a lifetime's work, for most human problems result from a failure to carry ourselves into adult life. That leaves us confronted with a world that refuses to meet the expectations and demands that had had a place in our lives when we were children.

Our experience of life gradually morphs as we grow from infancy toward adulthood, building better ego strength, a fuller, deeper self-sense. That means we don't change by changing our thinking, feeling and beliefs so much as our thinking, feeling and beliefs change as we get better at dealing with life. In short, we change by developing better ego strength. That's why the notion of rising above "egotism" doesn't really represent the process we go through. Egotism is a label we apply to childhood needs and expectations in an adult, and we change by moving forward, not by levitating.

Another way of describing our development out of childhood is that we all have ways of carrying a common mantra that at least silently chants: *My Way! It's supposed to be My Way!* Even as reasonably competent adults, that mantra will still be chanting in the background of our lives although it will have faded to whisper that no longer drives us like it once had. Rather, life demands that we learn to collaborate with the mantras chanting away in other people's heads while they learn to collaborate with ours.

As ever, it takes ego strength and emotional maturity to collaborate, and having things our way becomes less significant as we grow into this life. Life doesn't work anybody's way, and it doesn't owe us, for our job is to work our way into the world we find ourselves in rather than expecting the world to cater to us.

Said a bit differently, ego strength is a matter of developing our vehicle, the carriage with which to carry ourselves through life, for without it we'll have no true freedom and no true sense of choice. This is what we see in our current culture regarding, for instance, the COVID-19 pandemic where so many people see reasonable restrictions as denying them their rights. When we lack ego strength, as we do as children, we know only to give in or rebel, which can leave us looking for freedom in all the wrong places. Yes, there are valid complaints about losses of freedom, but an underdeveloped mind has a hard time grasping the difference between oppression and common sense.

In the same way, we have no true choices in life without ego strength, for we'll be driven by impulse far more than by reason, convinced our impulses define reality. The same applies to being open to change—a popular theme in the New Age culture—for true personal changes come from developing ego strength, not through high-minded philosophies. A large part of the process is that as we gain an increased sense of self, we need less—less attention, less control, less need to be right in order to prop ourselves up, and we're less likely to resent others for faults we all have.

Failing this, we'll typically want to solve anything from personal issues to world problems by trying to tell others how to think properly, telling them how and what to feel, or simply forcing them to behave by the rules we dictate. These are the three patterns Adler outlined, while the Enneagram breaks things down into finer detail, but the intention is the same—to show us our own pitfalls, which is never an easy or comfortable thing to do.

It's inevitable that we're challenged to reevaluate our past, which brings to mind a quote from Brendan Gill, who writes: "If the unexamined life is not worth living, the unexamined past is not worth possessing; it bears fruit only by being held continuously up to the light, and is as changeable and as full of surprises, pleasant and unpleasant, as the future."

Breaking out of old patterns means stepping out of our comfort zone, the conundrum being that it builds ego strength to do that, but it takes ego strength to even begin, which is why it's so hard for us to face as children, even as teens. Human psyches are slow to change in any case, but without enough ego strength to begin with, we'll fight against useful insights, feeling criticized, blamed and oppressed instead. This is why I've attempted to pose this material as a way of gaining personal awareness rather than as a way of blaming others.

A large part of the challenge is that the normal plan is to develop ego strength throughout the early decades of our lives, but the reality is that we do an incomplete job, then have to play catch-up when we're confronted with the weak links in our chains. And catch-up means we have to move more quickly than the earlier growing-up process, which is difficult.

Another way of describing our developmental process is with an old therapy analogy that an underdeveloped psyche is like a house with three walls, trying to create a sense of wholeness in ways that generally don't work. As children, we typically use our mothers as our fourth wall, then go on to glom onto lovers, political stances, philosophies and religion the same way we'd glommed onto Mommy. And it's not that any of those lovers, political stances, philosophies or religions are at fault, simply that we need to develop our psyches rather than trying to find solid ground outside ourselves. A truth fourth wall to our structure is created by engaging in the life going on around us, for that's how we develop ego strength, a more complete sense of self.

We have all heard the word "wisdom" used in many ways, but wisdom in its truest sense is not a matter of high-minded words, but simply a matter of mature ego strength, of having a self-sense not dependent on possessions, material or otherwise. There's an old Taoist saying that the Great Way is easy if we don't have preferences, which can be reworded to say that it's easy if we don't try to use the stuff of the world to create a fourth wall for us. In much the same way, the Buddhist stance that suffering is created by desire can be reworded to say that suffering results from trying to feel whole in ways that fail, that obsessive desire amounts to attempts to feel whole in ways that don't work. Along the same lines, the uplifting messages popular in today's spiritual marketplace do little more than convince us that wisdom is a matter of pretty words, which while lovely in themselves, fail in the long run. And none of it is ever enough, for most of our attempts to feel whole simply miss the mark as we aim at false targets.

We are all challenged to pay deep attention to life, to rein ourselves in and realize that our version of life is simply that: it's just our version of life, and no one is obligated to bend to it or tolerate it. One thing breaking down personality styles can show us is how the things that give us a sense of well-being can be the very things that drive others up the wall. At its worst, our habitual style is a trance state that we're likely to defend even as it undermines our life. We see the same thing on a cultural level, for every culture prides itself in itself while justifying its weaknesses by blaming others. As with the individual, so with the many.

It can be surprising, considering most of the notions we find in religious and therapy circles, that there are three powerful teachers in life that most of us want nothing to do with: fear, if not outright terror; anger, if not outright rage; and pain, if not outright trauma. But it's not about being scared, angry or in pain; rather that if we penetrate those experiences they can reveal deeper places in us that are difficult to access any other way. If nothing else, these extremes can break through the drone of our lives in startling ways.

Of course all this is an over-simplification, yet simplifications both reveal and conceal, and while discussions of this sort can deteriorate into blaming and complaining, everyone complains about everyone else anyway. Just as a culture's mythology explains and justifies that culture, our personal style is a mythology through which we view life, assuming all others to be bad, wrong, stupid, evil, or just plain crazy.

So, the intention is to reveal aspects of ourselves to ourselves, to create a level playing field where we're all equal in having faults, for personal growth only happens when we recognize there's a problem with our habits. Emotional maturity involves the ability to come to terms with our own worst traits while accepting human frailties in others, and perhaps the best we can do is to simply see humanity as humanity, which requires emotional intelligence, ego strength, emotional maturity or whatever name we wish to give it.

The process is an invisible one, and it's always a bit mysterious, something that's difficult to take in hand. In the old Grimm Brothers' fairy tales, a young prince or princess has to undergo seemingly impossible labors or wear out a hundred pairs of shoes wandering endless roadways, implying an unexplained and mysterious journey that takes decades. So, we're left facing new landscapes without much by the way of maps, and it's always a puzzle, one we can only live in and never truly solve.

And it has little to do with our conscious thinking or strongest feelings, for many of our habitual thoughts and feelings simply justify our maintaining an habitual stance. This is why many approaches to therapy and personal growth fail, for they fail to go to the heart of the matter, leaving us trying to dictate to a world we don't understand anywhere near as well as we like to think.

Generally, it comes down to a simple statement: Whatever you're used to doing, learn to do the opposite. It's tempting to say: Whatever you're used to doing, just don't do it! But that's a nearly impossible task, for the best we can do is to rein ourselves to some extent. Yet even the slightest interruption of our habits can have us experiencing life differently enough to loosen our hold on what we think will give us a sense of security and identity.

This is why anyone who claims to have far-reaching answers to the problems of humanity is not only fooling himself, but will likely make a fool of himself. The best we can do is to take long looks in the mirrors that life presents us and make some tough choices.

In the final analysis, it comes down to willpower and discipline, for we're required to have the strength of character to see our own lives clearly, and to have the strength of will to act on more mature dynamics, not on the familiar, habitual ones when they become a problem.

CHAPTER NINE

~THE ONGOING CHALLENGE~

> ... *the end of all our exploring*
> *will be to arrive where we started,*
> *and know the place for the first time.*
> ~T.S. Elliot, *The Wasteland*

> *Even monkeys fall from trees.*
> ~Japanese proverb

To repeat an earlier theme, the first great challenge of being human is the most obvious of all—that we get born as infants, and it doesn't stay that way. And the person who fails to face that most basic challenge will not only spend much of his time torturing everyone around him, but will fail to truly embrace his own life.

For all the negatives, the outstanding question is what it would be like if we consciously acted in a mature, reasonable and responsible manner. Yet even at our best we can find ourselves acting on immature impulses while our better nature takes a back seat. So, while people debate religion, philosophy and politics, each trying to change the other's mind and feelings, what truly changes our thinking and feeling is being forced beyond where we've been habitually rooted, and debate rarely does that.

As the old saying goes, good judgment comes from experience, and experience comes from bad judgment. So, it's not in changing the way we think that our lives change, although centuries of philosophical and religious rankling have tried to do just that, but in having a different life experience.

Another factor is that overpopulation affects us in ways we can barely comprehend. While in prehistoric times we wandered plains and forests, rarely encountering other humans, we now wander a wilderness of crowds and cars and buildings and telephone poles, all of it becoming a faceless blur. Moreover, in older times we lived for the most part in cultural enclaves where most people thought, felt and believed much the same way as each other, as opposed to the mish-mash of cultural blending we see today. So, it's little wonder that we tend to see each other on the sidewalks and highways as objects and obstacles rather than as people in their own right. But seeing others as people in their own right requires emotional and intellectual maturity, and in watching the impulses that so often rule the modern day, it's hard not to wonder if population density in itself doesn't inhibit our development. It's worth pondering, especially as our visiting Martian anthropologist may well conclude that crowded living drives us to stark raving madness.

One thing we learn as children is that the people who are the cruelest to kids are usually other kids, for one of the great shocks that hits us in preschool or kindergarten is running into other children who seem to be out to get us for reasons we can't understand. Perhaps this is why many of us have dreams of finding ourselves at school naked. In a moment of honesty, Steven King tells how he, too, had been one of the guys to torture the already suffering kid he later used as the source of his novel, *Carrie.*

Having that ruthlessness aimed at us by another child presents many of us with our first realization of the viciousness of the world, and many of us were ill-equipped to face it, feeling abandoned and betrayed by the adult world that failed to do anything about it. Then some of us learned that the way to survive was to become ruthless ourselves, while others of us learned to manipulate, evade and skulk our way through life. But the thing that forces us to grow up more than anything else is our participation in life with all its relentless demands and unforgiving sharp edges.

Nearly two and a half millennia ago, Plato wrote that our mind is like a charioteer driving two horses, one well-disciplined, the other rampant and wild, and it's clear that human nature hasn't changed in all that time, except that there are now more of us wanting to ride a wild pony and avoid paying a price for it. Actually, the old Greeks had some pretty fair notions about quite a few things. Beyond being a war story, Homer's *Iliad* is a tale about narcissistic rage and self-indulgence in which a cast of self-centered characters is challenged to come to terms with themselves, and they generally fail. Helen is just beginning to understand the responsibility she bears, Paris is an irresponsible punk, and Achilles is a spoiled brat out to prove he's the gods' gift to the world despite his one brief lapse into decency near the end. And before the tale even begins, the source of all the trouble is the intrusion of cosmic jealousy and discord into the human scene, as if it's simply human fate that the gods can and will undo us on a mere whim. Is that a reflection of a conflict between parents before their child was even conceived? Then there's the tale of Theseus working his way out of the labyrinth by retracing his steps like Hansel and Gretel, hinting at our dilemma in getting lost in this human maze and the challenge to work our way out of it.

Thoreau said a man must take responsibility for his face past the age of forty, for this is the point where we look in the mirror and ask ourselves, perhaps with a sense of horror: *What have I become?* In trying to prove himself, though, a young man will try at first to prove what he's not: *I'm not a geek. I'm not a number. I'm not a Lady Gaga fan.* But whether he feels like a cog in the machine isn't a result of how the world treats him so much as it's a result of how developed his self-sense is.

At any rate, we're all challenged to go beyond our comfort zones, for that's where we learn to embrace life more fully. That means taking decisive action, even if it means making a few stupid mistakes, for stupid mistakes can teach us quite a lot while taking no action at all will leave us to stagnate. That's the fate an immature person has to face sooner or later, looking back on a discarded life when it's too late to do anything about it.

Here's an excerpt from a something that came over the Internet one day:

Life is short, very short. Missing out on any of the joy life offers is a tragedy. Courage is the mental muscle that conquers fear. Like all muscles, the more you use it, the stronger it becomes. Courage is not something you are born with: it must be developed. Individuals who fail to develop courage remain confined in mental prisons and face each day as mental lightweights.

For years, I believed that courageous individuals had no fear. I was wrong. Eddie Rickenbacker put it very well when he said, "There is no courage without fear." We all have fear. However, not everyone becomes subservient to their fears. Remember, life is not a practice run. This is it. Observe those poor souls who are without courage. They merely tiptoe through life hoping they make it safely to death. You and I were never meant to live that way.

And here's a piece from a business in the Denver area, presented in a little pamphlet looking like the sort of thing you might find in a phone booth advertising some get-rich-quick scheme, entitled, "The Secret of How to Make Money:"

Go to work! If you are poor, work. If you are rich, continue to work. If you are burdened with seemingly unfair responsibilities, work. If you are happy, keep right on working. Idleness gives room for doubts and fear. If disappointments come, work. If sorrow overwhelms you, and loved ones are not true, work. When faith falters and reason fails, just work. When dreams are shattered and hope seems dead, work. Work as if your life were in peril: it really is. No matter what ails you, work. Work faithfully, work with faith. Work is the greatest remedy available. Work will cure both mental and physical afflictions. Thank God every morning when you get up that you have something to do which must be done whether you like it or not. Being forced to work and forced to do your best will breed in you temperance, self-control, diligence, strength of will, contentment, and a hundred other virtues which the idle will never know.

As Timothy Gallwey tells us, work isn't about being constrained, but about the freedom to learn, grow and gain a sense of fulfillment. And Alfred Adler tells us that right from early childhood we yearn for a sense of belonging and significance, a sense of usefully participating. Interestingly, students acknowledged for their intelligence generally aren't willing to face new challenges, while those acknowledged for their hard work are.

George Bernard Shaw topped them all with this often-quoted statement:

This is the true joy in life, being used for a mighty purpose; being a force of nature instead of a feverish selfish little clod of grievances complaining the world will not devote itself to making me happy. I am of the opinion that my life belongs to the whole community and as long as I live, it is my privilege to do for it whatever I can. I want to be thoroughly used up when I die; the harder I work, the more I live. I rejoice in life for its own sake. Life is no brief candle. It is a sort of splendid torch which I hold for the moment and I want to make it burn as brightly as possible before handing it on to future generations.

Adler emphasized three areas of life we need to address: personal intimate relationships, group social relationships and work, three areas that test us and pull us out of our childhood versions of life. In this we are challenged to develop both as individuals and as part of a social whole. Most of us remember our first faltering steps in each of these arenas, work being the one that compels us most strongly to stop focusing on our personal feelings and expectations. Yet this isn't to say that work alone matures a person, as there are plenty of childishly self-centered people in the workplace, nor is it a matter of the work-for-the-good-of-the-collective mantra of the failed Soviet Union, nor that we need to wear a hair shirt when it comes to our work ethic. It's simply that work is a way of putting aside our self-obsession and take to participating in the life around us. All work and no play may make Jack a dull boy, but all play and no work will keep him a boy. Besides, as Shaw also said, the more we work, the more we live. Or as Eugene O'Neill once said, work can be more fun than fun itself.

The overarching question is how to develop ego strength in an immature adult. One answer is to go against expectations we've held over from childhood, and one gift the world of work has to offer is that it provides us a way of acting as active agents in life rather than as passive subjects or targets of a hostile world. That means moving through cycles of setting goals, initiating actions and carrying through to accomplish and attain successes, then setting new goals, new plans and taking new actions. Even if the goals and successes seem small, it's the process that's important, for any way we can pull ourselves free from our habits can prove significant.

So, this isn't so much about working through past issues as it's about taking ownership of our lives and consciously moving forward. After all, as children our options were fairly limited, and even if we did have choices available to us, we typically didn't know it. And it brings to mind the traditional Japanese sword-making technique of subjecting steel to the fire, folding it over and beating it into itself, then repeating the process to produce a blade both flexible and strong. In the same way, life has a way of forcing us between the hammer and anvil, while lack of involvement keeps us resenting and distrusting the world around us. Besides, if we don't know how to maintain an income, adult life can be overwhelming, recalling the old Japanese adage that a man with money is a dragon, while a man without it is a worm. Above all, work is the best way for a man to overcome the damage done by emasculation and narcissistic parenting, because as another old adage says, the best way to get even with lousy parents is to succeed in spite of them.

While many of us feel intimidated by the corporate world, it's actually fairly easy to succeed there because the person who applies a reasonable degree of effort and responsibility will gain quickly respect. And if you are straightforward and admit to a mistake, your supervisor may fall off his or her chair in astonishment. The reason is that so few employees *are* diligent and straightforward that it's not all that hard to stand out. But then it's important to see supervisors and managers as people engaged in business rather than as adversaries or parental figures out to oppress us, for that single shift in attitude can change our entire world outlook, as it's now viewed through the eyes of an adult rather than those of a defiant child.

Going cold turkey from our habits means breaking with things that had given us comfort or a sense of power when we were young. Our natural process is to build upon bonds we'd developed in infancy so we can carry into adulthood an innate sense of security. The problem, though, is when we gain comfort and in ways that have kept us stuck, so that in order to move forward we have to break with at least part of our original security. Whenever our normal movement out of childhood has been stymied, we have to force ourselves to complete the process on our own, and that requires the psychological equivalent of a crowbar. That's what work and sort of constructive effort become—things with which to pry ourselves loose.

That's especially true for those of us raised under narcissistic parenting, for we have to break childhood bonds that right from the outset had undermined our development. One thing that can break a person loose is anger. Initially it's anger directed at him that jars him out of his complacency, making him realize why he compels others to want to take him by the scruff of the neck and shake him. And while his own anger may be initially at a parent, it's his anger about his own situation that will move him forward. Basically, he has to get pissed off about being stuck. And when a person can face his frustration with the imprints he carries, his frustration with the world around him diminishes, for he hasn't been fighting the world out there so much as he's been fighting his image of it.

We're also challenged to change how we carry ourselves in life.

This is one of the things about which the image-conscious are correct, that if we dress like a bum, we'll think and feel like a bum; if we dress like a kid, we'll act like one; if our house is a mess, our life will be one too. And if we insist on thinking like a teenager, we'll live a teenager's life—resentful, complaining and indolent. That's why we'll find it unsettling to see an adult's home full of childish images, anything from women's silly gewgaws to men's rock and roll memorabilia, for they can keep them stuck in childish attitudes. Yet, we see an embarrassing abundance of childish imagery in everything from computer clipart, advertisements and movies.

Moreover, if we feel chronically helpless, or if we go through life feeling suffocated, we've probably been creating ways to suffocate ourselves and make ourselves helpless. Going cold turkey from habits like that requires self-discipline in even the most trivial things. Even replacing an empty toilet paper roll instead of leaving it for someone else can say something about the attention we pay to our lives, for it's through addressing the little things that the big things change, countering the anti-incentives we've built up since childhood. Remember the movie scene where Jennifer Aniston's soon-to-be-ex-boyfriend asks her why would he ever *want* to do the dishes? The answer is more important than an immature person understands, for while high school and college may have failed to mature us, washing the dishes can work wonders.

Some tips for going cold turkey include cutting out of our lives anything that maintains our habits. For example:

* Give up your TV addiction: As one bumper sticker says, *Kill your television!* Even at its best, TV gives us an artificial experience of life, so stop it. At the very least, cut out the music videos, cartoons and mindless sitcoms. Above all, cut out all those movies that tell us it's cool to go through life as chronic teenagers. Sophisticated drama that requires insight and inspires deeper feelings may be alright, but sophisticated fantasy is still fantasy. Instead, the next time you turn on the TV, the stereo, or the computer game, ask what you could be doing instead. Seriously ask yourself if you want to use up your life in this way. And I really do mean *use it up*.

* By the same token, get rid of the computer games. Period. Just get

rid of them. Life happens outside the computer screen.

* Shut off the rock and roll and anything else that seems more appealing than the world around you. Especially get the ear buds out of your ears because they shut out everything else. Life is what's happening outside, and if you're on an artificial high most of the time, you'll miss the better part of everything.

* Look at all your relationships that have tanked in pretty much the same way. and stop blaming all those other people. We're all bound to find things about ourselves that we can't change, but we can at least take responsibility for them and stop inflicting ourselves on others.

* Look at your images of power, and look at the repercussions you've had on other people as you strive for it. What's the strength you need to develop instead of trying to be powerful? Do something constructive, creative or helpful, and watch for any part of you that doesn't want to.

* Listen to your language, and pay attention to how it affects your expectations. If you believe the adolescent hype that says there are no limits, you'll never have your feet on the ground. And if you philosophize about *the* heart instead of your own, you'll probably live in the clouds.

* We also need to take a hard look at our politics, morality, spirituality and philosophy with an eye toward asking how much of it is an expression of self-responsibility, and how much is little more than childish expectations in disguise.

* By the same token, pay attention to what you have taken in from TV and movies, especially paying attention to how much of it represents men either as mindless bullies or as incompetent little boys who have to sneak around and lie to their wives or girlfriends. We may not have a hand in writing that garbage, but we can refuse to

watch it.

* The next time you feel like complaining or criticizing someone, ask yourself what is it that you've been wanting that person to do for you that you really need to do for yourself. Or in what way are you asking that person to change so you don't have to?

* By the same token, no matter how confident you are in what you are doing with your life, ask who may be paying a price for it, who might be carrying the burden of your luxury, contentment or inactivity?

* Look for things that need to be done, and do them without complaining about whose job it's supposed to be. Pick up other people's litter, take back other people's shopping carts, wash the dishes and finish every task not because you want to, but because someone needs to do it, and it may as well be you. Yes, you're doing things for some slug who won't do it for himself, but get used to it. You'll spend the rest of your life doing it, anyway. Besides, it'll do you a world of good. Give other drivers a break rather than charging at them like a battering ram, and pay attention to the debris trail you leave for someone else to deal with.

* By the same token, learn to let others carry their own burdens when they need to, let them struggle when it serves their growth. This is especially important for those of us who grew up taking emotional care of a manipulative parent, taking their needs on as our burden. In that case, learning when to leave others to their own struggles can be one of the best learning experiences we can ever have.

* In any questionable situation, ask yourself what would a mature, responsible person do? To play on a New Age cliché, remember that maturity brings out everything unlike itself.

Growing Up

Teachers are my lessons done? I cannot do another one.
They laughed and laughed and said, 'Well, child?
Are your lessons done?'
~Leonard Cohen, *Teachers*

I never live with balance,
though I've always liked the notion
~Bruce Cockburn, *Open*

Yet another piece that came over the Internet one day goes like this:

Twenty-five Signs That Prove You've Grown Up:

1. Your houseplants are alive and you can't smoke any of them.

2. Having sex in a twin bed is out of the question.

3. You keep more food than beer in the fridge.

4. 6:00 AM is when you get up, not when you go to bed.

5. You hear your favorite song on an elevator.

6. You watch the Weather Channel.

7. Your friends marry and divorce instead of hook up and break up.

8. You go from 130 days of vacation to 14.

9. Jeans and a sweater no longer qualify as "dressing up."

10. You're the one calling the police because those damn kids next door won't turn down the stereo.

11. Older relatives feel comfortable telling sex jokes around you.

12. You don't know what time Taco Bell closes anymore.

13. Your car insurance goes down and your car payments go up.

14. You feed your dog Science Diet instead of McDonald's leftovers.

15. Sleeping on the couch makes your back hurt.

16. You no longer take naps from noon to 6:00 pm

17. Dinner and a movie is the whole date instead of the beginning of one.

18. Eating a basket of buffalo wings at 3:00 AM would severely upset rather than settle your stomach.

19. You go to the drug store for ibuprofen and antacid, not condoms and pregnancy tests.

20. A $4.00 bottle of wine is no longer "pretty good stuff."

21. You actually eat breakfast food at breakfast time.

22. "I just can't drink the way I used to," replaces, "I'm never going to drink that much again."

23. 90% of the time you spend in front of a computer is for real work.

24. You no longer drink at home to save money before going to the bar.

25. You read this entire list looking desperately for one sign that doesn't apply to you.

What stands out in these bits of web wisdom is that for all their flippancy, they're coming from guys who've had to face the climb from adolescence to adulthood, and have embraced it with a combination of pain, frustration and humor. So, it comes to this:

Think you're hot shit, kid? So did we at your age. Just wait 'til life rakes you over the coals for a few decades, then we'll sit down and talk. Okay?

Bette Davis once said that old age isn't for sissies. Well, life itself isn't, and if we can't face that, we'll resist and resent a good deal, blaming the world for not being the way it's supposed to be.

Dad

There's an old saying that a man isn't truly a man until his father has died, if for no other reason than it leaves him feeling that a large piece of his psychic support, or at least the hope for it, has fallen away forever. The thought is hardly a new one, as Shakespeare portrayed it in *Henry IV* where the dissolute young prince grows up in a hurry upon taking the throne. Nor is it limited by gender, as novelist Deborah Crombie has one of her characters (in *Dreaming the Bones*) relate how the death of her mother has forced her to grow up "kicking and screaming like a child."

Gabriel Garcia-Marquez writes that a man is old when he realizes how much he looks like his father—looks like, feels like, laughs like, sighs like, farts like. As kids we'll covet Dad's stuff, his guns and tools and fishing gear, maybe his house, but when we actually inherit all that stuff, we may find we don't want it anymore. What we'd really wanted was his adult maleness, and in having his stuff, we find it's just stuff, that the rest is something we'll still have to find for ourselves.

Past adolescence, we succeed or fail on our own merits, and we eventually need to succeed not at things expected by others, but at things demanded by life itself. And as we age, our fathers' lives become the Thoreau's mirror into which we wind up staring. But a father's lack of ego strength becomes a weak spot in the son's psyche as well. That's why feeling neglected by his dad and other men leaves a boy with a poor footing in life. The same is true for the boy who feels defeated by his dad, for a bullying father will generate either a child bent on beating the old man at his own game and learn to bully others, or one driven to passivity. But the bullying kid still doesn't have any true sense of his own maleness, only a sense that every other male is a threat.

On the other hand, most of the things a father gives his son are so intangible that it can take well into adulthood to appreciate them. In spite of their faults, fathers provide inner strength simply by being there, and lacking that support leaves a boy with an emptiness that can take him a lifetime to deal with. The old notion that the virility of the father shows in the health of his sons has practical value in that it's the psychological health of a father that's reflected in his sons' lives.

Ironically, the man who grew up as a geek is often compelled far more than others to gain an understanding of himself because he can't afford not to. He may have a hard time breaking out of that shell, but in the long run he'll be far ahead in being able to see the common faults we all share, having had to spend so much time facing his own. Besides, the football stars and beauty queens tend to become old geeks, while some who started out as geeks age like wine.

The father we internalize affects our sense of the future, as the traditional father wanted to build a legacy for his children and grandchildren. Unfortunately, that tendency has faded, for lacking the strength of character to take our focus off immediate gratification, many of us have become prodigal fathers, using up family resources just as we use up the environment, leaving no land, no businesses, no savings and no plan for coming generations.

The Chinese merchant classes understood this long ago, realizing that a man's wealth would be squandered by following generations, that unearned wealth can lead to decadence in the children unless something is ingrained into their culture to prevent it. Their solution was to live frugally, even dressing as if they were poor, and it worked for them to a fair extent, a lesson our profligate modern times could stand to learn.

An old story comes to mind in which an interviewer, probably expecting some sort of public relations statement, once asked Conrad Hilton if there was anything he would like to say to his hotel guests, to which he replied that, yes, he wanted to remind them to make sure the shower curtain stayed on the inside of the tub. The point is that people who create major businesses keep their minds on practical matters while the heirs who spend that fortune often have attention only for their narcissism.

A fitting metaphor is in the Greek fable of the man who, like an obstreperous child, cut down a sacred tree only to be condemned to such endless hunger that he wound up eating himself. That's what modern culture seems bent on doing, devouring itself along with everything else in sight.

The Rights of Man and Woman

One great outcry worldwide is of people demanding their rights, and though a noble cause in itself, demanding rights is the first line of defense for those attempting to live irresponsibly, even criminally, the cry of those first to deprive others of their rights. It's a tendency that's especially true in the West where few of us have ever had to face serious tyranny.

At issue is the question as to what is a personal right versus what's just a sense of entitlement, and that's an issue as old as philosophy itself. The democracy of the ancient Greeks was only for those deemed worthy of it, and to be a member of the Spartan senate you had to be at least sixty years old (the word "senate" translates roughly as a gathering of old men), and a man in Athens didn't have political power until he'd reached thirty. The Greeks were well aware of the capacity of rational beings to be irrational, which is why only those competent enough to behave responsibly were considered proper citizens, only those willing and able to work for the good of the *polis* qualifying for citizenship. Our modern notions of democracy would have horrified them, although they did fall short of their own ideals. Even the democracy of the founding fathers of the United States was nowhere near as generous as what we take for granted today.

So, we hear a criminal raging about his inalienable rights, declaring himself a political prisoner, the murderer raging at the court that no one has the right to treat him this way, a man shot to death while attacking the judge in the courtroom, a corporate executive accused of draining his company's resources and pillaging his employee's pension fund pouting: *How dare you accuse me?*

We see it in issues ranging from the trivial to the outrageous. I recently watched a woman raging at a man in a parking lot because he'd had the audacity to confront her for parking in a handicap space: *How dare you?* she'd stormed. And a foreign national who has overstayed her visa by several years and is threatened with deportation rages that she has a right to live wherever she wants, although in some countries she'd have been dragged to the border long ago, perhaps with a gun to her head.

It's human nature to justify whatever we want with overblown grandiosity and indignation. We've seen the likes of Slobodan Milosevic and Saddam Hussein declaring that no one has the right to take them to task for fomenting genocide, and we've heard North Koreans admitting they'd kidnapped and murdered Japanese citizens, that they'd broken international agreements, then demanding foreign aid to compensate for their incompetence.

Closer to home, an author noted that if we were to act on a personal level the way advertisers do, we would be shocked at each other's behavior, yet we accept it every day in our consumer culture. Imagine your friends and neighbors trying to bluff you at every sentence, trying to squeeze another obligation or another dollar out of you.

The culture-wide acceptance of childish expectations also shows up in the number of frivolous lawsuits we see, which is little wonder considering the outlandish awards handed out for some remarkably stupid things. One result is the Stella Awards (named for the woman who successfully sued the McDonalds restaurant chain after being burned by the cup of coffee she'd spilled on herself), addressing people who'd successfully sued people they'd tried to rob, people who'd been injured through their own behavior, the guy who sued the owner of the dog that bit him after he'd tormented it, people who'd successfully sued the manufacturers of products they had foolishly misused.

An immature mind always sees someone else as responsible, then complains about being disenfranchised, and although it's sometimes a valid complaint, an immature person will disenfranchise himself through his own fecklessness and incompetence. So, when we see leaders of impoverished nations spending fortunes on palaces, predatory governments driving their populations to despair, or executives spending recklessly while their corporations spiral into bankruptcy, we have to wonder. And it applies to the way we drive, for as a bumper sticker declares, safe driving is a civic duty, but try telling that to the kid tailgating you at seventy miles an hour with a cell phone to her ear.

There's a conservative versus liberal element in this in which two clichés are relevant. The first, attributed to Winston Churchill among others, is that if we're not liberal when we're young, there's something wrong with our hearts, while if we're not conservative when we're older, there's something wrong with our heads. The other cliché is that liberals fear power while conservatives fear powerlessness. But then conservatives are often seen as bullies contemptuous of others' needs while liberals are often seen as whiners playing at being helpless in order to get their way. Both extremes want to act without repercussions while blaming anyone trying to hold them accountable, and we're all caught between concerns that a few influential people will walk over everyone else versus concerns over the indolent using us for a free ride. And there's nothing new in any of it as these arguments go back to ancient Athens where plebeians and patricians went at each other with a vengeance.

Traditionally, liberals have complained that wealthy conservatives (not that all conservatives are wealthy, but that the wealthy tend to be conservative) make their luxury and privilege a burden on others, that they live with frat brat narcissism and yacht club naïveté, and undermine democracy by compelling the legislature and legal system to support their wealth. On the other hand, conservatives complain that liberals make their lack of incentive and their unrealistic idealism someone else's burden, that like children they want to be sheltered from harsh realities. Conservatives, moreover, are accused of lacking social responsibility while liberals are accused of lacking personal responsibility; conservatism is accused of striving for maximum freedom for the individual while giving license to abuse of power, while liberalism is accused of striving for maximum benefit of the many by taking the success of the hardworking and giving it to the indolent.

A liberal wag once compared wealthy conservatives to Winnebago RVs because they lumber along making their luxury a burden on everyone else on the road. Others bring up the example of the Johnstown Flood where a dam holding back a lake for wealthy vacationers was carelessly neglected until it let go, killing thousands of working class people in the town below—for which no one was ever held accountable. This was at a time when workers had to fight for things we take for granted today, such as the forty-hour work week and the eight-hour day. In more modern times, the notorious Love Canal and Bhopal, India situations demonstrate corporations attempting to avoid responsibility for their actions through legal maneuvering and political dodging.

On the other hand, conservatives see liberals as promoting a soup kitchen welfare state, and accuse the ultra-Left of using notions of democracy to justify making their sense of entitlement a drain on everyone else's bank accounts; of taking an attitude that if you have something I don't, then I deserve a piece of your success, maybe all of it. But if the implication is that liberal values are immature, ultra-conservatives are just as easily criticized for acting like selfish children, especially in the form of mega-corporations assuming the rights of individuals but without the liability or responsibility of individuals, using up natural resources for the sake of immediate gain and creating a corporate aristocracy, if not outright kleptocracy, that treats the needs and rights of others with contempt.

These are issues that date back to *The Federalist Papers* stating that while people are naturally self-interested, they are expected to behave responsibly. History tells us that some do and some don't, so while conservatives regard liberalism as an abdication of responsibility, liberals see conservatism as a flippant disregard of it, each seeing the other as the bloodsucker, the criminal violating others' rights, the self-centered child.

And so it goes. On one side is the cliché that the elephant that dances among the chickens is free to step wherever he wants, while the counter complaint is that too many people insist on getting underfoot, then complain about getting stepped on. Yet, conservatives feel they have to uphold the strength, dignity and character of the culture against egalitarian notions that would reduce everything to the lowest common denominator, while liberals feel they have to defend the vitality of free expression against the threat of conformist rigidity created by those who define society to their own advantage.

But we're all prone to that sort of thing, and our technologically-oriented culture, itself, has been accused of all these things and more, criticized for its sophistication that aims to rise above the basics of farming and common labor without which no society can survive, that like emperors of old, we scorn those upon whom we depend, leaving the question as to who is taking advantage of whom. The best we can say is that any political system or economic policy is helpful to some, hurtful to others, and that there will always be those who will devise ways of taking advantage at the expense of someone else.

We all make choices as to where to focus our attention and energy, yet we're all prone to living in pink bubbles defined by narrow notions of how life is supposed to be. Both sides of the congressional aisle are prone to it, as are both sides of every social argument.

But the system and the jargon used to describe it have deteriorated so badly that the more reasonable among us have a hard time defining ourselves as either liberal or conservative as those terms are used today. Anyway, our political leanings don't have to be conservative to appreciate the following piece accredited to Georgia State Representative Mitchell Kaye (in 2007), for in many ways it applies to adulthood in general:

> *We, the sensible people of the United States, in an attempt to help everyone get along, restore some semblance of justice, avoid any more riots, and keep our nation safe, promote positive behavior, and secure the blessings of debt-free liberty to ourselves and our great-great-great-grandchildren, hereby try one more time to ordain and establish common-sense guidelines for the terminally whiny, guilt-ridden deluded, and other bedwetters. We hold these truths to be self-evident: that a whole lot of people are confused by the Bill of Rights and are so dim that they require a Bill of No Rights.*
>
> *ARTICLE I: You do NOT have the right to a new car, big screen TV or any other form of wealth. More power to you if you can legally acquire them, but no one is guaranteeing anything.*
>
> *ARTICLE II: You do NOT have the right to never be offended. This country is based on freedom, and that means freedom for everyone, not just you! You may leave the room, change the channel, express a different opinion, etc., but the world is full of idiots, and probably always will be.*
>
> *ARTICLE III: You do NOT have the right to be free from harm. If you stick a screwdriver in your eye, learn to be more careful, do not expect the tool manufacturer to make you and all your relatives independently wealthy.*
>
> *ARTICLE IV: You do NOT have the right to free food and housing. Americans are the most charitable people to be found, and will*

gladly help anyone in need, but we are quickly growing weary of subsidizing generation after generation of professional couch potatoes who achieve nothing more than the creation of another generation of professional couch potatoes.

ARTICLE V: You do NOT have the right to free health care. That would be nice, but from the looks of public housing, we're just not interested in public health care.

ARTICLE VI: You do NOT have the right to physically harm other people. If you kidnap, rape, intentionally maim or kill someone, don't be surprised if the rest of us want to see you fry in the electric chair.

ARTICLE VII: You do NOT have the right to the possessions of others. If you rob, cheat, or coerce away the goods and services of other citizens, don't be surprised if the rest of us get together and lock you away in a place where you still won't have the right to a big screen color TV or a life of leisure.

ARTICLE VIII: You do NOT have the right to demand that our children risk their lives in foreign wars to soothe your aching conscience. We hate oppressive governments and won't lift a finger to stop you from going to fight if you like. However, we do not enjoy parenting the entire world and do not want to spend so much of our time battling each and every little tyrant with a military uniform and a funny hat.

ARTICLE IX: You do NOT have the right to a job. All of us sure want all of you to have one, and will gladly help you along in hard times, but we expect you to take advantage of the opportunities of education and vocational training laid before you to make yourself useful.

ARTICLE X: You do NOT have the right to happiness. You have the right to pursue happiness, which, by the way, is a lot easier if you are unencumbered by an overabundance of idiotic laws created by those of you who were confused by the Bill of Rights.

Political implications aside, the overall theme is familiar, that the key to adult life is to finally get it that our life is our own job, not someone else's, and there are repercussions for everything. The resentment built up over years is surfacing with a vengeance in contemporary society on both sides of the aisle, and we don't have to be liberal to appreciate some of the grievances put forth by the Occupy Wall Street movement such as demanding that elected officials and corporations so huge as to hold sway over us all act with greater responsibility. Legislating that level of responsibility may entail a disturbing degree of socialism, but that doesn't mean it's socialistic to expect individuals, corporations and governmental officials to act with maturity.

So, who's right? No one. Everyone. Actually, it's not a matter of right and wrong so much as it's a matter of learning to deal with life as best we can. Problems result when we ignore consequences, yet one of humanity's greatest yearnings is to act without having to experience any unwanted results. After all, that's the way it was when we were little, or so it had seemed.

Learning and Useful Effort

For better or worse, most who write books of this sort try to play a pundit role with recommendations for educators, therapists, parents, politicians and the like, but the best I can do is to stimulate others' thinking because the arena is so vast. For instance, the New Age cliché that it's all about love can be meaningful only if our notion of love is mature, for the care and concern we feel for others when we can carry our own lives is not the same we feel as dependent children, hormone-driven adolescents, or fragile adults. Rather, the challenge is to recognize that we're all just folks, all seven billion of us.

One great question is as to how we can influence our culture both to promote the developmental process and to reduce the influences that undermine it. It's been said before that the most helpful thing we can do is to engage children in constructive effort at as early an age as possible, for the kid who grows up assuming he's to do his share without having to think about it has a leg up on everyone else.

One thing Adler emphasized is that we yearn for a way to be a constructive part of society. That's why any boy needs to grow up knowing men's lives, whether in camping, hunting and cars, or in anything from music to stamp collecting, for what counts is involvement with adults. We see the boy in *How Green Was My Valley* watching his dying father struggle to the end, or the exuberant intellectual in *Dead Poet's Society* sharing his passion, and there we see what so many of us have missed. Instead, most of us grow up watching Dad drive off to a job we can't comprehend, and when that's all we see, we'll feel we're growing into an incomprehensible world that doesn't seem to want us any more than we want it.

In an interview with Chuck Palahniuk, the rock star Marilyn Manson, when asked what he would have said to the young men who carried out the Columbine High School massacre, replied that he wouldn't have said anything at all—he would have listened. He's right of course, because many of us grow up feeling like no one's even noticing except to hurt us now and then, although that alone doesn't explain the violence in our culture. And in his work like *Fight Club*, Palahniuk has expressed the frustration and rage that many young males feel toward the culture around them, resorting to random violence and vandalism, restaurant chefs masturbating into customers' food, all with a self-destructive fervor that sometimes borders on psychosis. Some of it is simply a rush of adolescent hormones throwing itself against the world, but some of it is the outrage of the guy who resents the ordinary demands of life invading his adolescent haze. But some of it is the rage of a damaged psyche trying to defend itself at any cost, some of it is the pain of being beaten down by prejudice and poverty in the midst of affluence, some of it is the vengeance of the black sheep who has been ridiculed and harassed for not fitting in with the flock, and some of it is revenge on a culture that seems to a young mind to expect mindless, lifeless conformity.

Well, teens and black sheep have always raged against the world. The Greeks wrote about it twenty-five hundred years ago, and there have always been races, cultural groups and individuals forced into the role of the downtrodden. No matter the reason, the bitter pill we're challenged to swallow is that raging against the machine can keep us trapped in the machine just as much as acquiescing to it does, that just because we're treated like a number doesn't mean we have to feel like one, for if we go through life that way, we'll be bound to stay trapped and enraged at "the system" for simply being what it is—a mass cultural tide that's not about to change for our sake.

Many of us grow up with parents pulling the rug out from under us every time we try to stand, then endure humiliation from the bullies and brats we go to school with, struggle to figure ourselves out, feeling ignored and disregarded by the people we look to for guidance, and retreat into the electronic haze of TV and computer games only to find all that junk sucks the life out of us instead. And if we complain that it's just not fair, we learn that, well, yeah. It's not.

If we're lucky, though, we'll discover that we've been missing the point all along, and what a surprise! The challenge is to step outside "the system" with creativity, for guys like Bill Gates and Steve Jobs did that and created systems the rest of us now have to comply with. And the guy masturbating into the soup in a restaurant kitchen can feel smug only until he gets caught at it.

So, one thing we can do is to find something productive, something inventive, something helpful, perhaps something insanely adventurous, but do *something*, because the guy who does nothing but sit around throwing his toys out of the pram might spend his entire life complaining. Yes, there are things to object to and confront, but it needs to be done intelligently and constructively.

Seeking Common Ground – The Rules of the Game

In a piece e-mailed around the internet several years ago, Bill Gates spoke about how feel-good, politically-correct messages have left kids with little concept of reality, setting them up for failure in the real world. So, in response, he came up with a list of eleven things high school and college grads need to learn that they didn't in school:

One: Life is not fair: get used to it.

Two: The world doesn't care about your self-esteem. The world will expect you to accomplish something before you feel good about yourself.

Three: You will not make forty thousand dollars a year right out of high school. You won't be a vice president with a car phone until you earn both.

Four: If you think your teacher is tough, wait till you get a boss. He doesn't have tenure.

Five: Flipping burgers is not beneath your dignity. Your grandparents had a different word for flipping burgers: they called it opportunity.

Six: If you mess up, it's not your parents' fault, so don't whine about your mistakes: learn from them.

Seven: Before you were born, your parents weren't as boring as they are now. They got that way from paying your bills, cleaning your clothes and listening to you talk about how cool you are. So before you save the rainforests from the parasites of your parents' generation, try delousing the closet in your own room.

Eight: Your school may have done away with winners and losers, but life has not. In some schools they have abolished failing grades; they'll give you as many times as you want to get the right answer. This doesn't bear the slightest resemblance to anything in real life.

Nine: Life is not divided into semesters. You don't get summers off, and very few employers are interested in helping you find yourself. Do that on your own time.

Ten: Television is not real life. In real life, people actually have to leave the coffee shop and go to jobs.

Eleven: Be nice to nerds. Chances are you'll end up working for one.

It's really a bit of tough love, and with an eye on deconstructing ourselves, here are a few of my own rules of the game:

*   What we are is not an ego, but we have to develop one to get around. That's the game. (This is for the rise-above-the-ego types out there.)

*   Human psyches are inherently at least slightly insane. That's a handicap we're all given. Some of us are given a bigger handicap than

others. No one knows why.

Corollary: the saner we think ourselves to be, the crazier we probably are.

* The most basic job in life is to grow up, to mature our ego structure. Everything else follows from that. Caution: we all fail to some extent.

* If we don't carry our own part in the game, we'll create a burden for other people to carry, then blame them for it. It's true whether we are in a power position or a power*less* position.

* If we don't carry our own part in the game, we'll use metaphysics, philosophy, economic theory or anything else at hand to justify why we don't have to.

* It's all done with mirrors.

Beyond this, the top ten rules are:

Rule #10: We can't win the game, but we have to play it anyway.

Rule #9: The human mind tries to change the game to make it easy for itself, but never works, no matter how good we are at convincing ourselves it does.

Rule #8: It's our own life, not someone else's. This gives us the freedom to not have to live someone else's life for them, and the responsibility to not expect others to live ours.

Rule #7: The best lessons we have to learn are the ones where we make really dumb mistakes.

Rule #6: Life isn't fair. Deal with it. (Yes, Gates had this one too.)

Rule #5: Most of the other seven-plus billion people in the world don't know we exist much less care about our feelings or our needs, and there's no reason they should. Deal with it.

Rule #4: What we want from life, and what life demands of us are usually in completely opposite directions.

Corollary: The help we want from other people is usually the opposite from what actually helps us.

Rule# 3: We have to be ruthlessly honest in telling ourselves the truth about what we are doing and feeling. Discontentment is a great motivator.

Rule #2: Don't be a twit.

Rule #1: We're all twits. Enjoy life anyway.

Rule #0: The freedom to choose is one of the heaviest burdens we can ever carry.

Life as Boot Camp

A few years ago there was a TV show in which problem teens were sent to a version of military boot camp where the idea was to drag them, kicking and screaming if need be, out of childhood—spare the drill sergeant and you'll lose the kid to crime, drugs and worse.

Too many of us, though, grow up with simply no place to be a meaningful member of the family or the community, no way to feel useful or appreciated. Then, as adults, we have to learn things others take for granted—changing the oil in the car, taking a trip on our own, or building some small thing for the first time, gradually developing competence and surprising ourselves by taking on challenges we'd always felt we couldn't handle. The feminist movement was encouraging women to do that sort of thing decades ago.

Children have a natural yearning to be a part of things, and when an adult habitually defeats a boy's sense of adventure, they defeat his emotional development, for if all a boy ever feels is being stopped from trying new things, he'll eventually give up. And when he gives up, something drains out of him, some piece of his developing self-sense slipping away, leaving behind a gnawing despair he can't understand. Even if he's never told *No!* in an outright way, but is simply left out of things, that gnawing feeling grows in him. Then when he does learn a skill, raising himself out of his chronic emptiness, he'll likely become vain, anyone from the chess champion to the carpenter to the intellectual to the religious zealot scorning all those morons out there. And that's not a good feeling, even if it does make him feel grand for a moment or two.

The challenge, then, is to keep taking on new adventures, new projects, new learning opportunities and new risks. One thing that can throw us into life's boot camp is the realization that we've moored ourselves to an anchor that's been dragging us down for years, and that recognition alone can be a great motivator once our adolescent bravado wears off. The broader our experience, the more mature our attitude will be, and that's something we hunger for. Yet no matter how sheltered our childhoods may have been, as a joke greeting card says: *A happy childhood is the worst possible preparation for life.* That's why some of us throw ourselves headlong into challenging experiences as if cutting a second umbilical, businesses like NOLS, Outward Bound and a swarm of trekking companies filling the void many of us grow up feeling. Others of us go into the military or anything else we can find to force ourselves out of our lingering childhoods, as if to pay a backlog of dues owed to life.

Physical challenges are important because our self-sense develops largely through physical experience, which is why intellectuals, computer geeks and the indolent can have such a hard time growing up. And because our sense of identity is a physically-felt experience, it will resist if forced to change too quickly, which is why we may have a seemingly life-altering experience, but if it isn't drawn out over time, our psyches won't fully absorb it. In fact, it's likely to reject the experience out of hand as something "not me."

Rediscovering Our Lives

The last of the human freedoms (is)
to choose one's attitude in any given set of circumstances,
to choose one's own way.
~Viktor Frankel

But there are victories far worse than defeats;
and to overcome an angel too gentle to put out all his strength
and ride away in triumph on the back of a devil is one of the poorest.
~George MacDonald, *The Lost Princess*

An essential question is what we are to do about any of it. What, after all is said and done, is the cure? The answer is for us to find a way do the opposite of our habitual way of being in this life, and there's no simple way to delineate how to do that. Actually, I feel that anyone who claims they have far-reaching answers to the problems of humanity is not only fooling himself, but will ultimately make a fool of himself. The best we can do is to take long looks in the mirrors life presents us with and make tough choices, and what we choose to do with this or any other mirror is where our personal power and responsibility lie.

While it has been said that it's more important to be a problem solver than a problem identifier, the problems confronting modern society are so deeply immersed in our culture that identifying them becomes of supreme importance. Beyond that, the process of personal change remains mysterious and generally has a life of its own down there in the subconscious layers of our psyches. So, for all the seemingly negative emphasis in this work, the aim is one of self-empowerment through recognizing that our habitual personality dynamics are not who we are, through seeing that we don't have to be victims of our own habits, and the expectation is that through bringing those habits to light we can engage in some deep personal change. And in that, we are challenged to let life teach us instead of trying to tell life the way things are supposed to be.

Researchers have noted that successful coaching can significant generate changes in our brains, indicating that the challenge is not just in changing our behaviors. Adlerian coaching presents a template for this through the ICA model; or, more correctly, IICCAA. We need to clarify the issues at hand, gain insights from those issues, make new choices based on those insights, commit to those choices, take action on those commitments, and be accountable for following through. This book focuses on the first two steps—the issue and insight arena—while implying the choices available. The rest each one of us has to find for ourselves, for the process tends to have a life of its own.

The basic hallmarks of emotional maturity and effectiveness as defined in the emotional intelligence arena are the ability to recognize and manage our emotions, and the ability to respond effectively to the challenges before us. The ultimate boot camp, the ultimate bitter medicine, then, is an ongoing demand to wake ourselves up from our habitual stances. Avoiders are challenged to reel themselves in when they start to drift away, clingers are challenged to stay put in their own space instead of trying to climb inside everyone else's, and pushers are challenged to face life without trying to dominate. Otherwise, we'll live with the "you're wrong for being different from me" stubbornness to which we're all prone.

We are all challenged to step outside our normal range of comfort, and that often requires us to face a complex stew of difficult feelings. Life is rarely easy, and, contrary to popular notions, we are challenged to develop invisible muscles through new, even uncomfortable, experiences. As men we are challenged to face the opposite gender equivalent of what Simone de Beauvoir posed to women, that one is not born a man, but becomes one; that there is no self to be discovered, but a self to be created. But we spend so many of our early years fighting against what we're not that it's only later that we discover, as if by accident, what truly fits for us. This is why so many of us stumble onto a true self-sense only after having been tripped up by a few disasters along the way.

The painter Thomas Hart Benton used to tell his students to stop trying to get in touch with their souls and just get down to painting, for the road to self-discovery is through living and work, not through self-obsession. Novelist Tom Robbins expresses much the same notion through one of his characters declaring that self-esteem is for sissies, a startling thing to hear if we've spent too much time in the self-help swamp. It's more to the point to say that self-esteem is a characteristic of ego strength, and ego strength results from hard experience, a bit like stumbling out the far end of the gauntlet, having gained from the beating we've taken.

Said differently, we have to take a hard look at the ground we've been standing on for so long, which is difficult to do until we've gained enough age and experience. Otherwise, we'll take our position for granted while condemning others for the ground they don't realize they're standing on. And we'll blame the world at large for not complying with our small piece of ground, assuming it's obligated to.

Yet there are many things that can impede us along the way, or at least convince us we've been impeded. I was recently following a driver on an open road when another car pulled abruptly up to the stop sign on a cross street. At that, the driver ahead of me overreacted, braked hard and swerved, then carried on down the road at twenty miles an hour as if something were about to leap out and crash into him, as if some obstacle, invisible to everyone else, was in his way.

Human psyches work like that at times, for we all have had difficult experiences, and are prone to going on as if paralyzed by obstacles that are no longer there, and perhaps never really were.

As a counter-example, we see Milton Erickson's case of the town punk who'd changed simply by discovering something he wanted more than the way he'd been. In other words, he made the choices he needed to make in order to have what he wanted, and although the story doesn't provide many details, we can guess that most of those choices happened unconsciously. After all, deep choices can make for deep changes.

On the other hand, I recently passed a family argument outside a restaurant where a teenager was storming her way across the parking lot in a fit of purple rage while her father called after her, "Susan, don't make this choice!" A family that no doubt had been exposed to a bit of therapy, but the question that struck me was as to whether Susan was really making a choice, or was she simply abdicating choice in favor of a child's notion of power, refusing to make any real choice at all.

Typically, as children or teenagers, even as adults, we don't believe we have other choices, which is one reason we tend to stay stuck in repeating the same behaviors, and the challenge to find other choices is likely to drive us to anger as a way of defending our stance in life and protecting ourselves from the fear that can grip us. Acting on habits we'd developed at age three is sometimes simply a habit, sometimes simply the best we can manage, but either way when we give in to glorious indignation, to hysterics, or resort to revenge, we're abdicating choice altogether. To have choice, we have to be willing to stop ourselves from taking off like a runaway train on tracks laid out in the human psyche since before our ancestors were born, thinking all the while we're being true to ourselves. On the other hand, the dad's challenge was to remind her that even in the midst of a tantrum, choice was available to her whether she wanted it or not.

Most of the time, though, we shoot ourselves in the foot because we simply don't know how not to. So, this is the question life challenges us all to answer: What do we want more than we want to live sensible lives? And what does it take to remake our choices?

Yet we can change even when we don't know how. In the example earlier, a homeless man was given consistent challenges, each a bit more difficult than the last, until he was able to engage with life in more fulfilling way. But that's what life confronts us all with throughout childhood, and one thing a story like that tells us is that we often don't know we have choices until we have to make one, that a victim stance will only keep us in a victim stance, and that ego strength is built through increasing challenges. And neither the man living in the drainage ditch nor the punk who wanted to date the girl had to get in touch with their inner feelings or address their childhood hurts, although they likely spent time considering things like that along the way. Rather, they took action based on the incentives driving them, for without that they would have gone on as they always had. Beyond this, the best we can say is that when change happens, it does so in mysterious and unpredictable ways.

In one of his film series, Joseph Campbell shows an ancient portrayal of the Eleusinian mysteries in which an acolyte holds a mirror in front of an initiate, turning away while the initiate stares with horror. The same theme is seen in a fresco in Pompeii's "Villa of Mysteries," where an acolyte holds a frightening mask behind the initiate as he looks into a mirror, as if a ghoul is peering over his shoulder. That takes us back to the old sci-fi show, *The Cheaters*, the implication being that it's no one else's business to know what we need to see about ourselves. For each of us, life itself is a ruthless mirror into which we are all challenged to stare, and for most of us there are at least a few ogres of our own making peering over our shoulders.

Those ogres are often the very things that challenge us to take a hard look at the assumptions we make about life, about others, and especially about ourselves, and find the choice we hadn't known had been available to us all along. In fact, many of us undermine our lives by clinging to a stance early in life, then trying to make life wrong for challenging us to move along in our psychological development.

So, what's the solution, what answers does this book propose? While some look for a formula or menu of strategies, it really just comes down to willpower and self-discipline, gaining the strength of character to see our own lives clearly, and having the strength of will both to act on more mature dynamics, not the familiar ones.

I started by saying that this book was never been intended to be likeable, especially as likeable books tend to be ineffective. But I've also joked about how we would all look to an alien anthropologist, so while this work may grate on our human sensibilities, I think the Martian anthropologists would get a kick out of it.

Again, we're challenged to find new possibilities in life rather than living by probabilities determined by our personality habits. Beyond that, it's important to ask how anything can be helpful, for there's no magic bullet. Rather, I would hope for this book to be a fulcrum against which we can lever many things in any number of directions. In the end, life remains a mystery just as we remain mysteries to ourselves, a mystery that can only be explored, not solved. As I'd also said at the beginning, there's a theme reflected in the Joni Mitchell song telling us to shine a light on all of it. There's more than enough pain and resentment to go around, and whenever we obsess on our personal idealism, we'll find all the excuses we could ever need to turn our personal resentment against the rest of humanity.

So, as I'd said at the outset, while so much of this work can strike us as negative, the most positive statement of all is that we have to learn to dance the great human dance, that while there's no one to teach us the steps, it's by stumbling through life that we learn. Otherwise we'll be stuck trying to instruct life to work our way rather than letting it teach us. And if we accept the challenge, eventually we just may stumble onto our authentic self like finding an old friend in the dark: *Oh! This is me. At last, this is really me.*

ABOUT THE AUTHOR

Rich Jewett MA is the author of *Dance on Fire—The Art of Radical Experiences: Upheaval, Crisis and Insight, Four Storms: True Confessions of an Insurance Adjuster, The Magpie Chronicles*, and the fictional works, *The Buddha and the Whale, Roger,* and *Weavers.*

Rich received his Master's Degree from the University of Colorado with a background in developmental psychology, object-relations theory and Adlerian Coaching. Rich and his wife Pamela live in in Colorado with 14,000-foot mountains in their back yard.

Thursday, October 6, 2022